Glossary

ARM Wing between body and carpal joint (often used in raptors).

BROWNHEAD Term applied to encompass female, juvenile and immature plumages of Smew, Red-breasted Merganser and Goosander.

CHUM Revolting mixture of dead fish, fish oil and popcorn poured onto the sea to attract seabirds on pelagic trips.

ECLIPSE Non-breeding plumage of male ducks in late summer.

HAND Wing between carpal joint and tip (often used in raptors).

LEUCISM Results from dilution of the normal pigmentation, so that, for example, blacks

by
ther

and

are
....u twitching).

Two Points to Remember

(1) Moustachial, Submoustachial and Malar Stripes: Do not confuse these terms. The moustachial stripe is the dark line from the bill below the eye, along the lower border of the ear-coverts. The pale line below this is the submoustachial, and the dark line below that, down the sides of the chin and throat, is the malar. (Many observers confuse the moustachial and malar stripes.)

(2) Tertials These are the elongated innermost secondaries that cloak the primaries at rest (the secondaries are often hidden or mostly hidden).

THE MACMILLAN FIELD GUIDE TO
BIRD
IDENTIFICATION

Alan Harris, Laurel Tucker and Keith Vinicombe

Laurel Tucker

Laurel died on 20 June 1986, having suffered a cerebral haemorrhage from which she never regained consciousness. She was 35. We had been together for nearly three years and she had embarked upon this book with her usual child-like enthusiasm, excited at the prospect of a joint project. In the event, she completed only 18 of the plates and the unfinished work on this page was her last, started the day before she died. Laurel was a remarkable woman, whose vivid and intense personality was somehow reflected in her illustrations. It is hoped that this book, and the forthcoming *Handbook of Bird Identification* by Steve Madge and Mark Beaman, will serve as a tribute to her remarkable ability, both as a bird artist and as a birdwatcher. It is, of course, dedicated to her memory.

K.E.V.

Published by Grange Books
An Imprint of Grange Books PLC
The Grange
Grange Yard
London SE1 3AG
First published in 1989 by THE MACMILLAN PRESS LTD
London and Basingstoke
This edition 1994

ISBN 1-85627-641-4
Printed and bound in Czech Republic

CONTENTS

* *Illustrations by Laurel Tucker (remainder by Alan Harris)*

Introduction

This book was born out of a meeting in 1985 between Laurel Tucker and Dr Tim Sharrock, the latter in his capacity as natural history consultant to Macmillan. The idea was to produce a book that would tackle in depth the problems of identifying 'difficult' birds. It was felt that the standard field guides, mainly because of lack of space and, in some cases, poor illustrations, could not do justice to the problem of separating similar species. The result is, in essence, a series of well-illustrated 'mini' identification papers.

Choosing the subjects was problematical, but it was decided to include mainly those regularly occurring British and Irish species that present a problem for the 'average birdwatcher' and to include only those rarities that are frequently confused with something common. Inconsistencies have, however, been inevitable. For example, it was difficult to discuss the problem of dull Melodious and Icterine Warblers without dealing with Olivaceous Warbler and, in turn, Booted Warbler. In other cases, for example the stints, discussion has been confined to the commoner species, as to have gone into detail on the extreme rarities would have been beyond the scope of this book.

It is hoped that the end result will appeal not only to relative beginners but also to those more seasoned observers with gaps in their knowledge. The author and artists certainly learnt a lot in the preparation of the book.

Acknowledgements

We are particularly grateful to Dr Tim Sharrock for all his help and guidance in the preparation of this book. All the text and plates have been scrutinised by the *British Birds* Identification Notes Panel and we are extremely grateful to Alan Dean, Peter Grant, Steve Madge, Dr Malcolm Ogilvie and Dr Tim Sharrock for their invaluable comments. We are also grateful to David Christie for expertly editing the text. The author and artist, however, take responsibility for any errors that may have crept in.

At Macmillan, we are grateful to Julian Ashby, Mary Ryder and Robert Updegraff for all their help. At the Wildfowl Trust, we should like to thank Martin Brown, James Godfrey and Nigel Jarrett for showing us around the breeding pens at Slimbridge and for discussing at length the ageing and sexing of wildfowl. Peter Colston at the British Museum (Natural History) at Tring was as helpful as always during our various visits to check skins.

A.H. would like to thank Alan Ball, Chris Dee, Kevin Osborn, Harry Sims, Aron 'Jinxie' Sapsford, Hadoram Shirihai, Bruce Taggart, Graham White and Barry Williams and members of the Rye Meads Ringing Group for many hours of useful (and not so useful!) discussion.

K.E.V. is particularly grateful to Grahame Walbridge, whose unparalleled knowledge was regularly tapped, and to the following, who helped in various ways: Andy Barber, Martin Cade, Tim Cleeves, Andy Clements, Andy Davis, Pete Fraser, Andy Hawkins, Pete Hopkin, Simon Horseman, John Marchant, Chris Newman, Ken McEntee, Tony Merritt, Andy Middleton, Tony Pym, Dick Senior, Chris Stone and Nigel Tucker. He is also eternally indebted to Chris and Theresa Stone and to Geoff and Sarah Upton for attempting to keep him sane.

How to Use This Book

In order to facilitate the efficient exposition of difficult identification problems, a rigid format has been abandoned. Each 'chapter' has been arranged in the form of a 'mini' identification paper so as best to suit the topic under discussion. As it is important to be aware of the likelihood of any particular species occurring in a given area or at a given time of year, each article is, however, prefaced with a short section entitled 'Where and When'. This sets out where and when you are likely to encounter the species under discussion, but it must be stressed that this is only a generalised thumbnail sketch which cannot account for every eventuality. Many accounts end with a list of references. These point the way to articles which contain useful additional information or which go into various aspects of identification in more detail. Only readily available references are cited, mainly those in *British Birds*.

Short Cuts to Identification

Knowing the Common Birds

The only way to become an expert birdwatcher is to spend as much time as possible in the field and, as in all things, practice makes perfect. The time should be spent, however, not in acquiring a huge life list, but in getting to know the common birds. The secret of identifying a rarity is the ability to eliminate the common confusion species: how, for example, can you identify a Ring-billed Gull if you have never bothered to take a close look at a Common Gull?

Keep an Open Mind

When faced with something unusual, do not automatically assume that it is a rarity. Consider all the other possibilities. Could its appearance be due to individual variation? Is it something common in an unfamiliar plumage? Is it aberrant? Is it a hybrid? Is it an escaped cagebird? If you are stuck, take a full description, but always try to get somebody else to look at the bird. This is especially important with rarities, as substantiated observations will have a much better chance of acceptance. On the other hand, try to make up your own mind about an identification, and do not be bamboozled by so-called 'experts' who are not.

Calls

Most good birdwatchers identify a large proportion of their birds by calls and songs. Unfortunately, there is no short cut to learning calls, but try to follow up all the unidentified bird calls you hear. Bird records may be a help, but they are no substitute for hearing the real thing within the context of its natural environment.

Ageing and Sexing

As the immediate problem for the beginner will be to identify the species, the idea of ageing and sexing may seem like an unnecessary complication. With many species, however, ageing may be an important first step to identification and in some cases it may, at a stroke, eliminate several confusion species. For example, many beginners are confused by small waders. This is often due to the fact that many of the old text books illustrate only summer and winter adults. The fact is that many waders have an equally distinct *juvenile* plumage. Is it any wonder that confusion arises when, in many cases, the most commonly occurring plumage type is not even illustrated?

Moults and Ageing Terminology Tied in with ageing and sexing is, of course, moult. As a general rule, most adult birds have two moults a year: a body moult in late winter/spring and a complete moult in late summer. This simple knowledge of moult times is surprisingly useful and, associated with this, so too is the correct use of ageing terminology to ensure that we are all speaking the same language.

A bird's first feathers, after it leaves the nest, are called *juvenile plumage*, and in most species this is retained until late summer, when there is a body moult (i.e. excluding the longer wing and tail feathers). Juvenile is then replaced by *first-winter plumage*. In most small passerines (e.g. Robin), this is basically adult plumage, but many species take longer to reach maturity and they go through a whole sequence of immature plumages before reaching adulthood. As a general rule, the bigger the bird, the longer it takes to reach maturity. Thus, a Black-headed Gull has a distinct first-winter plumage, but, in the following spring, there is another body moult, after which *first-summer* plumage is acquired; then, in late summer, when just over one year old, it has its first *complete* moult, and, thereafter, it is adult. The Common Gull, on the other hand, takes two years to reach maturity, so first-summer is followed by *second-winter* and then *second-summer* before adulthood is reached. It may be worth remembering, however, that, if any feathers are lost, they may be replaced by feathers of the subsequent plumage type.

First-year and Second-year First-winter and first-summer plumages are often lumped together as first-year. Similarly, second-winter and second-summer may be lumped as second-year, and so on.

Juveniles and First-winters in Autumn Most passerines moult out of juvenile plumage before they migrate in autumn, so late August–October migrants are largely in first-winter plumage, which in many cases (e.g. Willow Warbler) is not safely separable from adult winter in the field. On the other hand, many species

(waders and terns, for example) migrate in juvenile plumage and many do not moult to first-winter until they reach their winter quarters. Others (e.g. Dunlin) may start to acquire their first-winter feathering while still on migration, so that they have a patchy mixture of juvenile and first-winter plumages. It should be remembered that, compared with the adults, autumn juveniles are usually very neat and immaculate as their plumage is fresh: in many species (e.g. Curlew Sandpiper and Reed Warbler), the contemporary late-summer adults look very worn and 'tatty' in comparison. Svensson (1984) outlines the moult times for all European passerines, while *BWP* covers non-passerines and some passerines (at the time of writing, Volumes 6 and 7 are still to be published).

'Calendar-year' Ageing Some large species, such as many large eagles, undergo an almost continuous moult so that several different ages of feathers may be present at any one time. In such cases it is often sensible to age the bird by 'calendar-year'. The year in which the bird was hatched is termed the *first calendar-year*, the *second calendar-year* starting on 1 January of the next year (i.e. when the bird is about six months old) and so on.

'Immature' and 'Sub-adult' One particularly important point to remember is that *immature* simply means 'not mature' and so can be applied to any bird that is not an adult. Thus, juvenile, first-winter and first-summer plumages are all 'immature' plumages, but many observers confuse immature with juvenile. You should try to avoid using the term 'immature' in relation to any one individual bird, as it is usually possible to be more accurate. Similarly, *sub-adult* is also to be avoided if possible, as again more accurate ageing can usually be determined.

Feather wear When identifying birds and assessing ageing, bear in mind the effects of wear, abrasion and bleaching. Old feathers wear and fade and significant

SHORT CUTS TO IDENTIFICATION

plumage features (such as wingbars) can disappear through wear, while some species alter plumage tone (for example, fresh autumn Meadow Pipits have quite a green tint, whereas worn individuals are browner). Immature gulls are notoriously prone to wear and bleaching, and may look particularly 'tatty' and faded in summer, when their wing and tail feathers are nearly a year old. Some species have only one complete moult a year, in late summer, and their summer appearance is the result of feather wear (in the case of the Starling, the buff feather tips of 'winter plumage' wear off to produce the plainer black 'summer plumage').

Field Craft

Standards of field craft have declined in recent years, presumably because so many observers now birdwatch from hides or turn up at a 'twitch' to find their quarry already under observation. Remember the old rules of wearing sombre clothing and moving quietly and smoothly. Also, remember the benefits of patient stalking, and do not be afraid to crawl on all fours or to duck down below vegetation to avoid flushing the birds that you are pursuing. It is often possible to get close to birds by using even scanty vegetation as cover.

Note-taking

When faced with an unusual bird, take exhaustive field notes *on the spot* (this is much easier nowadays as most birdwatchers use a telescope and tripod). It is also useful to take notes on unfamiliar plumage types and on anything else that attracts the attention, as note-taking aids the learning process. The easiest way to take notes is to make an annotated sketch: if you cannot draw, just use two circles, one for the head and one for the body.

Drawing the bird ensures that all parts are checked. When drawing, it does not matter quite so much if you forget the names of the feather tracts as these can be checked when you get home, but try to familiarise yourself with how the feathers lie, particularly on the wing (it is essential to know which are the median coverts, the greater coverts, the tertials etc.). It may be an idea to practise drawing your garden sparrows or a pet Budgerigar to work out which feathers are which.

Description-writing

At some point you will need to convince a records committee of one of your sightings. This is when field notes are essential. Remember to organise your description into a logical sequence (start with the head and work back), and the use of accurate topographical terminology is essential. Remember that records committees have to look at large numbers of descriptions, so make your notes concise, readable and interesting. Start with an introduction, outlining the circumstances of the observation, and write a short summary of the bird's appearance, emphasising the salient features and the overall impression, before embarking on a detailed feather-by-feather account. Try to do a drawing if possible, as it is usually easier for a committee to visualise a bird from a drawing than from a description. Furthermore, describe what you actually saw, not what you think you should have seen, and don't trot out standard text book clichés: it is those descriptions that include a minor feature not mentioned in the books that are often the most convincing. Finally, do not forget the bird's behaviour, habitat and calls, as well as weather details, distance, optics, names of other observers and details of your previous experience. All these points are important if a record is to be accepted.

Divers

Where and When Red-throated Diver is the most widespread and, generally, the most plentiful diver, particularly along east coast of Britain. Black-throated Diver is least numerous and most localised. Great Northern Diver is most numerous in north and west, particularly in Scotland and Ireland. All three occasionally occur inland. White-billed Diver is a very rare winter visitor, mainly in Scotland.

Red-throated Diver *Gavia stellata*

Size, Structure and Bill The smallest diver, although overlaps with Black-throated. Shape usually distinctive, with rather rounded back, shallow breast, full throat and rounded head. Bill slender and usually held at an upward angle, forming continuous line with throat and accentuating upward-curved lower mandible. Bill generally pale greyish, may darken towards spring.

Plumage Much browner than others, with diagnostic white upperpart flecking (difficult to see at any distance). White of 'face' variable, generally extends up and around eye; classic individuals, with eye isolated in white face, appear rather white-headed from distance, perhaps suggesting Great Crested Grebe *Podiceps cristatus*. Compared with Black-throated, demarcation between dark nape and white neck is further to rear, producing narrower nape line when viewed from behind. Amount of white visible along flanks depends on bird's attitude on water; when at ease, generally shows strip of white along entire length of flanks. Before moult (generally in mid winter), juveniles have variable amount of fine streaking on sides of head and neck, fuzzing line of demarcation; on extreme examples, whole head can look greyish from distance. Also on juveniles, and some adults, eye may be almost completely enclosed within dark of crown, often with just a small pale area in front of eye. Juveniles may also show dark chestnut patch on upper foreneck. Difficult to age once juvenile plumage lost in late winter. (Adults have complete post-breeding moult in early winter, so any Red-throated in active primary moult at that time will be adult.)

Pitfalls Typical individuals, if seen well, readily identifiable, but not all are so straightforward. Specific points to remember are: 1 Red-throated not infrequently holds bill horizontally; 2 head shape may, in certain postures, appear more angular; 3 in certain lights upperparts can look very dark and contrast markedly with underparts, provoking confusion with Black-throated; 4 in certain positions, can show isolated white patch on rear flanks, again suggesting Black-throated. Identification of distant individuals demands caution.

Black-throated Diver *Gavia arctica*

Size, Structure and Bill Intermediate in size between Red-throated and Great Northern, but overlaps with both. Very sleek, streamlined, graceful, but fuller-breasted than Red-throated. Head gently, smoothly and evenly rounded, although in certain postures can show more abrupt forehead. Bill usually held horizontally (occasionally at upward angle), is slender, pointed and straight, with upper mandible gently downcurved towards tip; shape, however, variable (some slightly thicker-billed). Bill grey, with dark culmen and cutting edges (less obvious than on Great Northern), blackens towards spring.

Plumage A crisply clean, almost auk-like black-and-white diver. Dark of head is tinged velvety grey at close range (in late spring can look quite grey-headed), but usually looks strikingly black and white, with sharp and even demarcation running below the eye and down the middle of neck sides, thereby producing larger dark nape area than on Red-throated. Eye-ring thin so that, unlike most Great Northerns, eye does not stand out from dark head. Fore flanks blackish, so rear flanks often stand out as isolated white patch, a useful feature at a distance; depending on posture, this can be reduced to a small round spot (Red-throated may show similar pattern in certain postures, so this feature should not be used in isolation). Juveniles have noticeable pale mantle and scapular edges until moult in New Year. After moult, ageing less easy, but adult (unlike Red-throated) has complete *pre*-breeding spring moult, so any Black-throated in active primary moult in spring will be adult.

Great Northern Diver *Gavia immer*

Size, Structure and Bill A large, heavy, cumbersome diver. Inexperienced observers may confuse it with first-winter Cormorant *Phalacrocorax carbo*, but note latter's large, full tail as it leaps to dive. Small Great Northerns do occur, provoking confusion with Black-throated, so head structure important for separation. Great Northern has large head with steep forehead (often with distinct 'bump' where forehead meets crown), rather flat crown and another angle where crown merges into nape. When frightened or when diving, however, feather-sleeking may produce much more streamlined appearance. Heavy-headed effect accentuates thick, heavy, deep-based bill, which usually shows a greater gonydeal angle than Black-throated; bill pale grey, with dark culmen and cutting edges.

Plumage Essentially a black-and-white diver, but messier-looking than Black-throated, lacking latter's smart contrasts: demarcation between crown/nape and front duskier and less clear-cut, showing dark half collar on lower neck and white indentation above this. Pale eye-surround produces more isolated and

more obvious eye than Black-throated. Great Northern shows long, rather uneven flank line, invisible if bird low in water. Juveniles show prominent pale mantle and scapular edges until moult in mid to late winter. Thereafter, ageing more difficult, but moulting adults in late winter lose their flight feathers.

White-billed Diver *Gavia adamsii*

Size, Structure and Bill A large, heavy diver, slightly bigger than Great Northern. Usually shows distinct 'lump' where forehead meets forecrown. Large bill very long and ivory-coloured, with prominently up-tilted lower mandible (appears almost banana-like), is usually held up at angle, suggesting gigantic Red-throated. Unlike Great Northern's, *bill lacks any dark along culmen and along distal cutting edges*, although dark feathering protrudes into base of upper mandible to nostril. Note: pale-billed Great Northerns occur, but always show dark culmen and cutting edges.

Plumage Similar to Great Northern, but head rather paler and greyer than most (contrasting more with dark upperparts) and has noticeable pale surround to eye. Juveniles even duskier-headed than adults, often show diffuse dark patch on ear-coverts; prominent pale mantle and scapular edges, more pronounced than on juvenile Great Northern. Winter adult White-billed often retains traces of white spotting on upperparts.

Flight Identification

Identifying divers in flight is difficult; distant individuals should be logged as 'diver sp.'. All are long-necked, long-legged, hunch-backed; their plain wings instantly separate them from grebes. Great Northern has the largest, most prominent feet, and Red-throated has smallest. Great Northern's slower, more goose-like flight may be of use.

References Burn & Mather (1974), Appleby *et al.* (1986).

Adult winter Red-throated Diver
Note extensive white on 'face'
and uptilted bill. Rounded head.
Upperparts spotted white.
▼

Juvenile Red-throated Diver
◀ Darker on head and sides of
neck than adult. Often shows
reddish patch on throat

Note continuous white
flank line.
▲

Adult winter Black-throated Diver
Black and white, very contrasting,
but head and nape may be
greyer. Slender straight bill
▼

Juvenile Black-throated Diver
Note pale feather edgings to
upperparts. Black-throated
Divers often show white patch
◀ to rear of flanks

1st-winter Cormorant may
◀ resemble a diver. Note
angular head, bill held
upwards, orangy 'face'
and long tail.

Adult winter Great Northern Diver
Plainer above than juvenile
▼

Juvenile Great Northern Diver. Note
◀ heavy pale bill and large angular
head. Extensive black on head, and
dark half collar around front of
neck. Upperparts show pale
feather edgings.

Adult winter White-billed Diver ▶
Note all-pale uptilted bill
(no dark along culmen).
Greyish neck sides with dark
patch on ear-coverts

11

Slavonian, Black-necked and Red-necked Grebes

Where and When Both Slavonian and Black-necked Grebes are very rare breeding species, but are more widespread as coastal winter visitors and passage migrants. In Britain, Slavonian Grebe is locally common from September to April, mainly in Scotland and around the east and south coasts of England, frequenting sheltered bays, estuary mouths and harbours; it is scarce and local in Ireland. It sometimes occurs inland, mainly in late autumn and winter, often during spells of severe freezing. In winter, Black-necked Grebe is distinctly rarer than Slavonian, with a more southerly distribution, mostly along the south coast of England; it is rare in Ireland. It prefers more sheltered environments than Slavonian and is less likely to be seen riding out rough seas. It also turns up inland, particularly on the London reservoirs, but mainly from July to November and again in spring (March–April); it is rare inland in mid winter. Red-necked Grebe is generally the rarest and is an uncommon winter visitor from September to April, mainly to the east and south coasts of Britain; it, too, is rare in Ireland. In severe winters, however, it may be much more widespread, even inland: in 1978/79, for example, about 500 were recorded.

Slavonian *Podiceps auritus* and Black-necked Grebes *P. nigricollis*

Size and Shape Both are small black-and-white grebes intermediate in size between Great Crested *P. cristatus* and Little *Tachybaptus ruficollis*. The simplest way of separating them is by their overall shape and by the extent of black on the head (see below). In shape, Slavonian may suggest a miniature Great Crested, with rather a low forehead, a flat crown and a peak at rear of head. The back, too, is rather flat and rear end tends to taper off towards water's surface; it may, however,

appear rather more fluffed up and rounded when resting. Compared with Slavonian, Black-necked is altogether a more rounded, fluffier-looking bird, with high, steeply sloping forehead with a distinct peak at centre or front of crown. The back, too, is rather more rounded and rear end tends to be held higher and more fluffed out, the whole shape being strongly suggestive of a Little Grebe, with which it often associates.

Bill Slavonian has a straight, pale-tipped bill, whereas Black-necked has an up-tilt to lower mandible, but this may be surprisingly difficult to detect at any distance, particularly on juveniles.

Plumage Even at a distance, Slavonian is a small, strikingly black-and-white grebe, again suggesting a miniature Great Crested. The black cap is sharply demarcated from gleaming white cheeks and it extends straight back from bill, through (but not below) eye; often shows small pale patches on lores (these are usually lacking or at least very tiny on Black-necked). Breast is white and the upperparts dark, blacker than Great Crested, while flanks are mainly whitish. Variable amounts of dark shading may extend around upper foreneck (perhaps strongest on first-winters), but Slavonian is essentially a cleaner, more black-and-white bird than Black-necked. Early-autumn juveniles similar to adults, but rather less clean-cut and may show traces of head striping behind eye and on lower cheeks. Post-juvenile moult continues throughout early winter, so that first-winter and adult birds are soon indistinguishable (same is true of Black-necked). On Black-necked, black of head extends below eye, and ear-coverts and throat are generally dingier, with a lobe of white extending up into black of rear crown. The whitish face contrasts with a dull greyish neck, which in turn contrasts with white breast. The over-

Winter Little Grebe can be pale below, but essentially brown-buff, never black-white.

Winter Slavonian (above) and Black-necked Grebes (left). Note differences in head shape and extent of black on head. Black-necked Grebe puffs up body like Little Grebe.

Black-necked (left) and Slavonian Grebes when alert. Again, note head shape and head patterns.

Black-necked and Slavonian Grebes can be confused with ♀/immature Smew (left) and winter ♂ Ruddy Duck (right).

Note up-tilted bill of Black-necked Grebe (left) and pale-tipped bill of Slavonian Grebe (right). Both features can be difficult to see.

Winter Great Crested (right) and adult winter Red-necked Grebes (left). Note prominent yellow base to bill of Red-necked, and dark cap down to eye. Neck dusky, blackish back and white flank 'flash'.

Great Crested Grebe is much whiter below, has all-pink bill and white between bill and eye.

Great Crested (left) and Red-necked Grebes. Note latter's rounded dark cap and dark upperparts. Great Crested Grebe's head is pointed and shows white before and above eye.

13

Juvenile Red-
necked Grebe.
Rusty neck, remnants
of head stripes.

1st-winter Red-necked Grebe. Yellow
extending towards bill tip. May show
some head stripes.

◀ Juvenile Slavonian
Grebe shows traces
of head stripes.

◀ Winter Slavonian Grebe. Note
angular head and clear-cut
black cap down to eye.
Straight pale-tipped bill.

◀ Early 1st-winter Great Crested
Grebe. Pink bill, extensive
white before eye. Retains
traces of juvenile head
stripes.

Juvenile Black-necked Grebe has
◀ yellowy tint to ear-coverts.
Generally buffy on neck and
breast and may recall
Little Grebe.

◀ Winter Black-necked
Grebe. More clear cut
than juvenile, with
brighter eye. Note shapes
of head and bill and
extent of black on head.

Winter Little Grebe.
Very buff and
brown. Note ▶
stubby bill.

all effect is of a drabber, messier bird than Slavonian. This dingier appearance is especially true of autumn juveniles, which, as well as being slightly browner than winter birds, show dull orangy tint to ear-coverts (often misinterpreted as remnants of summer plumage) as well as dull orangy eyes. (Note that, in spring, winter plumage differences break down as both species start to attain breeding plumage.)

Flight Identification The two species are similar, but Slavonian shows variable amounts of white on inner forewing. On Black-necked, the white on rear of wing extends to inner four or five primaries (confined to secondaries on Slavonian), but differences may be difficult to evaluate on the rapidly-moving wing.

Other Confusion Species Beginners may confuse Slavonian and Black-necked Grebes with other species. Particularly contrasting winter-plumaged Little Grebes may be mistaken for Black-necked, but note Little's essentially brown upper-parts and buff underparts. Great Crested Grebes may be confused with Slavonians, but are larger, longer-necked, browner above, have prominent white superloral line and, most obvious of all, a pink bill. Also, although Great Crested has red eyes, they do not stand out and 'glare' as much as Slavonian's. Distant Slavonians may be confusable with auks, but note latter's short, thick neck, longer body, longer tail and distinctive open-wing diving action. Female and first-winter Smew *Mergus albellus* look particularly scrawny and grebe-like, but concentrate on Smew's larger, rounder head, chestnut crown and grey body plumage. Drake Ruddy Duck *Oxyura jamaicensis* is another species that has been confused in the past, but note small, rounded body, discrete white face patch and, when resting, long tail.

Red-necked Grebe *Podiceps grisegena*

Size and Shape Intermediate in size between Slavonian and Great Crested, but distinctly shorter-necked and stockier than latter.

Bill Has an essentially black, rather dagger-like bill, but the diagnostic feature is *a bright yellow patch at the base*, which is usually prominent, even at long range. On adult, the yellow is restricted to a well-defined, clear-cut patch at base of bill, whereas on juveniles and first-winters it extends more diffusely towards tip, particularly on lower mandible.

Plumage At a distance, perhaps as likely to be confused with Slavonian as with Great Crested, particularly with those Slavonians that show dark shading on neck, and also with spring birds that have started to acquire chestnut neck feathering. Like Slavonian, winter Red-necked has a black cap down to eye, but the cheeks tend to be dingier and greyer; the neck, although variable, is usually a rather dark brownish-grey. Compared with Great Crested Grebe, looks dull and scruffy. Great Crested is always gleaming white below, browner above, has a pinkish bill and an obvious white superloral line. Red-necked is much blacker above and usually shows a striking white flash along upper flanks. Autumn juvenile Red-necked, and even some winter individuals, are decidedly chestnut on neck, a dull reflection of their attractive summer plumage. Early-autumn juveniles retain vestigial head and neck striping.

Diving Actions When feeding in deep water, Red-necked often leaps well clear of surface, rather like Shag *Phalacrocorax aristotelis*. Slavonian and Black-necked tend to spring forward with a quick, dapper action; Great Crested usually submerges smoothly, without leaping. Such differences are not, of course, diagnostic and, in general, the deeper the water the more energetic the diving action.

Great and Cory's Shearwaters

Where and When Great Shearwater is a summer visitor from breeding islands in South Atlantic (principally Tristan da Cunha), reaching British and Irish waters from July to October, with most in August–September; although numerous offshore, it is rarely seen from land, even during strong westerly gales. Perhaps the best way to see them is by joining an organised Atlantic pelagic trip, when they can often be found following trawler fleets. Cory's Shearwater occurs from April to September, with most in July and August, principally off Cornwall and southern Ireland. Annual totals vary: eight in 1972, but 17,000 in 1980.

Great Shearwater *Puffinus gravis*

A large shearwater, nearly as big as Lesser Black-backed Gull *Larus fuscus*.

Flight Has easy, effortless flight, gliding on bowed wings. Tends to fly with quicker, stiffer wingbeats than Cory's, but flight varies with wind force and direction.

Plumage A smarter, more contrasting bird than Cory's, being dark greyish-brown above and contrastingly white below. Easily separated by following features (in rough order of significance). **1** CAP Sharply demarcated dark brown cap (appearing black at any distance), looks 'tipped forward' and contrasts smartly with white throat. **2** COLLAR White collar extends, or appears to extend, around nape. **3** BILL All-black bill. **4** BREAST PATCHES Dark patches at sides of breast (recalling winter or juvenile Black Tern *Chlidonias niger*). At closer range, supplementary features include: **1** brown of

Great Shearwater. Note dark shoulder patch, patterned underwing. ▶

Cory's Shearwater. Note ill-defined brownish crown and pale bill. Upperparts uniform, can show whitish uppertail-coverts. ▶

◀ Great Shearwater. Black cap, dark bill, white collar, contrasting upperwing pattern

Beware of confusing these four species in poor light. Note Cory's Shearwater's languid, gull-like flight. ▼

Manx Shearwater

Fulmar

Cory's Shearwater

Juvenile Gannet

wing-coverts contrasts with blackish wingtips and secondaries (latter browner on Cory's); **2** black markings on underwing-coverts form diagonal black bar across base of underwing; **3** has dark markings on axillaries; and **4** has blackish patch on belly, although this surprisingly difficult to see in the field. Note that, although white tips to uppertail-coverts form a horseshoe-shaped patch above tail, Cory's can also show this feature. Great tends to show more contrasting pale edges to median and greater coverts than Cory's, but, in July/August, moulting Greats may show white bands along upperwing, produced when missing wing-coverts expose white bases to underlying feathers.

Cory's Shearwater *Calonectris diomedea*

Flight Similar to Great in size and shape, but tends to have a slow more languid, gull-like flight on angled, bowed wings which are flexed downwards from carpals. Although it towers in high winds, Great may also do this (as can Fulmar *Fulmarus glacialis*).

Plumage Given a good view, easily separated from Great. A rather featureless shearwater, brown above and white below, but note that: **1** it lacks Great's black cap and white collar, instead showing dusky greyish-brown head that merges more gradually with white throat;

and **2** it has a pale bill (difficult to see at any distance). For other differences from Great see under that species.

Pitfalls Undoubtedly the greatest identification problems occur not with Great Shearwater but with other species. Being a rather featureless shearwater, Cory's is a notorious 'beginner's bird' and the less experienced seawatcher is urged to exercise caution and to claim only those individuals that are seen well. Fulmar provides greatest pitfall, particularly when silhouetted at long range or seen in inclement weather: in these circumstances, Fulmar's characteristic white head and pale primary bases may be impossible to detect, while 'blue-phase' Fulmars would not show these features anyway. In strong winds, Fulmars also bound in high arcs over waves, so pay attention to shape and flight: Fulmars have fat, cigar-shaped bodies and fly with a flap-flap-glide on stiff but slightly bowed wings, inter- spersed with periods of banking and gliding. Another pitfall is provided by Mediterranean Shearwater, which is slightly larger and bulkier than Manx. Paler examples are brown above and dusky-white below but their shape is similar to Manx; they also fly with rapid, stiff-winged shallow strokes, followed by a shearing glide low over waves, banking from side to side. The underwing is dusky-white with brownish tip, trailing edge and axillaries. At close range, the small bill is blackish. Silhouetted Gannets *Sula bassana* can also be confused, but are easily eliminated by their long, narrow, sharply pointed wings, long head-and-bill profile and long, pointed tail. Immature Herring Gull *L. argentatus* and Lesser Black-backed Gull also need to be considered, bearing in mind the rather languid, gull-like flight of Cory's Shearwater.
References Harrison (1983), Sharrock (1980, 1983).

Manx, Mediterranean and Sooty Shearwaters

Where and When Manx Shearwater is an abundant breeding species at selected sites in northern and western Britain and in Ireland; by far the commonest shearwater, and likely to be seen all around coast, mainly March–October. Western Mediterranean race of Mediterranean Shearwater *P. m. mauretanicus*, or 'Balearic Shearwater', is mainly a summer visitor in varying numbers, most likely to be encountered off southern England in July–August. Sooty Shearwater is an uncommon summer visitor from southern hemisphere, reaching British and Irish waters in July–October.

Manx Shearwater *Puffinus puffinus*

Easily identified: strikingly black above and white below, the demarcation being sharply defined. Flies with rapid, stiff-winged strokes, followed by period of shearing, gliding and banking low over waves, alternately revealing upperparts and then underparts. Long wings and the flight instantly separate it from auks, which can appear similarly patterned at distance.

Mediterranean Shearwater *Puffinus mauretanicus*

The taxonomic status of 'Balearic' and 'Levantine' Shearwaters from the Mediterranean has been the subject of recent debate. They have now been split from Manx to form a separate species: 'Mediterranean Shearwater'. Plumage of the western race – 'Balearic Shearwater' – varies quite considerably: most have pale underparts, but much darker individuals are frequent (see under Sooty Shearwater). Most are similar to Manx, but, when directly compared, there are subtle but quite definite differences in size and structure. 'Balearic' is slightly but distinctly larger, with thicker head and neck, shorter tail, bulkier body and longer wings; also, flight appears rather more fluttery. Such differences are, of course, less easy to evaluate without direct comparison with Manx. Paler 'Balearics' are brown above and dusky, brownish-white below, and have brownish, smudgy cap which tends to merge with paler throat. Depending on light, underwings appear whitish, dusky or even silvery, with thick, dark trailing edge.

'Levantine Shearwater' British claims of the eastern Mediterranean race – 'Levantine Shearwater' – *P. m. yelkouan* have never been officially accepted (some

paler 'Balearic Shearwaters' can very closely resemble 'Levantine'). Similar to nominate Manx (but slightly smaller) and shows similar sharp contrast between upperparts and underparts. Instead of being black, however, upperparts are brown, slightly paler than 'Balearic'. Dark head of 'Levantine' seems to lack the white crescent which, on Manx, intrudes into the black, behind ear-coverts.

Sooty Shearwater *Puffinus griseus*

On the face of it, easily identified: an all-dark shearwater with silvery centre to underwing. The problem, however, is dark 'Balearic Shearwaters', some of which are entirely dark grey–brown

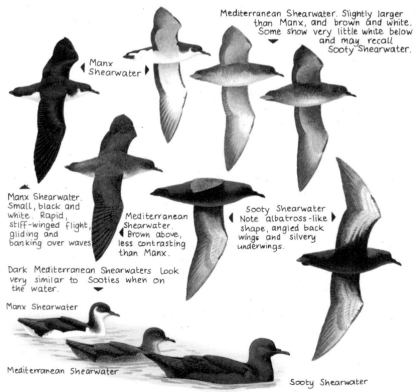

Mediterranean Shearwater. Slightly larger than Manx, and brown and white. Some show very little white below and may recall Sooty Shearwater.

Manx Shearwater

Manx Shearwater. Small, black and white. Rapid, stiff-winged flight, gliding and banking over waves.

Mediterranean Shearwater. Brown above, less contrasting than Manx.

Sooty Shearwater. Note albatross-like shape, angled back wings and silvery underwings.

Dark Mediterranean Shearwaters look very similar to Sooties when on the water.

Manx Shearwater

Mediterranean Shearwater

Sooty Shearwater

below, except for small dusky patch in centre of belly (can be difficult to see and is, of course, invisible when bird sitting on water). Easiest way to separate them is by shape: it is a rather fat, bulky-bodied shearwater, with long, narrow wings usually *angled back from carpals* (at distance, may vaguely suggest dark-phase Arctic Skua *Stercorarius parasiticus*). When flying with strong tail wind, rises high over waves in a series of arcs. 'Balearic' is closer to Manx in shape, so has proportionately thicker, shorter wings which are held more stiffly, less angled back. Although size comparisons particularly difficult at sea, note that, whereas 'Balearic' is only marginally larger and stockier than Manx, Sooty is about 25% as big again.

References Bourne *et al.* (1988), Dubois (1986), Yésou (1986).

Storm, Leach's and Wilson's Petrels

Where and When Storm Petrel is a numerous breeder on northern and western coasts, usually seen from shore only after gales. Leach's Petrel breeds in small numbers off western Scotland and Ireland, but migrants from larger North American colonies occur in late autumn and even winter (during strong gales, large numbers are occasionally 'wrecked'): recently, Merseyside has proved the area where they occur most regularly. During severe gales, Leach's more likely than Storm to be seen inland. Wilson's Petrel, once regarded as a very rare vagrant from southern hemisphere, recently shown by pelagic trips off Cornwall and southern Ireland to be reasonably numerous in western approaches in July–September.

The three are not difficult to identify, *given a good view*, but, since many sightings are during inclement weather, be cautious. Although seawatching experts can separate them by flight alone, less experienced birders should rely more on shape and plumage; also bear in mind difficulties of interpreting and accurately describing flight actions. Particular caution is demanded when identifying Wilson's: join a pelagic trip, when it can often be attracted close to the vessel by the use of 'chum'.

Storm Petrel *Hydrobates pelagicus*

Shape A small petrel (about two-thirds size of Leach's) with square tail and relatively short wings which lack definite angle at carpal joint. Unlike Wilson's, legs short and difficult to see.

Plumage Appears black, with contrasting square white rump. Unlike Leach's and Wilson's, has plain upperwing, lacking prominent pale grey panel across coverts (but *narrow* pale greater-covert bar may be visible at close range, most obvious on fresh juveniles). Most distinctive feature is prominent white line on underwing, obvious when looked for.

Flight Usually seen flying low over water like a bat or hirundine (inland Storm, unlike Leach's, can be quite difficult to pick out from hirundines). Flight fast and fluttery, with quick, flappy wingbeats and short glides. When feeding, patters on surface with wings noticeably raised.

Leach's Petrel *Oceanodroma leucorhoa*

Shape Noticeably larger than Storm; in size and shape resembles a small Black Tern *Chlidonias niger*. Colour and shape may also suggest miniature Arctic Skua *Stercorarius parasiticus* (is sometimes mobbed by Black-headed *Larus ridibundus* and Common Gulls *L. canus*). Has long, pointed wings, noticeably angled back from carpals, and longish forked tail (moulting adults can look slightly rounder-winged, while tail fork can be very difficult to see at any distance).

Plumage Slightly paler than Storm, appearing dark brown. Most distinctive feature is a thick, dirty grey band across upperwing-coverts, also visible at rest; this can, however, largely disappear on moulting adults. White rump narrower than on Storm, is V-shaped when seen from above; narrow dark central bar may be visible at close range, but is often hard to see at distance, when rump itself less obvious than on Storm.

Flight Slower and lazier than Storm, with easy action recalling Black Tern or Nightjar *Caprimulgus europaeus* (it is possible to count each wingbeat). In full flight, sheers up from surface to produce bounding flight, often with sudden changes in speed and direction (again recalls Nightjar). When feeding, hangs over surface with swept-back wings, slightly bowed and flatter than both Storm and Wilson's, then half flies, half walks across surface.

Wilson's Petrel *Oceanites oceanicus*

Shape When seen well, is not difficult to identify, but most observers unfamiliar with species initially find it difficult to pick out from Storm, with which it associates. Distinctly larger than Storm and, although basically similar in shape, wings are more rounded and hence rather paddle-shaped. When most occur (late summer), many are moulting and old outer primaries often project beyond still growing new inners, producing hooked effect to wingtips (most Storm at this time are fresh juveniles). Of particular importance is leg length: long legs prominent when feeding, and often trailed at 45° when flying short distances; in full flight, legs project quite prominently beyond tail (but yellow webs on feet incredibly difficult to see in the field).

Plumage Paler than Storm, looking more faded, but best feature is thick pale

Storm Petrel. Small and Bat-like. Relatively plain-winged. Square rump and tail.

Wilson's Petrel. Note diffuse grey wing-covert panel, paddle-shaped wings. Legs project beyond tail. Underwing bar reduced or lacking. Late summer birds may be in wing moult, giving hooked-wing effect.

Note Storm Petrel's diagnostic white underwing stripe.

Moulting Wilson's Petrel

Feeding Storm Petrel

Wilson's Petrel often dangles legs when moving from one feeding area to another.

Note Leach's Petrel's lazy Nightjar-like flight action on long pointed, angled wings. Note rump and forked tail.

Note long legs and highly raised wings of feeding Wilson's

Leach's Petrel holds wings relatively flat and bowed when feeding.

grey upperwing panel, as on Leach's (and unlike plain-winged Storm). Rump more obvious than on Storm, extends further onto sides, appears to be continuously on view. May show diffuse pale stripe on underwing, but lacks prominent white underwing line of Storm (being a 'negative' feature, lack of this character may not always be immediately apparent).

Flight Full flight vigorous and direct, with rapid wingbeats followed by short glides (recalling Swallow *Hirundo rustica*), often several metres above surface. When feeding, wings are raised high over back in a V (higher than Storm). Feeding flight slower and more butterfly-like than Storm, tends to skip over surface of waves with legs dangling and wings slightly bowed.

Reference Harrison (1983).

Cormorant and Shag

Where and When Cormorant *Phalacrocorax carbo* is common around all British and Irish coasts, as well as on inland waters and larger rivers. Shag *P. aristotelis* is essentially marine, commonest around rocky coastlines in north and west; rare inland. Separating them is not always easy, particularly at distance. Difficulties often arise with out-of-context Shags, particularly inland. A detailed description would then be essential for acceptance.

Size and Structure Most birdwatchers identify Cormorant and Shag by a combination of size, structure and 'jizz'. Cormorant is larger; although it towers above Shag at rest, height difference is emphasised by its tendency to hold head and neck higher. Note, however, that Cormorants exhibit considerable size variation: particularly small females can look remarkably Shag-like if seen in isolation. Cormorant is generally bulkier, heavier and more angular than Shag, particularly when out of water: has thick neck and heavy, angular head; lower forehead and more tapered bill produce rather more wedge-shaped head-and-bill profile overall, differing from Shag's thin parallel bill and steep forehead (although latter flattened when diving). Cormorant has 14 tail feathers, Shag has 12: a surprisingly useful difference when identifying corpses (unless in tail moult). In flight, Cormorant looks heavy and more massive, with relatively larger head, thicker, slightly kinked neck and slow, rather goose-like wingbeats. Shag is slimmer, more scrawny, with smaller head and thinner, straighter neck; its narrower wings and more tapered primaries produce quicker flight action.

Facial Pattern At close range, pay particular attention to facial pattern. On Shag, greeny-yellow bill extends backwards to produce conspicuous greeny-yellow or yellow gape line below and beyond eye; rest of face and throat is usually feathered (throat white in immature and nonbreeding plumages), and green eye isolated within feathering. Cormorant has extensive area of bare skin on lores, face and chin, extending narrowly above and behind eye; on immatures, whole of this area usually brightly coloured, yellow or orange, and individuals with extensive patches can be safely identified as Cormorant (note that Shags never show *orange* on face). Bare skin on Cormorant's lores, however, often obscured by minute black feathering, so some less distinctive than others and, consequently, look more Shag-like, especially at distance. Summer adults may have blackish skin in front of and behind eye, but readily identified by other features.

Plumage *Juvenile/first-winter* Both species very variable, problem compounded by fact that both undergo almost continuous body moult from first autumn until they acquire adult plumage two

Adult summer Cormorant. Heavy head, kinked neck. Goose-like flight. Note whitish 'face' and white flank patch

1st-winter Shag. Eye isolated within feathering. Note steep forehead, evenly slim bill and shape of gape line.

Adult summer Shag. Straight neck, narrow pointed wings. Flies low.

1st-year Shag when worn, shows pale panel across wing-coverts.

1st-winter Cormorant. Bare orange or yellow skin on 'face', enclosing eye. Note heavy wedge-shaped bill.

Winter Cormorant (left) and Shag (right). Note head shapes and back of Cormorant highest towards rear.

1st-winter Cormorants. Note size and head-shape. Underparts white or mottled white.

Two 1st-winter Shags. Small and slim. Note pale throat and uniform brown underparts.

years later. Juvenile/first-winter Cormorant blacker than Shag and *usually much whiter below* (an unidentified individual showing strikingly white underparts will invariably prove to be a Cormorant); some, however, are brown below, on others white is confined mainly to belly, and on many the white looks mottled and moth-eaten. Juvenile/first-winter Shag distinctly browner than Cormorant, often shows paler feathering on foreneck and breast, sometimes extending to belly, but lacks obvious whiteness of most young Cormorants. First-winter Shags with very white underparts are occasionally recorded, so differences not absolute. (Incidentally, Mediterranean race *desmarestii* of Shag normally has extensive white on underparts.) Juvenile/first-winter Shag lacks Cormorant's bronze tint to upperparts, but usually shows noticeable whitish edgings to median and greater coverts; these whiten with bleaching and abrasion so that, by first summer, these feathers can produce conspicuous pale upperwing panel, obvious in flight. Young Shags show pale flesh-brown to yellow-brown foot and tarsus (black on

Cormorant). *Adults and second-years* Adults in summer readily identifiable. Cormorant has yellow face, large white facial and flank patches, blue gloss to head and underparts, and bronze upperparts with dark feather edgings; white filoplumes on head may be conspicuous (see below). Shag has noticeable forehead tuft, yellow gape line and green-glossed plumage. Winter plumage of both is duller. Shags gain pale throat and lose tufts, but some may acquire tufts by early December, while even non-breeding adults (and even some first-winters) may show slightly ragged feathering on forecrown (Cormorants often show slightly ragged feathering on *back* of head). Cormorants lose flank patches and have less obvious white facial patch. Both species become darker with age, so that second-years similar to, but duller and browner than, winter adults.

'Continental Cormorants' Breeding adults of Continental race *sinensis* are whiter-headed than British breeders, but amount of white on latter varies, increasing with age. Older British Cormorants may be very white-headed, are not separable from their Continental counterparts by this feature.

Behaviour Although not diagnostic, behavioural differences useful. Shags tend to fly low over waves and avoid crossing land, whereas Cormorants often fly at some height. Shags often feed in large, dense flocks; Cormorants are rather more solitary when fishing, but roost communally. Both species jump clear of water when diving, but this is particularly marked in Shag (often enters water almost vertically). Shags are often very tame, and an unusually approachable 'Cormorant' is always worth a second look.

Purple Heron

Where and When Purple Heron *Ardea purpurea* is a vagrant in April–October, most in April and May, mainly along east and south coasts of England.

Habitat and Behaviour Much more dependent on reeds than Grey Heron *A. cinerea*. Secretive, often difficult to detect as it stands motionless on edge of reeds. Unlike Grey, often lands on tops of reeds, or in trees and bushes within reedbeds.

Size and Structure Smaller, slighter and narrower-winged than Grey Heron, compared with which looks positively scrawny and rakish. Long, dagger-like orangy-yellow bill appears as continuation of head, while neck long and snakelike. In flight, most obvious feature is deeply pouched appearance of neck, visible even from behind as bird flies away. Feet orangy-yellow, large and conspicuous, protrude prominently behind tail. Tendency for body movement during downstroke of wings.

Call Higher-pitched, quieter and more gruff than Grey's.

Plumage *Adult* At rest, looks dark purply-grey above. Predominantly chestnut head and neck and long black neck stripes should be obvious, allowing instant recognition. Note also chestnut patch at bend of wing, dark purply-chestnut underparts and chestnut thighs. In flight, purply-grey wing-coverts contrast much less with black remiges than on Grey, producing much more uniform impression at distance; chestnut neck should be obvious, but black neck stripes can be surprisingly difficult to detect. Other features include buff patches at carpal joint and reddish-brown panel on underwing-coverts, useful if bird seen from below. *Juvenile* Easily identified and aged by pale sandy-brown upperparts, lack of prominent neck stripes and predominantly brownish crown. In flight, confusion with Bittern *Botaurus stellaris* conceivable: note latter's mottled plumage, thick neck (lacking neck bulge) and generally owl-like appearance. ***First-summer*** Frequently occurs in this country. Following partial post-juvenile moult (body and some wing-coverts) from November to April more similar to adult, but neck stripes less well developed, being browner and less distinct. Wing-coverts remain decidedly brownish, most obvious in flight. ***Second-year and older*** Reaches maturity at three to five years. Older immatures similar to adult, but may show browny tint to greater coverts and poorly defined head plumes.

Melanistic Grey Herons Dark, melanistic Grey Herons (occasionally recorded) should be relatively straight-forward if careful attention paid to structural differences outlined above.

Reference Lansdown (1985).

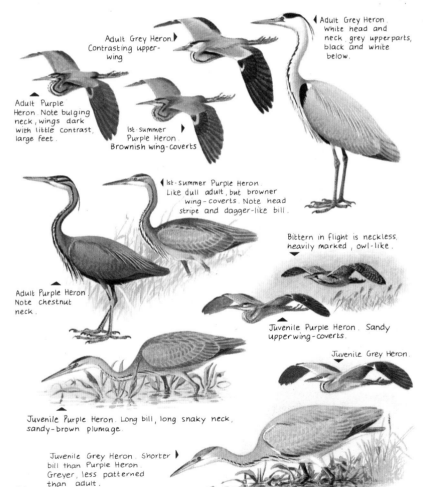

Adult Grey Heron. Contrasting upper-wing

Adult Grey Heron. White head and neck, grey upperparts, black and white below.

Adult Purple Heron. Note bulging neck, wings dark with little contrast, large feet.

1st-summer Purple Heron. Brownish wing-coverts

1st-summer Purple Heron. Like dull adult, but browner wing-coverts. Note head stripe and dagger-like bill.

Adult Purple Heron. Note chestnut neck.

Bittern in flight is neckless, heavily marked, owl-like.

Juvenile Purple Heron. Sandy upperwing-coverts.

Juvenile Grey Heron.

Juvenile Purple Heron. Long bill, long snaky neck, sandy-brown plumage.

Juvenile Grey Heron. Shorter bill than Purple Heron. Greyer, less patterned than adult.

Whooper and Bewick's Swans

Where and When Whooper Swan *Cygnus cygnus* has generally more northerly winter distribution than Bewick's *C. columbianus* and occurs mainly September–April, majority in Scotland (has bred) and Ireland. Bewick's occurs in increasing numbers, October–March, mainly in England and Ireland, with main concentration on Ouse Washes. Mute Swan *C. olor* is widespread resident.

Structure Bewick's is the smallest swan, with the most goose-like proportions. Compared with Whooper, head is more rounded, bill smaller, neck shorter and proportionately thicker. Whooper has long neck, large, wedge-shaped bill and tends to show more bulging breast. Most of these differences also apparent in flight, but great caution then demanded.

Bill Patterns Bewick's has smaller bill, at least half of which is black; amount and shape of yellow at base varies individually, but yellow generally rounder or squarer than on Whooper. On Whooper, yellow extends in sharp point towards tip, so most of bill appears yellow from distance. Bill patterns of juveniles and first-winters vary, generally pale creamy or ivory at base, shading towards flesh-pink at tip; at distance, therefore, young Bewick's can appear to have a large, pointed pale area, recalling Whooper. Bills of both tend to blacken during course of winter and some develop more adult-like bill by spring (particularly Whoopers; many late-winter Bewick's show no adult patterning). Juveniles and first-winters of the two best separated by size and structure, though identification usually facilitated by fact that young normally stay with their parents throughout first winter (many Mute families split up in autumn).

Plumage *Adults* Whoopers often show orangy head staining. *Juveniles* Juveniles are uniformly pale ashy-grey (Whoopers tend to be slightly the darker) and, even when white first-winter feathering appears, still look rather uniform because of overall paleness; indeed, young not always obvious among distant adults (particularly Whoopers, despite fact that they start off darker). Compared with juvenile and first-winter Mute, they are more uniform and much paler and smoother-looking. Juvenile Mute is darker and browner, and gradual appearance of white first-winter body feathering creates uniquely patchy appearance: amount of white attained varies (some still uniformly dull brown in late winter), but usually similar within a brood; in flight, such birds still show patchy contrast between whitish flight feathers and brown wing-coverts and body. Note young Mute's dark grey, black-based bill. Rarely, all-white juvenile Mute Swans (so-called 'Polish Swans') occur.

Calls Bewick's has variety of calls, most softer and more muted than Whooper; perhaps most characteristic is soft, pleasing, rather hollow *oop oop*. Whooper's calls typically louder, deeper and more trumpet-like. Mute occasionally gives deep but quiet, wheezy grunt, a goose-like honk and a loud hiss; in flight, its wings make distinctive rhythmic musical throb.

Distant Separation from Mute Swan Note Mute's generally more curved neck and, particularly, longer, pointed tail; orange bill with black knob visible at some distance. Bewick's and Whoopers are sleeker, do not arch wings in threat like Mute, but engage in trumpeting displays with outstretched necks and open wings.

'Whistling Swan' There are recent British records of Bewick's showing characters of nominate North American race, known as 'Whistling Swan' (bill almost entirely black, often with tiny amounts of yellow at base). When faced with a black-billed Bewick's, very detailed attention should be given to bill (to eliminate possibility of discoloration), and exact pattern of any yellow noted.

Bewick's Swan
Proportions are
goose-like

Whooper Swan. Note
very long neck.

Mute Swan. The
wings make a
rhythmic throbbing
noise in flight.

1st-winter Mute swan
Brown rather than grey,
becomes patchy ▶

Mute Swans ▶
Curved neck
and pointed tail
distinctive.
Arched wings of
'threatening' adult
diagnostic.

◀ Whooper Swans.
Note small head
on long neck,
bulging breast
Extensive yellow
on bill, ending
in point
Head and bill
wedge-shaped.

◀ 1st-winter Whooper Swan
Greyer than Mute Swan
and more uniform.

Bewick's Swans.
More goose-like
build than whooper,
with short neck.
Yellow bill patch
small and generally
more rounded.
1st-winter Bewick's Swans
are paler, greyer and more
evenly-coloured than Mute Swan.

1st-winter Bewick's Swan ▶

Grey Geese

Where and When When identifying geese, it is important to be aware of their main distribution patterns and traditional (separate) wintering areas. Greylag Goose is only species breeding in Britain (in northern Scotland, particularly Outer Hebrides, although introduced birds breed in many other areas, notably south-west Scotland, Lake District, Anglesey, and east and southeast England); wild winter immigrants (about 115,000) occur mainly October–April in north and east-central Scotland. Feral Greylags often occur on lakes, reservoirs and gravel pits. Almost 200,000 Pink-footed Geese winter, mainly in southern and central Scotland, northern England (particularly Lancashire), on the Wash and in north Norfolk; present late September–April, with stragglers into May (even June). White-fronted Goose has two distinct wintering populations. Some 30,000 of Greenland race *flavirostris* winter chiefly in Ireland (mainly the Wexford Slobs) and southwest Scotland (mainly Islay and Mull of Kintyre). Nominate Eurasian race occurs in southern Britain, mainly on inner Severn, and in selected sites in north Kent, Hampshire and Dyfed: about 4000–5000 winter, but numbers may increase considerably in severe winters. Both races arrive October; Russian birds depart mainly March, Greenland birds April. Much rarer Bean Goose winters October–March, mainly in Yare Valley in Norfolk (up to 485), less regularly in Stirling and Kirkcudbright; very small numbers elsewhere, especially during severe freezing. Lesser White-fronted Goose is a real rarity (just about annual), mostly in flocks of Whitefronts at Slimbridge, Gloucestershire. Geese may occur in non-traditional areas and scrutiny of flocks may reveal oddities. They also escape from captivity: always check out-of-context individuals for rings, wing-clipping and unusual tameness.

General characters

Concentrate on bare-part colours, structure and head and neck colour.

Greylag Goose *Anser anser*

The largest, heaviest and most thick-set of the grey geese. Pale, browny-grey with thick-based, heavy orange bill and pink legs. Eastern race *rubrirostris* (may escape) is a paler, cleaner grey, with slightly longer *pink* bill. Many Greylags show traces of black on belly and white feathering around base of bill (vaguely recalling White-front). Lone Greylags can be confused with juvenile White-fronts; note that Eurasian White-front has pink bill and orange legs, opposite to Greylag (Greenland White-front has orange bill and legs). White-front is smaller, slighter, smaller-headed, smaller-billed and generally browner than Greylag.

Pink-footed Goose *Anser brachyrhynchus*

Much smaller and more compact than Greylag, with short, thick neck, rounded head and short, triangular bill. Bill black, crossed with pink band; legs pink. Very dark brown head and neck contrasting strongly with pale, grey-suffused body facilitates distant recognition. Particularly dull and messy first-winters can look less distinctive, but should be identifiable by structure and bare-part coloration, although legs can appear rather duller than adult's. Some adults show traces of white feathering at base of bill.

Bean Goose *Anser fabalis*

Closely related to Pink-foot, but has bright orange legs. Dark bill crossed with orange band which on some extends back along cutting edge, while extreme examples may have much of bill orange. Note, however, that bare-part colour should not be too heavily relied upon (pink and orange

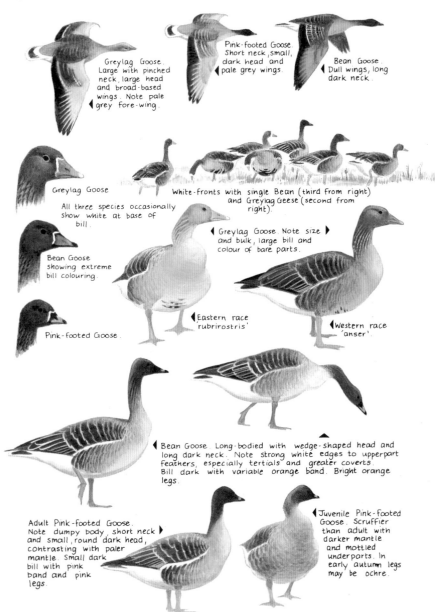

Greylag Goose. Large with pinched neck, large head and broad-based wings. Note pale grey fore-wing.

Pink-footed Goose. Short neck, small, dark head and pale grey wings.

Bean Goose. Dull wings, long dark neck.

Greylag Goose

All three species occasionally show white at base of bill.

Bean Goose showing extreme bill colouring.

Pink-footed Goose.

White-fronts with single Bean (third from right) and Greylag Geese (second from right).

Greylag Goose. Note size and bulk, large bill and colour of bare parts.

Eastern race 'rubrirostris'

Western race 'anser'.

Bean Goose. Long-bodied with wedge-shaped head and long dark neck. Note strong white edges to upperpart feathers, especially tertials and greater coverts. Bill dark with variable orange band. Bright orange legs.

Adult Pink-footed Goose. Note dumpy body, short neck and small, round dark head, contrasting with paler mantle. Small dark bill with pink band and pink legs.

Juvenile Pink-footed Goose. Scruffier than adult with darker mantle and mottled underparts. In early autumn legs may be ochre.

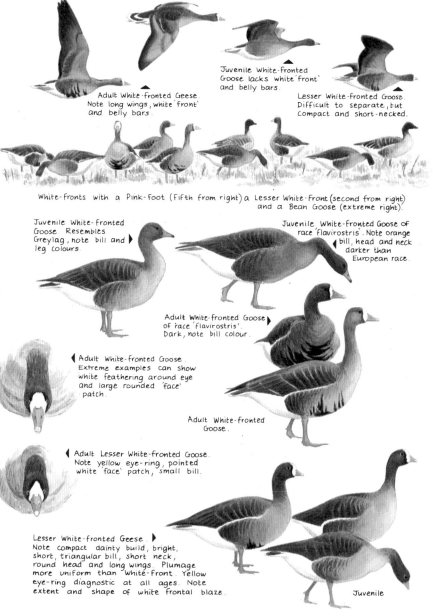

Adult White-fronted Geese. Note long wings, white 'front' and belly bars.

Juvenile White-Fronted Goose lacks white 'front' and belly bars.

Lesser White-fronted Goose. Difficult to separate, but compact and short-necked.

White-fronts with a Pink-foot (Fifth from right) a Lesser White-Front (second from right) and a Bean Goose (extreme right).

Juvenile White-fronted Goose. Resembles Greylag, note bill and leg colours ▶

Juvenile White-fronted Goose of race 'flavirostris'. Note orange bill, head and neck darker than European race.

Adult White-fronted Goose of race 'flavirostris'. Dark, note bill colour. ▶

◀ Adult White-fronted Goose. Extreme examples can show white feathering around eye and large rounded 'face' patch.

Adult White-fronted Goose.

◀ Adult Lesser White-fronted Goose. Note yellow eye-ring, pointed white 'face' patch, small bill.

Lesser White-fronted Geese. ▶ Note compact dainty build, bright, short, triangular bill, short neck, round head and long wings. Plumage more uniform than White-front. Yellow eye-ring diagnostic at all ages. Note extent and shape of white frontal blaze.

Juvenile

can look similar in dull light or at distance). More easily identified by plumage and structure. In contrast to Pink-foot, has long, slender, almost swan-like neck, and long wedge-shaped head-and-bill profile, latter emphasised by mainly dark bill and dark brown head. (Note that smaller tundra race *rossicus*, a regular vagrant, has shorter neck and shorter, deeper-based bill.) Unlike Pink-foot, at distance only head looks really dark and this merges more gradually with pale buffy-brown breast, thereby lacking abrupt contrast between neck and body shown by adult Pink-foot. Body feathers coarsely edged whitish, creating more scaly effect than other geese, while white-edged tertials can be useful for picking out back-on birds among White-fronts. Long 'rear end' gives bird more of a side-to-side swagger when walking. Can show traces of white feathering around base of bill.

White-fronted Goose *Anser albifrons*

Adult easily identified by white facial blaze and black belly barring. Greenland race rather darker than Eurasian but, despite different bill colour, can be difficult to separate except in favourable circumstances. Juveniles lack both facial blaze and belly barring and lone individuals can look bland, confusable with Greylag; concentrate on bare-part colours and structure. First-winters may acquire white 'front'.

Lesser White-fronted Goose *Anser erythropus*

Not only the rarest grey goose, but potentially the most problematical. To find Lesser White-front generally requires prolonged patient scrutiny of White-front flocks and, without previous experience, difficult to pick out. Adult's more extensive white blaze and yellow eye-ring can be obscured at distance, so other clues needed. Blaze extends well up forehead, but shape of the white may be of use: viewed front-on, is narrow and usually forms point on forehead (blaze more rounded on most White-fronts, but some do show more pointed blazes). Structure particularly important: smaller than White-front, with shorter and proportionately thicker neck (perhaps suggesting Pink-foot), while bill small, delicate, rather triangular, and generally brighter pink than White-front's. Head and neck slightly darker, with practice a useful character, particularly coupled with plainer body plumage and smaller area of black on belly. More subtle characters include slightly longer wings, quicker feeding action. Juvenile particularly difficult but, as with adults, combination of shape, structure, head and neck colour and yellow orbital ring is most useful. Most first-winters acquire white forehead blaze, similar in shape to adults', but slightly smaller. Before identifying Lesser White-front, essential to note *all* differences, particularly structural. Some White-fronts show particularly large white blazes, some even show yellow eye-rings; occasional individual shows white feathering around eyes which, at distance, may suggest yellow orbital ring of Lesser. Sleeping White-fronts reveal pale eyelids which, momentarily, can suggest the rarer species.

Flight patterns and calls

Geese can be identified in flight by combination of structure, forewing colour and calls, although latter require practice (since much variation). Greylags are heavy and thick-set with large head sometimes emphasised by 'pinched-in' neck; forewings strikingly pale grey, and loud honking calls recall domestic goose. Pink-feet look very short-necked and are rather small; dark head contrasts conspicuously with pale body, and forewings noticeably grey (but not so pale as Greylag); calls higher-pitched, include particularly distinctive, double *ang-ank*. White-fronts are rather evenly proportioned, have dull grey forewings; adults show black belly barring and white forehead blaze; calls yelping and rather musical, especially in flock. Bean have dullest forewings, lacking obvious contrast between wing-coverts and flight feathers; calls resemble those of Pink-feet, but lower-pitched.

Other Confusion Species

Beware escaped geese (such as blue-phased Snow *A. caerulescens*, Bar-headed *A. indicus* and Swan Geese *A. cygnoides*), as well as hybrids (such as Canada *Branta canadensis* x Greylag and Snow x Barnacle *B. leucopsis*) which may show peculiar combinations of plumage and bare-part coloration.

Reference Ogilvie & Wallace (1975).

Eclipse Male, Female and Juvenile Dabbling Ducks

Introduction: Moults

The identification of male dabbling ducks in full plumage is straightforward, but eclipse males, females and juveniles are more difficult and require considerable practice. Problem is most acute in late summer, when a bewildering amount of variation. In mid summer, adult males lose their distinctive finery and acquire an eclipse plumage that camouflages them during the period of flightlessness. Eclipse males, though similar to females, are easily separable in most species, but identification complicated because of individual variation and because different males are often in different stages of moult into and out of eclipse. Juveniles are generally similar to adult females, and their separation is not so easy as it is, for example, for most waders. Also, they remain in juvenile plumage for a relatively short period before starting a partial and variable body moult in which a certain amount of 'first-winter' plumage is acquired, prior to moulting into adult-like plumage usually in late autumn/early winter. First-year males moult into full plumage slightly later than adult males, and are usually less immaculate. Some species, for example Shoveler, do not acquire full male plumage until at least the following spring. It must be stressed, however, that moults and ageing of wildfowl have not been well studied, so details outlined below are, to a certain extent, tentative.

Wigeon *Anas penelope* and American Wigeon *A. americana*

Where and When Wigeon breeds mainly in Scotland and northern England, with small numbers in eastern England; Continental immigrants appear in late summer and, by mid winter, it is one of our most numerous dabbling ducks, congregating on coast and on lakes and floodwaters. American Wigeon is a rare vagrant, mainly in autumn and winter; occasionally occurs in small parties (as many as 13 were seen together in Co. Kerry in 1968).

WIGEON

General Features A stocky, short-necked duck with steep forehead, small grey bill (tipped black) and pointed tail. In winter, typically grazes on land, often in large flocks and often with Coots *Fulica atra*. Newly arrived late-summer migrants, however, tend to feed on water weed with Coots and Gadwall, when very white belly obvious when up-ending. Male has diagnostic, *wee-oo* whistle, female a grating growl.

Flight Identification Looks stocky and short-necked, with pointed tail. Often flies at some height, frequently in large flocks or bunches. Adult male easily identified by huge white patch on wing-coverts. Female's wing plainer, with obscure speculum faintly bordered with

♀ Gadwall. Broad-winged, white belly patch. ▶

♀ Mallard. Bulky body, dark belly. Blue speculum bordered white. ▶

♂ Gadwall. ▶ Greyish, black rump, small white wing 'flashes'.

♀ Wigeon. Wings centrally placed, stocky body, pointed tail. Lighter grey forewing. ▼

♀ Gadwall. White wing 'flash', plain-faced, greyer wings. ▶

1st-winter ♂ Wigeon lacks white wing-coverts of adult ♂. ▼

◀ ♀ Wigeon. Darkish underwing, white belly patch.

♀ Shoveler. Wings set well back, long bill. Belly brown. ▼

Eclipse ♂ Wigeon. Chestnut, white forewing ◀

♀ Shoveler. ▶ Grey forewing.

♀ Teal. Small, compact, short neck. Wader-like flight. Prominent white bar across greater coverts. ▶

♀ Teal. Note underwing pattern. ▲

◀ ♀ Garganey. Dark leading edge to underwing. Patterned head.

♀ Pintail. Long-bodied, narrow-winged. ▲

◀ ♀ Garganey. Paler upperwing than Teal, bold white wing stripes.

◀ ♀ Pintail. Pale, long thin neck and pointed tail. Obvious white trailing edge to speculum.

♂ Garganey. Pale forewing, bold white border to speculum.

white. Both female and first-year male lack white forewing patch, but may show paler area which intensifies with wear. White belly patch obvious.

Plumage *Adult female* Plumage tone varies considerably; most are predominantly dark reddish-brown, slightly browner or greyer on head. At close range, head is peppered blackish (difficult to see at any distance). Others have paler, more orangy-brown body and rather greyer head. Wing-covert feathers blackish or greyish with narrow white feather edgings, although they may whiten with age and wear. *Adult male eclipse* Similar to female, but head and body rich, deep rufous. Unlike female, shows grey vermiculation on mantle and may show hint of a paler forehead; also, tertials black, noticeably edged white (browner-edged on females and juveniles). Adult male easily sexed as retains white wing-covert patch. *Juvenile* Very similar to typical adult female, but slightly drabber and neater, with slightly paler, more fulvous breast and flanks, and with slightly narrower edgings to upperpart feathers. Mantle appears, therefore, darker and more uniform than on adult female, and breast more uniform and only lightly spotted. Differences, however, rather subtle in field. *First-year* Young males acquire adult-like plumage during first winter and most are largely in full plumage by New Year, although often less immaculate. Juvenile wing-coverts retained until one year old (although whiten with wear).

AMERICAN WIGEON

General Features Similar to Wigeon, but tends to look larger-headed, with steeper forehead, and slightly longer tail.

Plumage *Adult female* Superficially similar to Wigeon, but head has pale greyish-white background, and is liberally and quite noticeably peppered with coarse black spotting. A darker area around eye

may also be noticeable. Pale, spangled head contrasts quite noticeably with body, which, compared with most Wigeon, is rather paler, more fulvous-brown or orangy-brown. In comparison, darker head and neck of Wigeon do not contrast with the body and, because of the darker, browner background colour, dark peppering does not stand out in field. When faced with a potential American Wigeon, check axillaries: *on American they are gleaming white* (on Wigeon vermiculated grey, giving overall grey effect in field). Close examination essential, and detailed notes should be taken: prolonged close-range observation should reveal further subtle differences. **1** BREAST American has more coarsely mottled breast. **2** MANTLE AND SCAPULARS American has thicker feather edgings which, being slightly paler, make upperparts look more coarsely patterned. **3** WING-COVERTS On American generally much whiter, often forming subdued whitish patch on open wing, mirroring that of adult male. **4** RUMP Tends to be more contrasting on American, feathers being dark brown, edged whitish (on Wigeon, feathers usually dark brown, edged brownish, thus rump looks more uniform, but some also show pale feather edgings). **5** PRIMARY LENGTH On American, primary tips reach tip of uppertail-coverts (Wigeon is longer-winged, primary tips extending about 1cm beyond uppertail-coverts). *Eclipse male* Some look practically identical to adult female, but easily sexed by white wing-covert patch. Most, however, while similar to female, show subdued version of full-plumaged head pattern, with diffuse broad green band extending back from eye. Vermiculated grey feathering should be present on mantle and scapulars. *Juvenile and first-year* By time they reach Europe, young American Wigeon should have acquired 'first-winter' feathering and thus appear similar to adult female. Juvenile/first-winter female apparently

Eclipse ♂ Mallard. Resembles ♀, but yellowish bill, dark crown and rustier breast

♀ Mallard Note bill pattern rich brown coarsely marked plumage Orange legs.

Juvenile ♂ Mallard Bill quickly begins to turn yellow.

Differences in tail position of up-ending Mallard (left) and Gadwall (right) sometimes useful.

Gadwall shows whiter vent when up-ending.

Juvenile Mallard. Darker than ♀, neater markings on breast.

Juvenile Gadwall. Smaller than Mallard, plainer, greyer head. Note bill pattern. Breast neatly streaked, belly speckled.

Adult ♀ Gadwall Smaller, greyer than Mallard, coarse breast markings, white belly patch. Note bill pattern, white wing 'flash', yellow legs.

Eclipse ♂ Gadwall. Richer brown than ♀, greyer head and tertials. Note bill pattern.

Juvenile Pintails are very variable, some ♂♂'s resemble adult ♂ in eclipse.

Adult ♂ Pintail in eclipse. Note finely patterned plumage, rusty head. Belly almost plain. Note bill pattern and grey legs.

Adult ♀ Pintail. Plain, pale head, long slender neck, coarsely marked body. Bill blackish.

Wigeon shows small grey bill, steep forehead, rounded head, stocky body and pointed tail Note white belly patch in all plumages.

◀ Eclipse ♂ Wigeon Deep chestnut, retains white forewing

♀ Wigeon Variable. Breast and flanks dull chestnut to orange Head varies from brownish to greyish.
▼

♀ Wigeon ▶

Juvenile Wigeons are darker above, plainer, more orange on ▶ flanks Breast almost unmarked.

Adult ♂ American Wigeon in eclipse. Some very similar to ♀, but most retain green stripe behind eye, which contrasts with the whitish-grey head Orangy breast and flanks paler than ▶ ♂ Wigeon.

In flight, note diagnostic white axillaries of American Wigeon (left) The Wigeon (right) has greyish axillaries.

Adult ♀ American Wigeon Very similar to some Wigeons, but note pale greyish-white head peppered darker, dark shadow around eye, ▶ orangy breast and flanks Always check colour of axillaries.

has wing-coverts similar to female Wigeon, whereas young male shows more white, particularly on inner lesser and median coverts and on greater coverts. Like Wigeon, first-year males should usually start to show adult-like plumage by late autumn/early winter, but they also fail to acquire white forewing patch.

Wigeon x Chilöe Wigeon Hybrids When identifying American Wigeon, it is advisory to eliminate possibility of hybrids. Wigeon x American Wigeon has not been recorded in Britain and Ireland, but there must be a possibility of such birds eventually occurring. There have, however, been wild records of Wigeon x Chilöe Wigeon *A. sibilatrix* (a South American species, frequently kept in wildfowl collections). These hybrids involved males, and showed superficial resemblance to adult male American Wigeon, but forehead yellower and cut-off squarely, while green head bands coalesce on rear crown (on American, they meet on lower nape, the flecked creamy crown extending in point down back of head and nape). The hybrid also shows Chilöe's black-centred feathering on mantle and scapulars, although this may be inconspicuous.

Reference Harrison & Harrison (1968).

Mallard *Anas platyrhynchos*

Where and When A familiar, abundant resident throughout Britain and Ireland, numbers augmented in winter by visitors from northern Europe.

General Features Should act as a yardstick when identifying other members of genus. The largest and bulkiest dabbling duck, on the water appears rather round-backed. Head also rounded, and longish bill forms continuous curve with head. Most familiar call is female's *quack*, or variations thereof; male has soft, nasal *raab* and high-pitched whistle and grunt in courtship.

Flight Identification A bulky duck, with broad wings that produce soft whistl-ing; speculum bright blue, narrowly bordered with black and white. Underparts uniformly brown, lacking white belly patch (cf. Gadwall); creamy underwing-coverts contrast with darker remiges and brown body.

Plumage *Adult female* Basically a pale creamy-brown duck, boldly mottled and patterned with darker brown. Facial pattern variable, most have pale supercilium and narrow dark eye-stripe. Domesticated varieties may be plainer or, conversely, may show striking white supercilium and sometimes dark bar across lower lores. Bill colour also variable: most show orange across tip and often at base, but some show extensive orange sides to bill, recalling Gadwall (but rarely as clear-cut); some domesticated types may lack orange altogether. Tail noticeably white, and ventral region predominantly brown when up-ending (cf. whitish belly of Gadwall). *Eclipse male* Easily separated from adult female, as it retains wholly yellow bill (although a proportion have blue-green bill). Unlike female, crown and eye-stripe are blackish, glossed green. Underparts more cinnamon in tone, and breast rather rusty, strongly mottled with black. Rump and uppertail-coverts remain blackish (patterned brown and black on female). *Juvenile* Tends to look smaller and scrawnier than adult, shape can suggest Gadwall. Plumage similar to adult female, but generally fresher and neater, while overall tone a darker, deep orange-brown. Easily separated from adult female as 1 crown and eye-stripe are black (like eclipse male) and 2 underparts, particularly breast, are neatly streaked (more spotted or mottled on female, coarsely mottled on eclipse male). Juveniles have more extensive diffuse orange on sides of bill, sometimes including most of upper surface. Juvenile males soon develop adult-like bill colour, the bill turning dull green, greeny-yellow and then yellow.

Gadwall *Anas strepera*

Where and When An increasingly common resident in much of Britain, the population stemming mainly from escapes and introductions; scarcer in Ireland. Small influx of Icelandic and Continental immigrants in winter. Occurs mainly on lakes and gravel pits.

General Features Superficially similar to Mallard, but smaller, less bulky, shorter-necked, flatter-backed and squarer-headed. Bill shorter and narrower, projecting from steeper forehead. Both Mallard and Gadwall usually bend tail away from wingtips when up-ending, but Gadwall sometimes holds wings and tail together in a vertical plane, producing different profile when viewed from side. Male's call a peculiar nasal *angh* and also a high-pitched wheezing whistle; female gives a quack, quieter and slightly higher-pitched than Mallard.

Flight Identification White speculum obvious on male, but often reduced to two inner secondaries on female, or occasionally even lacking; on male, speculum virtually surrounded by black, and has thick chestnut panel across median coverts. Looks smaller and slighter than Mallard, with obvious clear-cut white belly (except on juvenile). When courting or defending territory, engages in high aerial pursuits, often accompanied by male's whistling call.

Plumage *Adult female* Similar to Mallard, but less buff, colder and greyer, particularly about head. White speculum may be visible at rest, but note that moulting Mallards in late summer may occasionally show white feathering in this area. Conspicuous clear-cut orange sides to bill distinctive (unusual on Mallard). Tail shows very little white compared with Mallard. When up-ending, belly noticeably white, contrasting with browner undertail-coverts (whole of underparts browner on Mallard). Legs yellower than

on Mallard. *Eclipse male* Similar to adult female, gaining orange sides to bill. Head pattern rather more diffuse (crown and eye-stripe greyish), and tertials pale grey (blackish-grey on female). Easily sexed by reference to open wing, which retains chestnut and black of full plumage. *Juvenile* Quite easy to age by rather orangy breast, which is neatly and evenly *streaked* black, forming lines (mottled on female). Crown and eye-stripe clear-cut and black (usually less well defined and greyer on female); delicately speckled greyish face contrasts markedly with breast. Overall, looks darker and more uniform and has neater, fresher plumage than adult female (messy and mottled in comparison). Lacks female's clear-cut white belly, which instead is heavily spotted. Sexing of juveniles not easy, as juvenile male's open wing similar to female's, having less black and chestnut than adult male's.

Pintail *Anas acuta*

Where and When A rare breeding bird, mainly in northern and eastern areas. Finished breeders start to reappear July onwards; numerous in winter, with largest concentrations on various estuaries, particularly in northwest England.

General Features Rather slim, with long pointed tail projecting well beyond wingtips. Neck long and slender compared with Mallard and Gadwall; head rather rounded, and bill longish and slim. Male has distinctive disyllabic nasal whistle in display; female rather silent, but has high-pitched quack.

Flight Identification Looks a rather slim-bodied, long-necked duck with long, pointed tail, wings set towards rear of body. Speculum obscure, green on male, brownish on female, bordered by dark buff in front and white behind, *latter forming conspicuous white trailing edge to secondaries*. Wing-coverts plain grey on male, mottled buff on female.

Plumage *Adult female* At distance, a pale buffish duck with plain, featureless head (often strongly tinged with ginger). Upperparts and flanks thickly spangled with whitish or golden, latter showing strong dark chevrons; belly whitish. Bill blackish-grey, with some diffuse grey at base. *Eclipse male* Easily sexed by clear-cut grey sides to bill. Plumage variable, some paler and greyer overall than female, with finer, more delicate markings, particularly on breast and flanks. Mantle vermiculated grey, and long, pointed rear scapulars black, often thickly edged with grey; tertials also predominantly grey. Others have breast and flanks more coarsely patterned like female's. Males starting to acquire full plumage may look plainer and greyer at distance. *Juvenile* Similar to adult female, but variable, some more neatly patterned and less coarsely marked. In particular, mantle and scapulars generally more uniformly blackish, less coarsely patterned with buff; breast and belly whitish, tend to be finely streaked or spotted compared with adult female, while flanks may be neatly patterned with dark chevrons. Bill paler than adult female's, dull greyish, but juvenile male soon starts to acquire adult pattern, although less clear-cut. Sexed by reference to open wing (corresponds to adults').

Teal *Anas crecca*

Where and When A numerous breeding bird (scarcer in southwestern England); abundant in winter, large concentrations on coast and inland. American race *carolinensis* ('Green-winged Teal') is a vagrant, mainly in autumn, winter and early spring.

General Features A very small dabbling duck with short neck and small, narrow bill. Rather grey and featureless, but note short, narrow white streak on outermost undertail-coverts, immediately adjacent to tail. A quick, lively, nervous duck, often seen dabbling on mud or in shallow water,

frequently among partially submerged vegetation. Male has diagnostic high-pitched *crink crink* call, female a quiet quack.

Flight Identification Easily identified by small size, short neck, compact body, narrow pointed wings and quick actions. Often forms tight flocks that twist and turn like waders. Open wing has *thick white bar across greater coverts*, immediately in front of predominantly bright green speculum, white trailing edge to which narrower and less obvious; male's forewing dull grey, female's brown.

Plumage *Adult female* Featureless, with plain head, relieved only by obscure dark eye-stripe. Plumage tone varies from greyish to brown, coarsely mottled. Bill grey, but may show small amount of orange or yellow at base. *Eclipse male* Not readily separable from female except by open wing (see above), but some show strong ruddy tint to head. Others have slight cinnamon tint to head and underparts; can be more spotted with black on lower breast. Like female, may also show orange at base of bill. *Juvenile* Similar to female, but plumage immaculate, neatly streaked or spotted on breast and neatly patterned on flanks; belly smooth and creamy, not so well defined as adult. Adults in comparison look messy and rather coarsely patterned.

'Green-winged Teal' Full-plumaged male easily identified by vertical white stripe down side of breast; lacks horizontal white stripe on scapulars shown by nominate race. Shows less of a buff border to green head patch.

Garganey *Anas querquedula*

Where and When Unlike other members of genus, a summer visitor and rare breeder (mainly in eastern England); more numerous (though by no means common) on migration, in March–May and July–September, with stragglers into November and rarely in winter.

Adult ♀ Teal Small, dark grey·brown duck. Featureless 'face'. Usually shows slight orange at base of bill Note white stripe down sides of undertail-coverts.

Juvenile Teal Similar to ♀ but darker with neater streaking below.

Dull Garganey (left) and Teal (right). Note subtle differences in shape

Adult ♀ Garganey Note pale supercilium, pale loral spot and dark line across 'cheeks'.

Eclipse ♂ Garganey. Note grey forewing and white speculum border.

Juvenile Garganey Similar to ♀ but darker and neatly streaked below, often with cinnamon tint to underparts. Some virtually lack dark 'cheek' bar

Blue-winged Teal

Cinnamon Teal

♀ Blue-winged Teal Plain 'face', white eye-ring and pale loral spot. Thin dark eyestripe.

Juvenile ♀ Cinnamon Teal may show head pattern similar to ♀ Blue-winged Teal. Note warmer plumage tones, finer breast streaks, long spatulate bill.

Adult ♀ Cinnamon Teal. Very plain 'face'. Note bill shape and plumage tone.

39

General Features Slightly but distinctly larger, bulkier and longer-bodied than Teal, and, on water, rear end is held higher. Bill also longer than Teal's. Feeds mainly by head-immersion, with little up-ending. Rather silent, but male has distinctive rattling burp in breeding season, female a short, sharp quack.

Flight Identification Similar to Teal, but looks longer-bodied. Male easily identified by pale chalky-grey forewing; green speculum is thickly and evenly bordered with white, forming two parallel white lines. Juvenile male similar, but forewing slightly duller and white lines slightly narrower. Female less distinctive, with dull grey forewing; also has white borders to speculum, but front bar usually (not always) faint, and hind bar wider, *forming distinctive white trailing edge to secondaries, recalling Pintail*. Note that, on Teal, front bar is the wider and more conspicuous. Has darker leading edge to underwing-coverts than Teal. Distinctive head pattern may be obvious in flight, while juveniles may show distinctly fulvous underparts.

Plumage *Adult female* Similar to Teal, but generally paler and buffer and more coarsely patterned. Easily identified by head pattern. Unlike plain-faced Teal, has *prominent, clear-cut whitish supercilium*, highlighted by dark crown and eye-stripe. Also has noticeable whitish loral spot and throat patch, separated by a dark line across lower lores, which often extends back to form dark bar across cheeks: *on some, however, bar inconspicuous or even lacking*, thus prompting confusion with Blue-winged Teal (see below). Tertials blackish, thinly but noticeably edged pure white (thus appear quite contrasty). *Adult male eclipse* Very similar to adult female, but easily sexed by open wing. Unlike most other dabbling ducks, remains in eclipse for a long time, first signs of new feathering not appearing until late October (full plumage not acquired until mid winter). *Juvenile* Similar to adult female, but less

well-defined belly patch; whole underparts usually tinged orangy-brown, neatly streaked down breast and neatly patterned on flanks (patterning bolder than on Teal). Overall, plumage fresh and immaculate, less coarsely patterned than adult female. White borders to speculum narrower.

Blue-winged Teal *Anas discors*

Where and When An American vagrant, mainly in April–May and Aug–Oct.

Identification In many ways intermediate in appearance between Teal and Garganey; longer-billed than Teal. Overall plumage tone greyer than Garganey, but strongly patterned with buff particularly on flanks. Head pattern distinctive: prominent whitish loral spot (generally larger and more prominent than on Garganey), and note in particular that *Blue-winged has noticeable broken white eye-ring* (which Garganey lacks); has weaker supercilium than Garganey and lacks latter's dark bar across lower lores and cheeks (bar is, however, a variable feature on Garganey, and lacking on some). Before identifying Blue-winged, check open-wing pattern and leg colour. 1 OPEN WING On Blue-winged, wing similar to that of Shoveler. Male has bright blue forewing (thus brighter and bluer than chalky-grey forewing of male Garganey), with thick white greater-covert bar; unlike Garganey, *has no white trailing edge to secondaries* (this should always be clearly established). Female's wing similar to male's, but blue slightly duller, greater-covert bar is obscure (feathers grey, edged white) and speculum is blacker. 2 LEG COLOUR Yellowish on Blue-winged (brightest on male; grey on Teal and Garganey), but can be dull, particularly on young birds. Juvenile Blue-winged is unlikely to occur in this country, as most have at least some female-like 'first-winter' feathering by the time they turn up. Like Garganey, this plumage is retained for several months; adult males do not start to acquire full plumage until early winter, and first-year males not until at least mid winter. First-year male has white greater-covert bar, with small dusky spots on feather tips.

Cinnamon Teal *A. cyanoptera* Before identifying Blue-winged, this important pitfall species must be eliminated. A western North and South American duck which has escaped from waterfowl collections and caused confusion. As Blue-winged, but even females, eclipse males and juveniles *show distinctive pale cinnamon tint to whole plumage* (very intense on some adult females and eclipse males, becoming almost ruddy on breast); belly, too, has cinnamon tint, so less clear-cut than Blue-winged. Like Blue-winged, has conspicuous white eye-ring, but otherwise head plain. Some lack dark eye-stripe, while others show relatively faint one (sometimes more obvious before eye, sometimes behind). Even strongly patterned individuals look plainer-headed than Blue-winged, and always have bland, pleasant and gentle facial expression. Because of relative lack of eye-stripe, it lacks obvious supercilium. Pale loral spot smaller and less obvious than on Blue-winged, but diffuse pale coloration sometimes extends to upper lores, before the eye. Bill slightly longer, broader and more spatulate than Blue-winged. Adult male has orange or reddish eye (even in eclipse); Blue-winged always dark-eyed.

Shoveler *Anas clypeata*

Where and When A widespread but localised breeder, commonest in eastern England. Much more numerous outside breeding season, with first returning breeders arriving in mid summer; peak numbers in October/November, rather than mid winter.

General Features A rather dumpy, short-necked duck, about three-quarters size of Mallard. Easily identified by huge spatulate bill. Bright orange legs always conspicuous on land. Feeds by dabbling on surface, often in large packs, or by up-ending, when combination of slightly orangy-brown underparts and distinctly pointed tail are noticeable differences from Mallard, Gadwall and Pintail. May persistently dive in shallow water, using open-wing action. Very distinctive deep, throbbing wingbeats on take-off. Rather silent, but male gives quiet *took*, while female makes quacking noises.

Flight Identification A scrawny duck with long bill and narrow neck; wings narrow, set far back. Often flies at some height, like *Aythya* ducks. Male has bright blue forewing, offset by thick white bar across greater coverts, and lacks prominent white trailing edge to secondaries. First-year male has slightly duller forewing. Female's forewing dull grey, and white greater-covert bar may be virtually absent. Note dark belly.

Plumage *Adult female* Pale, coarsely patterned buffy-brown duck. Buffish head rather plain, eye-stripe petering out behind eye. Eye dull greenish or yellowish; faint eye-ring. Bill orange at base and diffusely across upper surface. Tail predominantly white. *Eclipse male* Completely different from female, with *rich orange-buff tone to flanks and belly*; at distance, underparts may appear deep orange. Head greyish, *manic yellow eye standing out conspicuously* (female eye dark). Upperparts plain, blackish, while two narrow white edgings to black tertials also stand out conspicuously. Bill develops orange at sides in summer. Later in autumn, some males develop 'supplementary' feathering, acquiring variable amounts of white on breast and rear flanks, large whitish crescent before eye. *Juvenile* Looks drabber than adult female, less buff and less coarsely patterned, plumage neat and immaculate. Mantle darker and more uniform, with narrow feather edgings; head greyish with

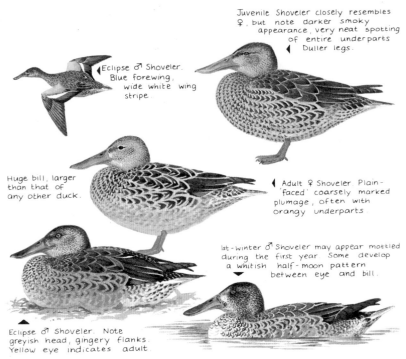

Juvenile Shoveler closely resembles ♀, but note darker smoky appearance, very neat spotting of entire underparts. Duller legs.

Eclipse ♂ Shoveler. Blue forewing, wide white wing stripe.

Huge bill, larger than that of any other duck.

Adult ♀ Shoveler. Plain-'faced' coarsely marked plumage, often with orangy underparts

1st-winter ♂ Shoveler may appear mottled during the first year. Some develop a whitish half-moon pattern between eye and bill.

Eclipse ♂ Shoveler. Note greyish head, gingery flanks. Yellow eye indicates adult.

pale eye-ring; underparts dark orangy-brown, delicately and neatly spotted or streaked with black. Bill smaller than adult's, and may suggest Cinnamon Teal. *First-year* Unlike other common first-year dabbling ducks, male Shoveler retains much immature plumage throughout winter, gradually acquiring adult-like plumage towards spring (some retain traces of immaturity even later). 'First-winter' male similar to eclipse male, but has dull eye colour; also, head buffer and underparts less orange, more cinnamon in tone. Blue forewing duller than adult's.

Aythya Ducks: Scaup, Ring-necked Duck, Ferruginous Duck and Hybrids

Where and When Scaup is a localised winter visitor, mainly in northern coastal areas, though small numbers occur right around coastline, and a few inland (particularly October–December and March–May); very rare in summer. Ring-necked Duck is a very rare North American vagrant throughout Britain and Ireland; it currently averages some 17 records a year (mainly October–May). Ferruginous Duck is very rare East European visitor, usually in winter and mainly in eastern England.

The Problem of *Aythya* Hybrids

Identification of unusual *Aythya* ducks is complicated by the frequent occurrence of hybrids. These vary greatly, but tend to fall into distinct categories: those illustrated represent the main types, and it must be stressed that many different plumage and structural combinations occur. In most cases an educated guess at a hybrid's parentage can be made: many are more or less 'half-and-half', some show distinct characters of one parent but not the other, but a few resemble a different species altogether. Remember also that some hybrids are escapes from captivity: one seen on an English reservoir was thought to have been a Tufted Duck *A. fuligula* x New Zealand Scaup *A. novaeseelandiae*. Before identifying an unusual *Aythya*, thorough familiarity with all plumages of the three commonest species – Tufted Duck, Pochard *A. ferina* and Scaup – and an awareness of individual variability are essential. Never claim a rare *Aythya*, no matter how distinctive it may appear, without having checked your notes against detailed texts and photographs. Better still, visit a good wildfowl collection and familiarise yourself with the more obscure confusion species. When faced with a difficult *Aythya*, concentrate on bill-tip pattern, bill-and-head shape, overall size and structure, eye colour, back and flank colour, and wingstripe. The less common *Aythya* species and their potentially confusable hybrids are outlined below. Female hybrids are less well known and tend to be overlooked; details of hybrids therefore refer to adult males unless otherwise stated.

Scaup *Aythya marila*

General Features A large, bulky, broad-beamed *Aythya*, obviously larger than Tufted and about size of Pochard. Bill long and broad, and head evenly rounded at rear with no hint of a tuft. White wingstripe fades to grey on outer primaries, similar to Tufted. When diving, often leaps more strongly than Tufted.

Plumage *Adult male* Very pale whitish-grey mantle (delicate vermiculations visible only at close range) and white flanks create very whitish impression at distance. Pale blue bill has small black tip restricted to oval nail (inconspicuous in the field). *Eclipse male* Like very dull full male. Blacks duller, back and flanks greyer and less even. Large pale crescent develops on lower ear-coverts. *Adult female summer* Rather a paler, richer brown than Tufted, especially on flanks. Large white facial blaze striking (some female Tufted show white blaze, but never as large as on adult female Scaup). Large whitish patch on lower ear-coverts is another conspicuous difference from Tufted. Bill less blue than male's, but also shows small black nail. *Adult female winter* Strong grey vermiculations appear on mantle and flanks. White ear-covert patch usually lost (some retain trace). *Juvenile* Many autumn migrants are juveniles (plumage retained into October–November). Similar to adult female summer, but large white facial blaze replaced by dull white or buffish-white oval patch on lores; on some, loral patch extends over bill and, on first-winter females, it increases in size and whiteness after post-juvenile moult. Often shows traces of pale ear-covert patch. Bill blacker than adult female's, becoming greyer during winter; because of darker base, black nail difficult to see; some show tiny black extensions from nail around extreme tip of bill. Eyes duller than adults'. *First-winter male* From early winter, young males start to attain adult-like plumage. Black head feathering soon appears, together with large grey patches on scapulars. Early in winter, transitional birds show messy combination of adult male and juvenile characters. By New Year, most are similar to adult males, although limited dark feathering may persist within the grey.

Confusable Hybrids Male Tufted x Pochard and Tufted x Scaup hybrids are frequent; Pochard x Scaup do not seem to

Adult ♂ Scaup ▼

Shape and structure are important in identifying Scaup. Note large size, broad-beamed, heavy-breasted body. Bill wedge-shaped in profile, broad front-on. Head shape very rounded at rear. Compare with Tufted Duck.

1st-winter ♂ ► Scaup.

Adult winter ♀ Scaup. ▼

Juvenile Scaup show more black on bill tip, smaller, duller 'face' patch confined to lores, and duller eyes.

Juvenile/1st-winter ♀ Scaup.

Adult summer ♀ Scaup. ► Note white ear-coverts.

Juvenile/1st-winter ♀ ► Scaup.

♀ Tufted Duck.

♀ Tufted Duck showing large white facial blaze. Compare general shape and colour with Scaup. ►

Adult ♂ Scaup

♀ Tufted Duck ► showing large white 'face' patch.

Hybrid ♂ Scaup × Tufted Duck.

Three Scaup-type hybrids. Note head and bill shapes. ► Most show vestigial bumps or tufts. One ♀ has orange eye and whitish band near bill tip. ▼

♀ Tufted Duck × Scaup ► hybrid (February).

Adult ♂ Tufted Duck × Scaup hybrid (resembling Lesser Scaup). ▼

♀ Scaup-like ► hybrid.

Adult ♂ Lesser Scaup. Note head and bill shape, strongly vermiculated upperparts and darker lower scapulars. Note bill tip.

Adult ♂ Tufted Duck x Pochard hybrid. Note bill pattern and finely vermiculated grey upperparts. Head very faintly tinged brown ▶

Adult ♂ Ring-necked Duck x Tufted Duck hybrid. Tuft, bill and flanks not quite right for Ring-necked Duck. ▶

▲ Two adult ♂ Ring-necked Ducks. Note bill shape and pattern, head shape and shape of flank panel.

All sexes and ages of Ring-necked Ducks have 'boxy' body shape, rather flat back, finely tapering bill, longer tail than any other Aythya. The wing-stripe is grey.

Juvenile/1st-winter ♂ Ring-necked Duck. (late October). Eye dull, wispy crest due to mouit. ▶

◀ Adult winter ♀ Ring-necked Duck.

Adult ♂ Ring-necked Duck in eclipse (August) ▶

Adult ♂ Tufted Ducks moulting out of eclipse. ▼

▲ Adult ♀ Ring-necked Duck in summer (August).

♀ Pochard-like hybrid (July). Body plumage and all-dark bill similar to Pochard; tail length and 'face' pattern similar to Ring-necked Duck. ▶

Adult ♂ Ring-necked Duck ▶ moulting out of eclipse. Note tail.

occur. *Tufted x Pochard* Male generally smaller than Scaup; has peaked head, often with slight tuft; bill smaller and less broad, and eye tends to be darker. Pochard influence makes mantle and flanks darker, greyer and more solid-looking than Scaup's, while head may show brown tint at close range. Unlike Scaup, bill shows large black tip. Wingstripe often shows grey coloration (a Pochard character). *Tufted x Scaup* A greater pitfall than Tufted x Pochard. Males often very similar to Lesser Scaup *A. affinis* (a North American species first recorded in Britain and Ireland in 1987: see page 45). Most have squarer head than Scaup, often with slight tuft. Tufted influence darkens grey-vermiculated mantle, but flanks remain white. Black bill tip small, but Tufted influence produces larger black tip than on Scaup or Lesser Scaup, covering more than just nail. Wingstripe extensively white, similar to Scaup and Tufted Duck (Lesser Scaup has pale grey primaries). Lesser Scaup is flatter-backed and longer-tailed than Scaup and Tufted. *Female hybrids* With female or immature Scaup, check overall shape, bill pattern, eye colour and any hint of a tuft: any discrepancies may indicate a hybrid. A Scaup-like female hybrid seen on one English reservoir is illustrated on page 44.

Ring-necked Duck *Aythya collaris*

General Features Similar in size to Tufted, but with squarer body, longer bill and longer tail (often half cocked). Most obvious shape difference is pronounced peak at back of head, but juveniles, first-winters and even eclipse males rather flatter-crowned. Wingstripe always grey.

Plumage *Adult male* Easily identified by black head, breast and upperparts, and rounded grey flanks with striking white 'spur' at front. Grey bill has broad white subterminal band and narrow white basal band. Beware moulting male Tufted with greyish flanks. *Eclipse male* By late June,

males begin to lose white basal bill band. By August, are in full eclipse, like severely dulled version of full plumage: blacks are browner and flanks become rufous-tinged with slightly whiter fore flanks, replacing white 'spur'. Eye remains yellow (no eye-ring) and distal bill band becomes duller. Pale loral patch and whitish undertail-coverts develop. Full plumage reappears September–October. *Adult female winter* Brown, with rather rufous flanks, dark crown, conspicuously pale buffish lores and throat, white subterminal bill band, dark eye and prominent pale eye-ring, sometimes with pale extension (or 'tear line') running back towards ear-coverts. Facial pattern suggests Pochard rather than Tufted. *Adult female summer* White subterminal bill band may be reduced or virtually absent; face pattern may be duller. *Juvenile* Similar to summer female. *First-winter male* By late October, many juvenile males attain blackish head feathering and pale eyes, may be surprisingly inconspicuous among Tufted, particularly since crown less peaked than adult's. By late November or December, mantle and breast have turned black and grey flank feathering starts to predominate. By mid winter similar to adults.

Confusable Hybrids Most vaguely similar male hybrids (Tufted x Pochard and Tufted x Scaup) are grey-backed. Confusion possible with Ring-necked x Tufted, which are black-backed, but they fail to show all obvious Ring-necked features adequately: lack of prominent bill band, lack of well-defined flank 'spur', hint of a tuft and white in wingstripe are instant give-aways. Female Tufted x Pochard may cause problems, but attention to structure and wingstripe should reveal any discrepancies.

Ferruginous Duck *Aythya nyroca*

General Features A compact duck, similar in size to Tufted, but with rather steep forehead, pronounced central peak to crown and rather slender bill. White wingstripe more extensive than on Tufted and particularly stunning on males, extending right across outer primaries. Some female Tufted show large white undertail-coverts, but not so extensive as on Ferruginous.

Plumage *Adult male* Distinctive, with bright burgundy head and breast, slightly browner flanks and black mantle. White eye fairly conspicuous. Bill generally blue-grey (blacker on some), fading to pale grey subterminal area, before small black tip (restricted mainly to nail). *Eclipse male* Duller, with browner flanks and mantle. Retains pale eye. *Adult female* Rather like a duller, browner male with dark eye. A subtle orangy loral patch inconspicuous. Bill blackish, with faint pale subterminal band before variable dark tip (often more extensive than male's, extending to either side of nail). *Juvenile* Similar to female, but brown flecking in undertail-coverts. *First-winter male* By mid winter, difficult to separate from adults. Any apparent Ferruginous showing dark within undertail-coverts is more likely to be a hybrid.

Confusable Hybrids *Ferruginous x Pochard* Relatively frequent. Some so similar to genuine Ferruginous that they produce severe identification problems. When faced with a potential Ferruginous, pay particular attention to bill pattern, head-and-bill shape, size, undertail-coverts and wingstripe. Hybrids reveal Pochard parentage by rather sloping forehead, longer, deeper-based bill and, consequently, more wedge-shaped head-and-bill profile; usually larger and bulkier than Ferruginous. Mantle may show faint grey vermiculation, and undertail-coverts may be impure, with extensive dark feathering (Ferruginous should lose such mark-

ings by mid winter, following post-juvenile moult). Hybrids have larger black bill tip, sometimes with noticeable pale subterminal band curving back towards bill sides; wingstripe usually shows certain amount of grey coloration. *Ferruginous x Tufted* Seem genuinely rare compared with Ferruginous x Pochard.

Pochard-like and Redhead-like Hybrids

Pochard-like hybrids are frequent. Parentage not always apparent (most are probably crosses with Ferruginous). Tend to resemble male Pochards but have greyer bill, often crossed with pale subterminal band, darker mantle and flanks, and yellowy or orangy eyes. Such features strongly suggest Redhead *A. americana* (North American species, never recorded in Europe: page 48). Male Redheads similar to Pochards but darker grey, with very rounded head, yellow eye and different bill pattern (see below). Unlike female Pochards (greyish in winter plumage), female Redheads are brown all year, with distinct pale eye-ring and whitish lores (reminiscent of female Ring-necked). Pochard-like hybrids which resemble Redheads have more wedge-shaped head-and-bill profile, reddish or orange tint to eye, and whitening of wingstripe. Note particularly bill: male Redhead has blue-grey bill with narrow white subterminal band and large black 'dipped-in-ink' tip (female's similar, but with blacker base); hybrids generally have darker-based bill, and black tip and pale subterminal band are more U-shaped or irregular, lacking clean-cut 'dipped-in-ink' appearance of genuine Redhead.

Reference Gillham *et al.* (1966).

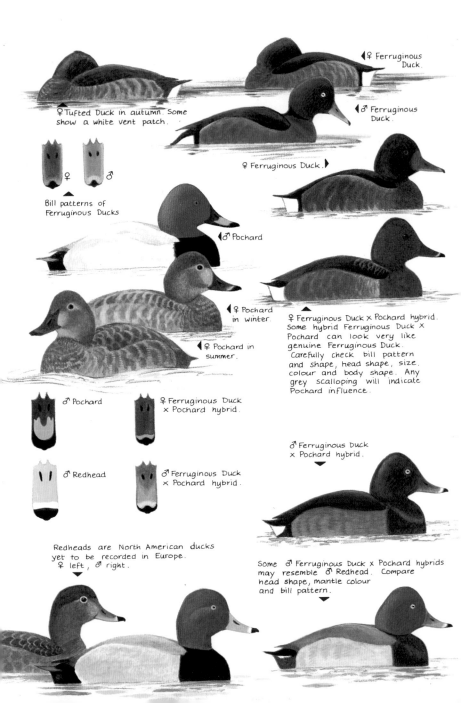

♀ Ferruginous Duck.

♂ Ferruginous Duck.

♀ Ferruginous Duck.

♀ Tufted Duck in autumn. Some show a white vent patch.

Bill patterns of Ferruginous Ducks

♀   ♂

♂ Pochard

♀ Pochard in winter.

♀ Pochard in summer.

♂ Pochard

♀ Ferruginous Duck x Pochard hybrid.

♂ Redhead

♂ Ferruginous Duck x Pochard hybrid.

♀ Ferruginous Duck x Pochard hybrid. Some hybrid Ferruginous Duck x Pochard can look very like genuine Ferruginous Duck. Carefully check bill pattern and shape, head shape, size, colour and body shape. Any grey scalloping will indicate Pochard influence.

♂ Ferruginous Duck x Pochard hybrid.

Redheads are North American ducks yet to be recorded in Europe. ♀ left, ♂ right.

Some ♂ Ferruginous Duck x Pochard hybrids may resemble ♂ Redhead. Compare head shape, mantle colour and bill pattern.

Scoters

Where and When Outside breeding season, essentially marine. Only Common Scoter breeds here (small numbers Ireland and Scotland), but from late summer to spring is locally common around coast. Velvet Scoter is much rarer, but can often be found in Common Scoter flocks; largest concentrations in eastern Scotland. Small numbers of Common occur inland on migration, particularly in March–April and mid June–August, latter mainly males on moult migration; Velvet very rare inland, but may appear during freezing weather. Surf Scoter, a very rare North American visitor, averages some 20 records a year; has occurred all around coast, usually in Common Scoter flocks, with a few inland records.

Scoters vary in size and males average larger than females. Identification of adult males straightforward, but females and immatures more similar. Juveniles resemble adult females, but tend to be slightly paler and whiter-bellied. Young males gradually acquire adult bill colours and black feathering during first winter, but progression varies individually. Eclipse males duller than full males.

Common Scoter *Melanitta nigra*

General Features Often gathers in large rafts and may migrate low over sea in large flocks. Generally the smallest and slightest scoter; compact, with squarer head, thinner neck and smaller bill than the others. Tail relatively long and pointed, held cocked when asleep. Wings plain and dark, but undersides of remiges distinctly greyer. Usually dives with closed wings (Velvet and Surf usually open wings), but occasionally with open wings, so differences not absolute. When wing-flapping, has unique downward S-shaped head movement.

Plumage *Adult male* Entirely black, with round black knob at the base of other-wise mainly yellow bill. *Female and juvenile* Readily distinguished from other scoters by pale, brownish-white face. Juvenile browner than adult female, with whitish belly barring. *First-winter male* Juvenile males moulting into first-winter plumage may appear variegated, with mixture of faded brown and dull black feathering, though some predominantly black by January. When moulting, may show dusky patches on sides of head (can suggest Velvet and Surf).

'Black Scoter' There are British records of Common Scoters showing characters of North American and eastern Siberian race *americana* ('Black Scoter'). Similar to nominate, but base of bill shows more gentle swelling which is extensively yellow-orange. Close-range views and *detailed* description of bill are essential for acceptance.

Velvet Scoter *Melanitta fusca*

General Features Largest, bulkiest scoter; size, coupled with long, wedge-shaped head-and-bill profile, may suggest Eider *Somateria mollissima*. Tail proportionately shorter than Common's. Unlike other scoters, has stunning white secondaries in all plumages but, at rest, these may not be visible or may appear as small white triangle or as narrow crescent on rear of wing. When diving, usually (but not always) opens wings like Eider (but see above). Tends to be more approachable than Common; on occasion exceptionally tame.

Plumage *Adult male* Most of bill yellow, and has inconspicuous crescent-shaped white patch under white eye. *Female and juvenile* Unlike Common, have two whitish facial spots, one before eye and one behind (some adult females may virtually lack these). Juvenile whiter on belly than adult female. *First-winter male* By January, advanced first-winter males appear uniformly dull black, but lack adult's white eye-crescent. Yellow on bill much duller than adult male.

Surf Scoter *Melanitta perspicillata*

General Features Rare, should be identified with caution. Averages larger and bulkier than Common, but heavy, deep-based bill produces wedge-shaped head-and-bill profile (recalls Eider). Easily separated from Velvet by its all-dark wings. Usually opens wings to dive.

Plumage *Adult male* Easily identified by large white patch on nape and smaller one on forehead. Bill intricately patterned with white, red and yellow, appearing mainly orange at distance. *Female and juvenile* Juveniles and most adult females show two white spots on face (on some juveniles these may run together). Slightly paler face, particularly on juveniles, produces slight capped effect. Some adult females show whitish patch on nape. Juveniles whiter on belly than adult females. Note that moulting juvenile/first-winter male Common can show dusky patches on sides of head, recalling Surf (see above). *First-winter male* May start to show adult bill patterning by December and, by spring, advanced birds show diagnostic white nape patch, but white forehead not attained until second winter.

Other Confusion Species Beware confusing Velvet and Surf with immature Eider and juvenile Scaup *Aythya marila* (see pages 44 and 51), or Common with female and juvenile Red-crested Pochard *Netta rufina*.

Goosander and Red-breasted Merganser

Where and When Both species breed in Scotland and northern England. Red-breasted Merganser *Mergus serrator* also breeds in North Wales and in Ireland, while Goosander *M. merganser*, an expanding species, now also breeds in central Wales. In summer, both are found on fresh water but, in winter, Red-breasted Mergansers are mainly coastal whereas Goosanders occur mainly inland (although note that Goosanders are rare in Ireland). This ecological split is a good clue to identification, but exceptions do occur: migrating Mergansers occasionally occur inland, particularly in late autumn and early winter, and also during periods of severe freezing, while the occasional Goosander may appear on coast. Paradoxically, the largest concentration of Goosanders is coastal, on the Beauly Firth in Scotland (over 2000 have been found in winter).

Structure Both are long, slim, thin-billed fish-eating ducks. Goosander is much the larger and bulkier (10–20% bigger), with large head, thick neck and large, full crest at back of head. Compared with Goosander, Merganser is distinctly smaller, slimmer and thinner-necked; its crest is thinner and wispier, generally forming two distinct tufts on back of head (Goosander has fuller, more even 'lump'). Despite its smaller size, Merganser has a longer, thinner bill, which shows more of a gentle up-curve than Goosander's.

Plumage Full-plumaged males easily separated. The best way to separate females and immatures is by the border line of the reddish-brown of head: on Goosander, reddish-brown ends abruptly, forming clear demarcation with obviously whitish breast; on Merganser, it gently merges to create dingier, more uniform impression to front of neck. Also, Goosander shows clear-cut white throat patch, while Merganser has more pronounced whitish loral line (although note that juvenile Goosander shows whitish loral line). Adult female Mergansers often show variable amounts of black on lores and around eyes. Mantle and flanks of Red-breasted Merganser show distinct

Diagnostic head
jerking flap

◄ Adult ♂ Common
Scoter.

Advanced 1st-winter ♂
Common Scoter

Adult ♀ Common Scoter

Advanced 1st-winter ♂ Velvet Scoter.
No white fleck behind eye as
in adult ♂. Wing-bar not
always visible at rest. ►

Compare head and neck
shapes, and bill, tail
and body lengths.

♀ Velvet Scoters. Note
variable head pattern

◄ 1st-winter ♂ Surf Scoter.
Note head pattern and
bill shape

◄ 1st-winter ♀
Surf Scoter.

Juvenile Scaup sits
higher on water than
Scoters. Note short
tail.

Note Red-breasted Merganser's thinner
bill, browner back, wispier crest and
less clear-cut neck line.

Eclipse ♀ Goosander

◄ ♀ Red-breasted
Merganser

♀ Goosander
in winter.

51

brownish cast, compared with clean grey plumage of Goosander. Eclipse males of both species resemble females but retain the large areas of white on forewings. Beware occasional 'brownhead' Goosander, particularly in autumn, which may show an atypically obscure line of demarcation on neck (perhaps caused by moult). **Ageing** Adult females and first-winter birds are similar. First-winter Goosanders have slightly less well-defined throat and loral line than adults, and slightly browner upperparts. Juvenile Mergansers have underparts suffused with greyish-brown. Juvenile males of both species gradually attain traces of adult plumage during first winter, but amounts attained are generally small, at least until late winter and spring. Males showing mixture of adult and 'brown-head' plumage *early* in winter will, therefore, be adults moulting out of eclipse.

Kites

Where and When Red Kite is resident in Wales, but winter dispersal produces occasional records elsewhere (particularly southwest England), while Continental visitors sometimes turn up in eastern areas. Black Kite is very rare but increasingly regular spring and summer vagrant, mainly to eastern England.

Red Kite *Milvus milvus*

Structure and Flight A stunning raptor, at distance can look like a flying cross. Long, rather narrow wings are often angled back from carpals. Unlike Buzzard *Buteo buteo*, holds wings flat or arched when soaring or gliding (tips may be slightly upturned). Wingbeats deep and elastic. Tail long and deeply forked, often twisted in flight. When fully spread, tail looks much squarer, though usually retains noticeable notch; tail fork can be briefly lost through heavy abrasion although tail corners always appear pointed.
Plumage Rich rufous-brown, with noticeably paler head. Following features particularly obvious: large, square white patch across inner primaries and bases of outer primaries; beautiful pale orangy tail; striking pale panel across median upperwing-coverts. Juvenile as adult, but slightly paler below and slightly better patterned above, with wider and paler median-covert panel, pale tips to greater and primary coverts, and paler uppertail-coverts.

Black Kite *Milvus migrans*

Structure and Flight Similar to Red Kite, but smaller, more compact and altogether less impressive. Like Red, wings comparatively narrow and angled back from carpals, but proportionately shorter. Flight is also flappy, with deep, elastic wingbeats; glides and soars with wings held flat or slightly arched. Tail long, but fork distinctly shallower, although depends on tail spread: when tail fully closed, fork deep and prominent; fully or even partially spread tail looks square, with sharply pointed corners.
Plumage Much drabber. Darker, rather chocolate-brown (often tinged rusty on breast and belly), with somewhat greyer head. Large pale patch at base of primaries less conspicuous, although variable (on some virtually lacking). Pale panel across median coverts on upperwing is also generally duller. Juvenile tends to be somewhat brighter than adult and shows well-marked creamy edgings to upperpart feathers.
The Marsh Harrier Problem Perhaps commonest confusion arises with high-flying female or immature Marsh Harriers *Circus aeruginosus*. Like all harriers, soaring or gliding Marsh hold wings in shallow V (which separates them from Black Kite), but when directly overhead, or in steadily flapping flight, wings can look flat (even at lower levels, Marsh can, over short distances, look flat-winged). High-flying

Red Kites. Wings of kites are arched in normal flight, tail frequently twisted.

Red Kite. Deeply forked cinnamon tail, pale upperwing-covert panel, long narrow wings.

Black Kite. Dark brown above, pale upperwing-covert panel and shallow tail fork.

♀ or juvenile Marsh Harrier. All Harriers fly with wings held in a shallow 'V'.

Black Kite. Dark below with less contrasting plumage than Red Kite. Note squarer tail.

Juvenile Marsh Harrier. Some are uniformly dark.

Red Kite. Reddish below with pale primary bases. Forked tail often appears pale.

♀ Marsh Harrier. Note head pattern 'V'-shaped wings may not be apparent when overhead.

♀ Marsh Harrier

1st-summer ♂ Marsh Harrier showing new grey inner primary feathers. At distance may recall Black Kite.

Black Kite

1st-summer ♂ Hen Harrier may recall ♂ Marsh Harrier.

Structure very similar when soaring overhead. Note Black Kite's tail may look square-ended when spread.

1st-summer ♂ Marsh Harrier.

53

Marsh look uniformly dark and any yellow/ golden on crown and throat can be difficult to see. In addition, female and immature can show slightly paler patch at base of primaries, while first-summer male can show grey feathering which can be misinterpreted as pale primary patch of Black Kite. On high-flying Black Kite, the following features should be carefully checked to eliminate Marsh Harrier: 1 in normal flight, should always show dis-

tinct tail fork (tail square only when spread); 2 wings often angled back from carpals; 3 has deep, supple, rather elastic wingbeats; 4 persistently soars and glides on flat or arched wings; 5 often twists tail, particularly when soaring; 6 usually shows distinctly paler patch across inner primaries and base of outer primaries; 7 if upperparts visible, e.g. when banking, usually shows noticeable pale panel across median coverts.

♀ Hen Harrier. Broad wings and blunt wing tip suggests an Accipiter.

♀ Hen Harrier. Note shorter, broader wings with four prominently fingered primaries.

♀ Montagu's Harrier. Note strong facial pattern and more falcon-like shape.

♀ Montagu's Harrier. Longer, more tapered wings three prominent primaries.

Juvenile Montagu's Harrier. Typically deep rufous below. Dark under-secondaries.

Juvenile Hen Harriers. Most show a slight orange tint below, but some (left) are strong orange below and may suggest the race 'hudsonius' of North America.

Hen and Montagu's Harriers

Where and When Hen Harrier *Circus cyaneus* breeds mainly on upland moorland and in young conifer plantations in Scotland, Ireland, Wales and northern England; widespread in winter, frequenting all kinds of open country, particularly moorland and coastal marshes (perhaps

most numerous on English east coast), but numbers of Continental immigrants depend largely on severity of weather. Montagu's Harrier C. *pygargus* is a rare passage migrant and summer visitor, mainly April–September; small numbers breed, mostly southern England.

Adult Females Very similar in plumage, best identified by shape. Hen is rather bulkier than Montagu's, with proportionately shorter, broader and more rounded wings. Four or five fingered primaries produce broader wingtip, but note that, at times, Hen Harrier's wingtips can look quite pointed. Montagu's is slimmer, more elegant, with long, narrow tail and long, narrow wings, latter with only three or four prominently fingered primaries that produce distinctly more tapering wingtip. Hen often recalls a giant *Accipiter* (particularly overhead), Montagu's an oversized falcon. The long, supple wings of Montagu's produce slow, easy flight action recalling Common Tern *Sterna hirundo*. Plumage differences subtle, and both species have either barred or solidly dark under secondaries. At close range, most useful difference is facial pattern: Hen shows rather plain, owl-like face, whereas Montagu's has whitish area behind eye which contrasts noticeably with dark cheek patch.

Juveniles Juvenile Hen is similar to adult female, but underparts tend to show slight but distinct ginger tint. (More intensely coloured individuals are discussed below under American Hen Harrier.) Juvenile Montagu's distinctive, with breast, belly and underwing-coverts intensely coloured dark buff to rufous.

Adult Males Easily separated. Hen is very pale grey, with white rump, plain tail and variable dark trailing edge to rear of wing. Montagu's is slightly darker grey and shows: **1** black bar across base of upper secondaries; **2** dark flecking on underwing-coverts and one or two dark bars across base of under secondaries; **3** rusty streaks on flanks; **4** whitish belly; and **5** lightly barred sides to tail.

First-year Males In both species, a variable post-juvenile body moult in first year produces mixture of juvenile and adult feathering. Following complete moult when one year old, young males are more like adult males, but generally duller.

Melanistic Montagu's Harriers Both sexes have rare melanistic form. Melanistic males are sooty-grey above and blackish below, with silvery area at base of primaries and pale, unbarred tail. Females are dark chocolate, with paler, barred tail and whitish primary bases.

American Hen Harrier There have been a number of British records of juvenile Hen resembling American race *hudsonius*, juveniles of which have dark, hooded effect, and are dark rufous below with little streaking. Their identification is, however, complicated by occasional occurrence of juvenile *cyaneus* with rufous underparts. For more detailed discussion, see Grant (1983).

Sparrowhawk and Goshawk

Where and When Sparrowhawk *Accipiter nisus* is common throughout Britain and Ireland, but less abundant in eastern England. Goshawk *A. gentilis* is a very rare resident (about 50–70 pairs), likely to be found in extensive tracts of coniferous woodland, particularly in Scotland and northern England. Goshawk is a notorious 'beginner's bird' (many up-and-coming birdwatchers pass through a phase of seeing 'Goshawks'): it is very rare in Britain, so identification requires extreme caution.

Size, Shape and Flight To evaluate correctly the size of a high-flying raptor is difficult, as there is usually nothing in the sky for comparison. Nevertheless, Goshawk is very big. Although measurements often of little value in the field, compare following (from *BWP*):

	length	*wing length*
Sparrowhawk	28–38cm	196–256mm
Goshawk	48–62cm	306–366mm
Buzzard	51–57cm	368–419mm

According to Marquiss & Newton (1982): 'Most Goshawks in Britain are of the large northern type . . ., so many females are larger even than Buzzards *Buteo buteo*, while all males are considerably larger than any Sparrowhawk, and three times as heavy'. It must be emphasised that Goshawk is not simply a 'big Sparrowhawk': important differences in shape should be obvious. It is a large, powerful, deep-chested raptor, proportionately longer-winged and slightly shorter-tailed than Sparrowhawk. Wingtips are less rounded, more tapered; they often look rather pointed, even sharply so when stooping (confusion with large falcon possible). Sparrowhawk, too, can look pointed-winged in a stoop or a downward glide, but normally looks round-winged. Overhead, Goshawk shows more of a bulge to secondaries (producing more S-shaped curve to rear wing); its head protrudes more than Sparrowhawk's and the tail is thicker-based and has broader, *rounded* tip (Sparrowhawk's tail tends to look narrow at base and broadens to square tip). Goshawk's flight is rather more crow-like.

Plumage Goshawk's upperparts are brown on females, greyer on males. At distance, adults' underparts look uniformly cold greyish-white compared with Sparrowhawk. Goshawk's dark face gives hooded appearance, while white supercilium may be visible at close range; white undertail-coverts may be obvious. Juvenile, unlike juvenile Sparrowhawk, has heavy drop-like *streaks* below, and often orange wash to breast and underwing-coverts.

Behaviour Goshawks may sit conspicuously in tree tops (unlike more furtive Sparrowhawk), but can be remarkably secretive; often best seen in early spring when, like Sparrowhawk, they indulge in spectacular display flights.

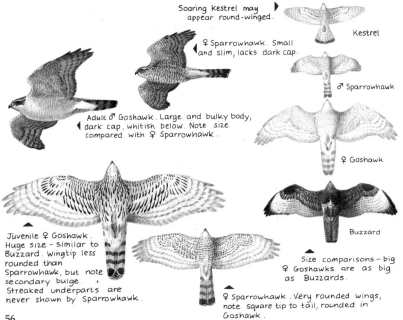

Soaring Kestrel may appear round-winged.

Kestrel

♀ Sparrowhawk. Small and slim, lacks dark cap.

♂ Sparrowhawk

Adult ♂ Goshawk. Large and bulky body, dark cap, whitish below. Note size compared with ♀ Sparrowhawk.

♀ Goshawk

Buzzard

Juvenile ♀ Goshawk. Huge size – similar to Buzzard. Wingtip less rounded than Sparrowhawk, but note secondary bulge. Streaked underparts are never shown by Sparrowhawk.

Size comparisons – big ♀ Goshawks are as big as Buzzards.

♀ Sparrowhawk. Very rounded wings, note square tip to tail, rounded in Goshawk.

Other Pitfalls High-flying female or immature Hen Harriers *Circus cyaneus* can appear quite *Accipiter*-like. Note harrier's slimmer proportions, rounded, well-fingered wingtips, square tail and heavy barring across primaries and secondaries (three thick bars, compared with four or five thinner ones on juvenile Goshawk).

Prolonged views should reveal Hen Harrier's V-shaped wing attitude (flat on Goshawk) and white rump. May also be confused with Buzzard and, particularly, Honey Buzzard *Pernis apivorus* (see page 59): note differences in shape and plumage, and Goshawk's flap-flap-glide flight. *Reference* Marquiss & Newton (1982).

Buzzards

Where and When Buzzard is a common resident in Scotland, Wales and northern and southwestern England (rare or uncommon in eastern England). Rough-legged Buzzard is a rare winter visitor, mainly to coastal areas of eastern England (sometimes, eastern Scotland); usually fewer than 20 records a year, but periodic influx years (in winter 1974/75, about 100 were present). Honey Buzzard is a very rare summer visitor to selected woodlands in southern England, also a rare spring and autumn migrant.

Buzzard *Buteo buteo*

Our only common large raptor, but rare in eastern England.
Structure and Flight A rather stocky, evenly proportioned broad-winged raptor, typically seen soaring over hillsides and woodland, often calling a plaintive, mournful *mew*. Usually soars with wings held in shallow V; glides on either raised or flat wings, but occasionally with hand slightly drooped (like Honey Buzzard).
Plumage Usually unremarkable and, unfortunately, extremely variable. Most have dark brown upperparts, head, breast and underwing-coverts, but bases of primaries slightly paler and greyer. Juveniles similar to adults. Some Buzzards, however, are very dark, others are very pale. Latter may be mainly white on head and underparts, provoking confusion with Rough-legged Buzzard or even Osprey *Pandion haliaetus* (note Osprey's thick black eye-stripe and long, narrow,

almost gull-like wings which are distinctly down-kinked, never raised).
'Steppe Buzzard' There have been several British claims of Buzzards resembling migratory eastern race *vulpinus* ('Steppe Buzzard'). This race has rather consistent appearance: very pale flight feathers on underwing (with black trailing edge) and pale orangy tail. See Porter *et al.* (1976) for further details.

Rough-legged Buzzard *Buteo lagopus*

The English east coast in October–November is the most likely place to see this species, but winterers may linger into April or May. Elsewhere or at other times of year, identification of Rough-legged requires extreme caution; note that, in western areas, pale Buzzards are far more likely.
Structure and Flight Similar in shape to Buzzard, but slightly larger, longer-winged, sturdier, more 'eagle-like'. Soars on slightly raised wings, and glides with arms raised and hands held level. When flapping, wingbeats deeper and more elastic, less stiff than those of Buzzard. A typical view of Rough-legged would be of a large, pale buzzard persistently hovering or hanging motionless over coastal fields or marshes, tail twisted and turned like a kite's. Buzzards also hover, but less persistently.
Plumage *Juvenile* Most of our Rough-legged Buzzards are juveniles, which are, on average, paler than adults. They stand

out through following characters (in rough order of importance): **1** white tail, with thick black terminal band; **2** predominantly whitish underparts; **3** large black carpal patch; **4** blackish belly (although exceptionally is pale); **5** black tips to under primaries and secondaries; **6** pale area across median upperwing-coverts; **7** large pale patch at base of upper primaries. *Adult* Adults average darker, lacking (unlike Buzzard) warm chestnut tones, with dark head, breast and underwing-coverts, more heavily barred flight feathers (especially secondaries), and darker upperwings with less conspicuous pale area across base of upper primaries. Note in particular that adult Rough-legged often shows whitish U on upper breast, between dark throat and black belly. Best age character is tail band: on adults, black and sharply defined, but with two or three narrower bands towards base; on juveniles, wider, duller and less clear-cut.

The Problem of Pale Buzzards Some pale Buzzards can look remarkably similar to Rough-legged: objective evaluation of size and structure and consideration of behaviour, date and locality are essential. Pale Buzzards, however, rarely show **1** clear-cut black-and-white tail (any white is *usually* restricted to uppertail-coverts) and **2** pale patch at base of upper primaries; they do often show creamy-white areas on upperwing-coverts and 'shoulders'.

Honey Buzzard *Pernis apivorus*

Structure and Flight Similar in size to Buzzard and plumage similarly variable. Concentrate on structure and flight and establish clearly following features (in rough order of importance): **1** Honey soars (and glides) on *flat* wings, tips often slightly *drooped* (never Buzzard's shallow V); **2** *small* head protrudes prominently, effect strongly recalling Cuckoo *Cuculus canorus*; **3** wings proportionately longer and narrower than Buzzard's, widest at wrist and with rather bulging secondaries

(although appear straighter in flapping flight), and have 'pinched-in' effect where secondaries meet body; primaries often look narrower than Buzzard's, but can look broad and rounded when spread; **4** wingbeats deep and rather elastic, with wings noticeably bowed on downstroke; **5** tail looks proportionately long and narrow and rather paddle-shaped when closed; **6** overall effect often recalls a huge *Accipiter*, particularly viewed from side.

Plumage *Adult* Note following important plumage features: **1** thick black trailing edge to underwing and black bars crossing bases of secondaries and underwing-coverts and curving forward across base of primaries, creating (when present) very characteristic pattern; and **2** thick black band across tip of tail and one or two narrower, less obvious bands towards base. Most show barring across breast, belly and underwing-coverts, but some look dark and rather uniform, while a minority have these areas very pale, almost white, and are hardly patterned at all. Unlike Buzzard, sometimes shows pale panel across median coverts on upperwing, rather like a kite. *Juvenile* Underwing differs from adult's in having more black on primary tips, darker secondaries (with less well-defined barring) and paler inner primaries, but lacking clear-cut trailing edge. Juveniles also lack clear-cut terminal band to tail, but instead show three or four evenly spaced but less noticeable dark bars. Many have whitish head, *pale* brown upperwing-coverts, whitish rump and uppertail-coverts. At close range, shows yellow cere and dark eye (blue-grey cere and yellow eye on adults). **Display** Adults have diagnostic display in which they rise high and descend in a series of loops, raising wings in steep V over back and wiggling them backwards and forwards (sometimes, clap wings over back in normal flight). This display facilitates even long-range identification. *Reference* Porter *et al.* (1976).

Some Buzzards are pale below and may show a paler rump and tail base. ▶

Buzzard Stocky but evenly proportioned. Typical birds are brown with paler primary bases. ▶

◀ Buzzards. Pale and dark examples. ▶

Adult Rough-legged Buzzard ▶ Usually darker than juveniles. Note dark bands towards tail base.

Juvenile Rough-legged Buzzard. Shape more 'eagle-like' than Buzzard. Note dark carpal patch, belly and tail band. ▼

Juvenile (left) and adult Rough-legged Buzzard. Note paler ◀ primary patch. Juveniles are paler above with clear-cut tail band.

▲ Typical Honey Buzzard is heavily barred below.

▲ Adult Honey Buzzard. Note protruding 'Cuckoo-like' ▶ head. Long narrow wings widest at mid-wing. Wings show pinched-in effect at base. Note uneven spacing of tail-bars.

Honey Buzzards show vast variation in plumage. ▼

Juvenile Honey Buzzard tends to show darker under secondaries, more black to wing-tip and evenly barred tail. The ◀ upperwing-coverts are often pale

Falcons: Peregrine, Merlin, Hobby and Red-footed Falcon

Where and When Peregrine breeds mainly on cliffs in coastal and upland areas of Ireland and northern and western Britain; in winter, some disperse to coastal areas, particularly estuaries, and even inland where abundance of suitable prey; much rarer in eastern half of England. Breeding distribution of Merlin resembles that of Peregrine, but it breeds on moorland and is more widespread in winter, when a more general dispersal and some immigration. Hobby is a summer visitor, mainly late April to early October, breeding almost exclusively in southern England; largest populations occur on southern heathland, but also breeds widely in agricultural areas. Red-footed Falcon is a spring, summer and, occasionally, autumn vagrant, currently averaging about 14 records a year; although, remarkably, about 150 seen in spring 1992. Most occur in southern and eastern England, but has occurred throughout Britain; very rare in Ireland.

General Identification Problems

Given a good view, separation of Peregrine, Merlin and Hobby not difficult but, when seen poorly, all three can be confused. Problems occur when falcons are high in air and size cannot be accurately judged, or when sighting very brief: identification then hinges on correct interpretation of size, structure and flight, and depends largely on experience.

Peregrine *Falco peregrinus*

Flight, Structure and Behaviour A large, spectacular falcon. Shape distinctive: heavy, thick-set and deep-chested, with broad-based pointed wings (although extreme tips can appear rather blunt, particularly when soaring); has medium-length tail. Viewed from the side, body looks rather cigar-shaped. Likely to be seen high in air, hanging in wind or circling upwards before stooping at great speed into flocks of waders, pigeons, thrushes or other suitable prey. Compared with Merlin and Hobby, is rather stiff-winged with shallow wingbeats in which only tips are obviously moved; flight can recall Fulmar *Fulmarus glacialis*. When soaring and gliding, wings often slightly bowed below horizontal.

Plumage *Adult* Blue-grey above, with variably barred, darker tail. Underparts look pale whitish-grey at distance, an effect produced by delicate black barring on white background. Thick black moustachial stripes stand out strongly against white face and throat. *Juvenile* Browner above and darker below. Underparts have heavy brown streaking, and dark moustachials stand out strongly against creamy face. Shows slightly paler forehead and sometimes pale supercilium which curves back towards nape. Cere blue (yellow on adults).

Calls May be quite vocal at nest, adults having variety of calls including *kiyaa kiyaa kiyaa* . . . In winter, a gruff, barking *archk archk* may be heard.

Pitfalls Besides confusion with both Merlin and Hobby, identification of Peregrine and other large falcons complicated by not infrequent occurrence of falconers' escapes such as Lanners *F. biarmicus*, Sakers *F. cherrug*, Laggars *F. jugger* and even hybrids. When faced with an odd falcon, in particular with possible dark-plumaged Gyrfalcon *F. rusticolus*, be sure to eliminate these various escapes. A complicated subject; see Porter *et al.* (1976).

Merlin *Falco columbarius*

Flight, Structure and Behaviour A small falcon. Male only about size of Mistle Thrush *Turdus viscivorus*, but female nearly as big as Kestrel *F. tinnunculus*. Compact; the relatively short, sharply pointed, angled wings and medium-length tail produce distinctive silhouette that

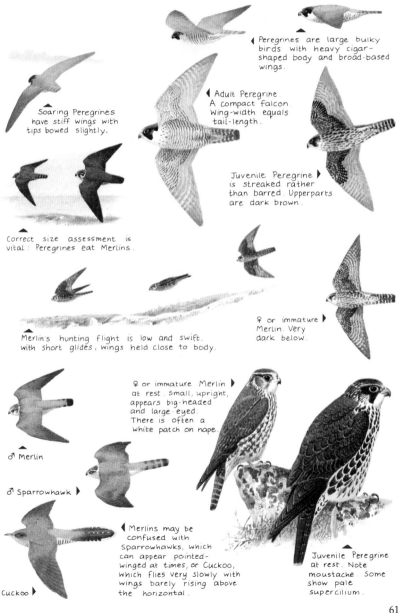

Peregrines are large bulky birds with heavy cigar-shaped body and broad-based wings.

Soaring Peregrines have stiff wings with tips bowed slightly.

Adult Peregrine A compact falcon. Wing-width equals tail-length.

Juvenile Peregrine is streaked rather than barred. Upperparts are dark brown.

Correct size assessment is vital: Peregrines eat Merlins.

Merlin's hunting flight is low and swift, with short glides, wings held close to body.

♀ or immature Merlin. Very dark below.

♀ or immature Merlin at rest. Small, upright, appears big-headed and large-eyed. There is often a white patch on nape.

♂ Merlin

♂ Sparrowhawk

Merlins may be confused with Sparrowhawks, which can appear pointed-winged at times, or Cuckoo, which flies very slowly with wings barely rising above the horizontal.

Cuckoo

Juvenile Peregrine at rest. Note moustache. Some show pale supercilium.

61

readily separates it from both Hobby and Kestrel. Most likely to be seen flying low over moorland or coastal marshes with fast, dashing flight in which sharply pointed angled-back wings produce rather 'flicking' flight action. Will, however, also rise to some height and fly at speed towards unsuspecting prey, wings often intermittently closed into body to produce flight action strongly reminiscent of fast-flying Mistle Thrush. When pursuing prey at close range, follows every twist and turn of quarry. Frequently sits on prominent perches, such as posts and stones.

Plumage *Adult male* (Adult males are in the minority.) Blue-grey above, with thick, dark subterminal tail band (some also show narrower dark barring towards base). Underparts vary from beige to orangy. *Adult female and juvenile* (Most winter Merlins seen in lowland Britain are juveniles, which resemble adult females.) Dark brown above; well streaked below on whitish to orangy background. Show white throat, but lack strong moustachial stripes (unlike Peregrine and Hobby), but sharply defined ear-coverts help to produce hooded effect. Neat white line over eye. Tail strongly barred. According to *BWP*, juveniles not certainly separable from adult females: it seems, however, that they are generally creamier on throat, have more diffuse moustachial stripes, less clear-cut ear-coverts, a pale crescent below eye, more diffuse creamy supercilium, and pale patch on nape; underparts tend to be duller. Cere bluish on juveniles (yellow on adults).

Calls On breeding grounds, calls include shrill, chattering *kik-ik-ik-ik*, recalling Kestrel.

Pitfalls Confusable with both Hobby and Peregrine, but note that by October, when migrant Merlins appear in force in lowland Britain, Hobbies are decidedly rare. A notorious beginner's bird; claims of Merlin in atypical situations often involve male Sparrowhawks *Accipiter nisus*, which occasionally bunch primaries to produce pointed wing shape. Another potential confusion species is Cuckoo *Cuculus canorus*, but this has long, graduated tail, pointed head/bill profile and slower, unhurried flight with stiffer, shallower wingbeats.

Hobby *Falco subbuteo*

Flight, Structure and Behaviour Arguably the most beautiful of our commoner falcons. Distinctive silhouette: slim, with very long, narrow, pointed scythe-shaped wings and shortish/medium-length tail; shape can suggest gigantic Swift *Apus apus* or, when hawking insects over water, Black Tern *Chlidonias niger*. Far more conspicuous in its aerial feeding behaviour than Merlin, is likely to be seen hawking flying insects over heathland, downland or lake edges, twisting and turning as it snatches dragonflies and other insects in talons before transferring them to bill. Also pursues birds and, like Peregrine, spends some time circling to great height before turning and stooping into flocks of Swifts and hirundines, its favoured prey (anguished shrill *shrip shrip* bird-of-prey alarm call of House Martin *Delichon urbica* is often first indication of presence of Hobby). Does not habitually sit out on prominent perches, but prefers to land within tree canopy; occasionally will, like Red-footed Falcon, feed in shrike-like manner from fence posts.

Plumage *Adult* When seen well, grey above and heavily streaked on breast and belly, with rufous thighs that may 'flash' at distance. Black moustachial stripes stand out against prominent white face. *Juvenile* Browner than adult, with paler feather fringes on upperparts and less rufous vent. *First-Summer* Faded brown above, buffer vent; may be paler on head.

Calls A deep, slow, *pew pew pew . . .*

Pitfalls Less likely to be confused with Peregrine because of latter's greater bulk and broader wings, but high-flying Merlin

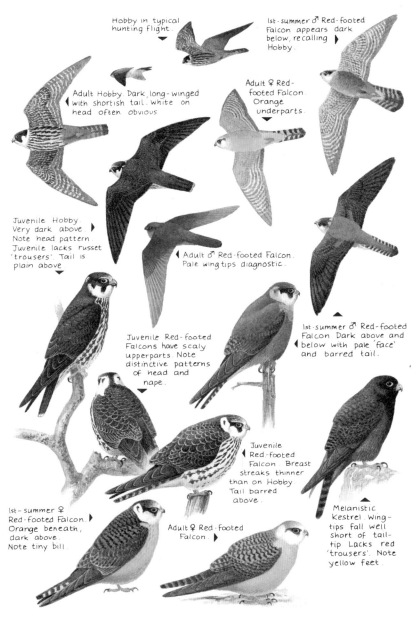

Hobby in typical hunting flight.

1st-summer ♂ Red-footed Falcon appears dark below, recalling Hobby. ▶

Adult Hobby Dark, long-winged with shortish tail. White on head often obvious

Adult ♀ Red-footed Falcon Orange underparts. ▼

Juvenile Hobby Very dark above. ▶ Note head pattern. Juvenile lacks russet 'trousers'. Tail is plain above. ▼

◀ Adult ♂ Red-footed Falcon. Pale wing tips diagnostic.

Juvenile Red-footed Falcons have scaly upperparts. Note distinctive patterns of head and nape.

1st-summer ♂ Red-footed Falcon Dark above and ◀ below with pale 'face' and barred tail.

◀ Juvenile Red-footed Falcon. Breast streaks thinner than on Hobby. Tail barred above.

1st-summer ♀ Red-footed Falcon. ▶ Orange beneath, dark above. Note tiny bill.

Adult ♀ Red-footed Falcon. ▶

Melanistic Kestrel. Wing-tips fall well short of tail-tip. Lacks red 'trousers'. Note yellow feet.

63

often misidentified as Hobby. Kestrel will, on occasion, hawk flying insects just like Hobby, so be cautious when identifying distant individuals.

Red-footed Falcon *Falco vespertinus*

Flight, Structure and Shape Similar in shape to Hobby, for which could be taken in brief view. Wings not quite so long as Hobby's, look slightly more Kestrel-like in shape. Unlike Hobby, persistently hovers, but with noticeably deeper wingbeats than Kestrel. Often hunts from telephone wires or fence posts in rather shrike-like manner; alternatively, may hunt from ground, flapping short distances or awkwardly leaping and hopping after prey; also hawks flying insects. Often sits on fence posts and wires in Cuckoo-like manner, often with partially drooped wings. Can be remarkably tame.

Plumage Great care required when identifying poorly seen Red-footed Falcons, records of which are always carefully scrutinised by *British Birds* Rarities Committee (Hobby superficially similar in shape, and in certain lights can look uniformly dark below; therefore, essential to obtain good, prolonged look at a potential Red-foot.) Four basic plumage types occur here: adult male, first-summer male, female and juvenile. *Adult male* (Generally one of rarest plumage types to occur in Britain and Ireland.) Uniformly blackish-grey, but, importantly, *on upper-wing primaries and secondaries always conspicuously pale silvery-grey*. Rufous thighs, red feet, and orange-red cere and eye-ring. *First-summer male* (Occurs more frequently than adult male.) Lacks strong silvery-grey of upper primaries and secondaries, instead shows obvious traces of immaturity in form of: 1 off-white throat, and orange coloration on sides of neck and upper breast (exact colour individually variable); 2 strongly barred tail; 3 barring on greater coverts and tertials; 4 heavily barred underwing; and 5 orange-yellow (not red) legs, cere and eye-ring. Since most first-summer males have paler throat/upper breast, this age/sex is the one most likely to be confused with Hobby. *Adult female* Perhaps most likely to be passed off as Kestrel, as crown and underparts orange-buff. Has black moustachial stripe and a line through eye. Mantle and wings grey, barred black. Both tail and under primaries/secondaries are barred, but underwing-coverts conspicuously orange-buff (although this may be restricted to leading underwing coverts). Bare parts orange. *First-summer female* Apparently separable by 1 is streaked on crown and nape (plain on adult); 2 larger dark mask; 3 is streaked below (little or no streaking on adult); 4 browner above with plain outer greater coverts (barred on adult). Beware confusion with browner first-summer Hobby. *Juvenile* more similar to juvenile Hobby, but more scaly above, has more obviously barred tail (barring more obviously barred tail (barring confined mainly to inner webs on Hobby, so not readily apparent), has paler forehead and more extensive white collar around sides of neck.

Pitfalls Besides Hobby (outlined above), another pitfall with males is melanistic Kestrel. The bird portrayed on page 63 is loosely based on one such individual seen near Cardiff in July 1986: it had blackish head and underparts and very dark upperparts, but was easily identified at rest by the wing/tail ratio (on Kestrel wingtips fall 1–2cm short of tail tip at rest, on Red-foot wingtips project about 0.5cm *beyond* tip of tail); in addition, it showed typical Kestrel bare-part colours, lacked rufous thighs of Red-footed Falcon and showed traces of barring right across upperparts.

Reference Porter *et al.* (1976).

Ringed, Little Ringed and Kentish Plovers

Where and When Ringed Plover is a widespread, mainly coastal, breeding and wintering bird, with numbers greatly inflated in spring and autumn by passage migrants (mainly Greenland breeders); on migration also occurs inland, sometimes in reasonable numbers if water levels low. Little Ringed Plover is a recent colonist (first bred in 1938), now a widespread summer visitor, mainly frequenting English gravel pits; occurs more widely on migration in March–May and July–October, although uncommon away from England. Kentish Plover (a former breeder) is now a rare passage migrant, mainly to south and east coasts; very rare elsewhere and unlikely to be seen inland.

Ringed *Charadrius hiaticula* and Little Ringed Plovers *C. dubius*

General Features Little Ringed Plover is smaller and slighter than the dumpy Ringed Plover, with distinctly more attenuated rear end. Such differences are, however, best appreciated when the two species are alongside each other. Best distinguishing feature is Little Ringed Plover's lack of a wingbar: Ringed has conspicuous broad white bar, whereas Little Ringed shows at best only tiny pale tips to greater coverts, difficult to detect in flight.

Calls Totally different: Ringed gives soft, mellow *poo-ip*, with upward inflection, whereas Little Ringed gives thin, abrupt, rather whistling *tee-u*, with second syllable inflected downwards.

Plumage *Adults* At rest, Little Ringed has dull horn or flesh-coloured legs and fine black bill (a tiny pale patch at base of lower mandible is difficult to see in the field). In contrast, summer Ringed Plover has bright orange legs and stubby black-tipped orange bill; winter bare-part colours are much duller. Further differences include Little Ringed's obvious

yellow eye-ring and thinner breast band. Female Little Ringed often have extensive brown feathering on otherwise black ear-coverts. Winter adults of both species have the blacks largely replaced by dark browns. *Juveniles* When identifying juvenile Little Ringed at rest, concentrate on the head: unlike on Ringed, forehead is buff, often golden-buff, merging *gradually* with rest of crown; the buff supercilium is faint or virtually lacking, and the ear-coverts are more or less concolorous with crown, creating a hooded effect which Ringed Plover lacks; there is a fine, inconspicuous pale eye-ring. Juvenile Ringed Plover has clear-cut white forehead and supercilium, and darker ear-coverts, producing far more contrasted pattern overall. Like adults, juvenile Little Ringed have narrower breast band, while paler, sandier upperparts may be surprisingly obvious when the two species are together (but variations in both species, for example those caused by bleaching, should be borne in mind).

Kentish Plover *Charadrius alexandrinus*

Size, Structure and Behaviour Intermediate in size between Ringed and Little Ringed, but with rather a front-heavy 'chick-like' shape. May appear rather long-legged, particularly when plumage is sleeked down in hot weather. Tends to be rather active, often running along beach like a Sanderling *Calidris alba*.

Call The call is rather Sanderling-like *fwit*, sometimes sounding faintly disyllabic but, occasionally, sounding rather more of a metallic *tip*.

Plumage Individuals of all ages are easily identified by their sandy plumage, blackish or dark grey legs, fine black bill and narrow patches confined to sides of breast. Females and juveniles are pale sandy-brown and white, juveniles having

Juvenile Ringed Plover.
Bulky with upright stance.
Note short thick bill,
clear cut white forehead-
patch and supercilium.

Adult summer
Ringed Plover.

Adult winter
Ringed Plover

Adult summer Little Ringed Plovers, ♂ left,
and ♀ right. Note slim black bill, yellow
eye-ring, flesh coloured legs and slim
build.

Juvenile Little Ringed
Plover. Smaller and paler
than Ringed Plover, more
horizontal and attenuated.
Note thin, longish bill, lack
of supercilium and buffy
ill-defined forehead giving
a hooded effect. Pale eye-ring.

Adult Little Ringed Plover
lacks wing-stripe.

Adult Ringed
Plover. Strong
wing-stripe

Adult ♂ Kentish Plover
shows head pattern at
its brightest.

♀ Kentish Plover.
Long black legs
set well back.
Note stumpy rear
end and small
breast-patches.
The palest of the three species.

Adult Kentish
Plover. Short tail
shows more white.

pale feather edgings and less well-defined head pattern. By late summer, males attain female-like winter plumage, but close scrutiny usually reveals slightly darker breast patches and eye-stripe. Males acquire breeding plumage early, and by the New Year are rather dandy with neat black breast patches, thick black eye-stripe and black forecrown bar. The rear crown is variable, but most males show at least some bright cinnamon-orange coloration; some have whole rear crown this colour and are very striking. In flight, Kentish Plover shows narrow white wingbar (narrower than Ringed) and white sides to tail.

Large Plovers: Grey, Golden, American Golden and Pacific Golden Plovers and Dotterel

Where and When Grey Plover is a common coastal winter visitor and passage migrant, some remaining throughout summer; small numbers occur inland, on passage and in winter. Golden Plover is a familiar farmland species in winter, but breeds on moorland in northern and western Britain and Ireland; occurs on passage in wide variety of habitats, and in winter will feed and roost in more saline environments. American Golden Plover is a rare vagrant, mainly to western areas in September–October (spring and late-summer adults also occur, often on English east coast). Pacific Golden Plover is a very rare vagrant (some 17 records up to 1991), more likely than American to occur in winter; seems to prefer to feed in saline habitats, whereas American tends to occur in fields and freshwater environments. Dotterel breeds in Scotland and northern England (sometimes in north Wales), but occurs more widely on migration, often on hilltops or coastal fields and moorland; in some areas, small flocks turn up in same favoured fields year after year.

Grey Plover *Pluvialis squatarola*

General Features A large, bulky, rather hunched, long-legged plover with large dark eye and hefty, thick, blunt bill, latter particularly useful when separating distant individuals from Golden. Compared with Golden, Grey is a pale, colourless, grey-and-white wader, but note that juveniles are distinctly buffer. If in doubt, wait until it flies.

Flight Identification A large, grey plover with prominent white wingbar that contrasts with black primaries and primary coverts. Easily separated from Golden by its square white rump and its prominent black axillaries, which contrast with white underwing-coverts. Call a diagnostic clear, evocative whistle: *wee-oo-eeee*.

Plumage *Adult summer* Easily identified by pale grey upperparts, spangled with white (lacking yellow tones of Golden), striking white forehead and supercilium, which runs down sides of neck and bulges on breast sides. Underparts black, but with white rear belly and undertail-coverts. In full plumage, females slightly browner below and show white feathering within the black. First-summers remain in winter quarters and do not acquire full breeding plumage; may become very bleached and worn. *Winter* Essentially a pale grey plover with diffuse whitish upperpart spotting. Rather subdued supercilium, and darker patch through eye. *Juvenile* Potentially more confusing. Essentially pale grey-buff, with upperparts neatly and beautifully spangled. Underparts look smooth and uniformly grey-buff at distance, but closer views reveal delicate breast streaking. Buffish tone may provoke confusion with Golden or American Golden. Compared with latter, Grey has browner crown, less distinct supercilium and larger bill.

Golden Plover *Pluvialis apricaria*

General Features A medium-sized plover, similar in shape to Grey, but slightly smaller with narrower, weaker bill. Easily identified by yellow plumage tones.

Flight Identification Looks rather uniform above, lacking Grey's white rump. Wingbar less conspicuous, confined mainly to base of primaries. Underwing-coverts silvery-white, lacks Grey Plover's black axillaries. Forms large flocks, often with Lapwings *Vanellus vanellus*, which tend to fly at some height where they bunch together and fly fast and

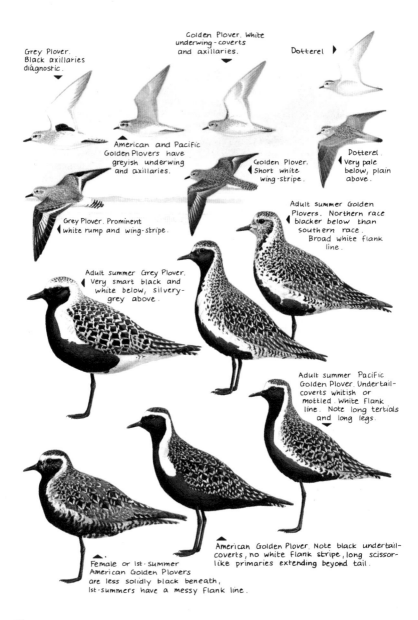

Grey Plover. Black axillaries diagnostic.

Golden Plover. White underwing-coverts and axillaries.

Dotterel ▶

American and Pacific Golden Plovers have greyish underwing and axillaries.

Golden Plover. Short white wing-stripe.

Dotterel. Very pale below, plain above.

Grey Plover. Prominent white rump and wing-stripe.

Adult summer Golden Plovers. Northern race blacker below than southern race. Broad white flank line.

Adult summer Grey Plover. Very smart black and white below, silvery-grey above.

Adult summer Pacific Golden Plover. Undertail-coverts whitish or mottled. White flank line. Note long tertials and long legs.

American Golden Plover. Note black undertail-coverts, no white flank stripe, long scissor-like primaries extending beyond tail.

Female or 1st-summer American Golden Plovers are less solidly black beneath, 1st-summers have a messy flank line.

Juvenile American Golden Plover. Strong white supercilium, dark cap, plainer breast, much greyer than Golden Plover - lacks yellow tones.

Juvenile Golden Plover. Yellowy tint to head and breast. Large dark eye. Yellow-spangled upperparts. Wingtips equal tail length.

Note tertials cover less of the primaries and fall well short of the tail.

Juvenile Pacific Golden Plover. Yellow plumage tones and obvious supercilium. Note longer tertials equal to tail length.

Juvenile Dotterel. Prominent white supercilium, buff below, scalloped above, yellow legs.

Both American and Pacific Golden Plovers are smaller, slighter and longer-legged than Golden Plover.

Adult winter Grey Plover. Plumage essentially grey. Note heavy bill.

Juvenile Grey Plover. Spangled above with pale buff, often suggesting Golden Plover.

69

direct; from below, wings look long, narrow and pointed. Easily identified by call: most usual is a soft, rather mournful *too-lee* or *tloo*, distinctive, yet unobtrusive and peculiarly evocative of frosty winter mornings; calls vary in length and composition, and large flocks are rather conversational. On breeding grounds, male sings a beautiful, mournful *poo-wee-oo* (rising on middle syllable).

Plumage *Adult summer* Varies according to range. Northern individuals are completely black from face to belly, but with broad white supercilium extending down sides of neck, broadening on sides of breast before continuing down flanks to vent/undertail-coverts. Southern individuals are grey and more mottled on face and throat, with black only in centre of belly, so the white on sides of neck and breast is more extensive. Upperparts are tinged yellowish. *Winter and juvenile* Brownish upperparts are liberally spangled with yellowish, while dingy underparts have a streaked yellow-buff breast and a whiter belly. Tends to look rather plain-faced, supercilium being ill-defined (although variable, is stronger on some). Large dark eye and often a darker area on rear of ear-coverts. Winter and juvenile plumages are very similar, but juvenile neater, slightly more streaked on breast, and slightly greyer on belly.

American Golden Plover *Pluvialis dominica*

General Features Distinctly smaller and slighter than Golden. Rather similar in shape at rest, with head hunched into shoulders, but when feeding can look totally different and this is often the most obvious initial difference from accompanying Golden. Can appear very slim, sleek and attenuated, with small head, slim, rather pear-shaped body and long legs; usually looks more upright and rather gangly. *Note in particular length of primaries*: they extend well beyond tail (by

about 1cm), whereas on Golden they extend only *just* beyond tail. Four primaries are visible beyond overlying tertials and exposed primaries are approximately equal in length to tertials, tips of which fall well short of tail tip (on Golden, usually three primaries are visible and tertials fall only just short of tail tip). Often very tame.

Flight Identification Similar to Golden, but smaller and slighter. Most important is *underwing colour*: coverts and axillaries are grey (silvery-white on Golden). Call distinctly different: a *tchoo-ik*, strongly suggestive of Spotted Redshank *Tringa erythropus*; also gives variety of monosyllabic or disyllabic calls, less mellow, more incisive than those of Golden. Apparently higher-pitched than Pacific with stress on first syllable.

Plumage *Adult summer* Upperparts rather blackish, with prominent buff and golden speckles and feather edgings. White supercilium extends to breast sides where it bulges prominently and provides smart contrast with black underparts. In full plumage, whole underparts black and, unlike Grey and Golden, *this includes vent and undertail-coverts*. Some adult females and first-summers of both sexes, however, are not wholly black below, thus show messy whitish line down flanks and predominantly whitish vent and undertail-coverts, although close inspection usually reveals at least some black mottling (same is true of transitional adults). *American Golden usually retains much of its summer plumage until it reaches winter quarters*, so autumn adults often conspicuous among winter adult or juvenile Goldens: summer-plumaged 'Golden Plover' in late autumn is always worth a second look. *Juvenile* Easily distinguished from Golden and, when seen together, they are really very different, both in shape and in plumage. Crown very dark blackish (often forms capped effect) and curves down to form grey crescent before eye. The dark cap accentuates strong white supercilium, which Golden lacks. Eye looks large, and there is a narrow dark line behind eye and a blackish smudge on rear of ear-coverts. General plumage tone is colder and greyer than Golden, lacking yellowy tones, thus rather more similar to juvenile Grey. Upperparts grey-brown, liberally and neatly checkered with whitish-buff. Underparts completely pale whitish-buff, lacking Golden's conspicuous well-streaked breast band, although close views reveal fine mottling and barring on breast. Note, however, that very grey Golden Plovers occasionally occur, so it is essential to check not only plumage features, but also structural differences outlined above, as well as underwing colour. *Winter* (Virtually unknown here in winter.) Similar to juvenile, but rather greyer above with less well-defined spotting.

Pacific Golden Plover *Pluvialis fulva*

General Features Superficially similar to American Golden. Separated from Golden in same way as is American (in particular, by differences in size and shape, and by colour of underwing). Pacific Golden, however, is in some ways more similar to Golden, being distinctly yellower in winter and juvenile plumages. Primaries distinctly shorter than those of American (thus Pacific's rear end not so attenuated), but key feature is length of primaries in relation to overlying tertials. On Pacific Golden, *exposed primaries are only about quarter to half length of overlying tertials* (equal on American) and only about 2½ primary tips are visible (4 on American). Incidentally, about three primary tips are visible on Golden. American completes primary moult in winter quarters, so problem of partially grown primaries unlikely to occur. If in doubt, check positioning of tertial tip in relation to tip of tail: on American, tertial tip falls

well short of tail tip, whereas on Pacific it is approximately level with tip of tail (it falls *slightly* short on Golden). Although photographs usually show Pacific Golden with very long legs with long, exposed tibia, most are taken in Far East where hot weather induces feather-sleeking; vagrants at higher latitudes may appear more fluffed out and, consequently, shorter-legged.

Plumage *Adult summer* Similar to American Golden, but rather yellower on upperparts, and white at sides of breast tends to bulge less conspicuously into the black. Tends to show more white along flanks and vent/undertail-coverts (thus not solidly black in this region) but, because of problems of first-summer and transitional adult American Goldens (see above), differences not absolute. Female in full breeding plumage tends to have more white feathering mixed with the black, while first-summers may not acquire full blackish underparts. Adults tend to retain traces of breeding plumage during southward migration. *Juvenile and winter* Juvenile quite different from juvenile American Golden, being much yellower and more coarsely patterned and, therefore, more similar to Golden. Upperparts brownish, heavily spotted and tinged yellow. May also show Dotterel-like chevrons on leading scapulars and wing-coverts. Supercilium prominent, yellowish-white or white, and there is a dark patch at rear of ear-coverts. Breast and flanks buffish, mottled yellow, but belly whitish. Winter plumage similar, but less neat and less crisply patterned.

Hybrids Several presumed hybrids between Golden and Pacific Golden have occurred. One seen in Avon superficially resembled Pacific Golden, but had white axillaries and underwing-coverts. It is, therefore, essential, to check for evidence of hybridisation when faced with a potential Pacific Golden Plover.

Dotterel *Eudromias morinellus*

General Features Smaller and stockier than previous four species and easily separated, particularly in summer plumage. Unlike the three 'golden plovers', legs are pale, yellow or yellowish-brown. Often very tame, but larger flocks may be more timid.

Flight Identification Resembles a small Golden Plover and, similarly, looks narrow-winged. High overhead, may not be readily identifiable if smaller size not apparent. Upperwings and rump plain, but tail noticeably blacker, with white edges. Underwing-coverts white, as Golden Plover. Call a distinctive, abrupt, ringing, slightly mournful *ski-er*, vaguely resembling Golden Plover; also gives plaintive *pew* and low, purring note, rather odd, but distinctive.

Plumage *Adult summer* Easily identified. At all ages has stunning, broad white supercilia, starting above eyes and meeting in a V on back of head. In summer, these offset by dark brown crown and dark line through eye. Throat white and upper breast grey, separated from orange underparts by narrow white band across breast. Upperparts brown, with buff feather edgings. Females are very bright, but males are less black on crown and duller below (some may be difficult to sex). *Juvenile* Rather buff-looking. Prominent creamy-buff supercilium contrasts with dark brown crown, which in turn curves down on to lores. Underparts rich buff, with fine grey streaking across breast and narrow pale band across lower breast, which is bordered below by a thicker, more diffuse dark band. Back streaked black and buff, but scapulars and wing-coverts blackish, with broad buff edgings. *Winter* Similar to juvenile, but grey-brown upperparts fairly plain, show faint feather edgings.

References Pym (1982), Vinicombe (1988).

Little Stint, Temminck's Stint and Sanderling

Where and When Little Stint is a rather scarce passage migrant, mainly in late April to early June and July–October, numbers of autumn juveniles varying annually; a few winter, mainly in southern England. Temminck's Stint is a much rarer migrant, mainly in May and August–September, mostly in eastern England; it occasionally breeds in Scotland and very rarely winters. Sanderling is a winter visitor to sandy coastlines, but larger numbers of Greenland migrants pass through western areas mainly in May and July–September; small numbers occur inland on migration.

Little Stint *Calidris minuta*

General Features A tiny wader, whose small size should always be apparent, even if no other species present for comparison. Has quick, energetic, rather jerky feeding actions, but at other times can be slower and even plover-like. A dumpier, longer-legged, more upright bird than Temminck's. Primaries are rather long, extending just beyond tail. Short bill easily separates it from Dunlin *C. alpina* and the black legs are an important difference from Temminck's. Looks very small in flight and is easy to pick out from Dunlin flocks.

Call A distinctive yet unobtrusive *tip* or *tip tip tip*.

Plumage *Adult summer* A bright and well-patterned stint compared with Temminck's. Upperparts are mottled with rich buff or chestnut, and there is a noticeable breast band. Pale edgings to mantle form a V when viewed from rear, although this is rarely as obvious as on juveniles. Has a variable supercilium. Spring migrants very variable as acquisition of summer

Winter Little Stint. Grey above with variable dark feather centres.

Adult summer Little Stint. Upperparts patterned with chestnut and buff. Variable breast band. Short black bill and legs.

Juvenile Little Stint. Richly scalloped upperparts. Note white mantle 'V's.

Little Stint ▶

Temminck's Stint. Note white outer tail feathers.

Juvenile ▶ Temminck's Stint recalls miniature Common Sandpiper. Pale legs.

Adult summer Temminck's Stint. Note pale legs, dull upperparts patterned with black. Tail projects beyond wings.

Juvenile Sanderling. White below, beautifully spangled above.

Adult summer Sanderling. Note short bill and black legs. Upperparts variable, patterned with grey or rich buff. Noticeable breast band.

◀ Adult summer Sanderling. A bright individual.

Adult winter Sanderling. Very pale, grey above, white head, dark at bend of wing.

Winter Sanderling ▶ Note thick white wing-stripe.

73

plumage produces a variety of plumage tones and patterns. On some, breast band peters out in middle, the patterning being confined mainly to breast sides. Note that summer-plumaged Little Stints can look rather uniform at a distance, thereby prompting confusion with Temminck's. *Winter* Upperparts become uniformly grey, although some show dark feather centres. Breast sides also grey, but on some this forms a complete band. Has an indistinct supercilium. Some may acquire winter plumage by late summer, and presence of such grey individuals among the more familiar juveniles often perplexes the inexperienced. *Juvenile* Most autumn Little Stints, from mid August onwards, are juveniles. They are neatly and immaculately patterned with golden, chestnut and buffish feather edgings. Most distinctive is characteristic white V formed by pale edgings to edge of mantle. Has a whitish 'split supercilium'. Underparts white, with shading and streaking confined to breast sides. By late autumn, juveniles fade considerably and look much greyer: the white mantle Vs may be much less obvious. Acquisition of first grey winter feathering reinforces impression of drabness.

Temminck's Stint *Calidris temminckii*

General Features An unobtrusive, secretive stint that is easily overlooked. Occurs almost exclusively in freshwater habitats. Tends to be rather solitary and creeps around on flexed legs in slow, furtive, mouse-like manner. Body looks long, low and horizontal, while, unlike Little Stint, tail projects beyond primaries to produce rather attenuated effect to rear end. *Key feature* is leg colour, which varies from yellowish through green to brown (always black on Little Stint), but beware effects of mud staining. Plumage always looks dull and plain compared with Little, and at all ages general appearance recalls a diminutive Common Sandpiper *Actitis hypoleucos*. Head and upperparts are dull grey-brown, and there is an obvious grey-brown breast band. Head is relatively plain but with traces of a faint supercilium and a narrow eye-ring. Flight fast and twisting with swept-back wings and flicking wing action, recalling House Martin *Delichon urbica* at distance; frequently towers when flushed. Pure white sides to tail are a feature not shared by any other Calidrid: can be obvious on take-off or landing, but frustratingly difficult to see in normal flight.

Call Completely different from Little Stint: a soft, mouse-like trill *si-si-si-si-si*. Note that Little Stint sometimes strings several *tip* calls together, but sound is harder and dryer and, therefore, quite different in quality.

Plumage *Adult summer* Close views reveal black feathering on scapulars, feathers of which are edged with buff or chestnut, and narrow buff edgings to median coverts. *Winter* Similar to summer, but plainer and greyer, lacking black scapular feathering and obvious pale edgings to median coverts. *Juvenile* Similar to winter but, at close range, upperparts are neatly and finely fringed with black and buff.

Sanderling *Calidris alba*

General Features Although quite different from previous two species, Sanderling does, nevertheless, recall an oversized stint. The traditional image of Sanderling is of a very pale hyperactive clockwork toy that chases waves up and down beach. In such circumstances, it is easily identified but, in less familiar summer and juvenile plumages, may be far more confusing, particularly if seen out of context at, for example, an inland reservoir. In such atypical situations may be far more lethargic but, nevertheless, still prone to run off at speed. Unlike other waders, it lacks a hind claw (close-range views are required to establish this). Easily identified in flight by very broad white wingbar (much broader than Dunlin). Winter Sanderling looks very pale in flight.

Call A hard, monosyllabic *kik* or *pit*.

Plumage *Winter* In its most familiar plumage, a very white-headed wader with pale grey upperparts and contrasting black bill and legs. *Adult summer* Rich golden-chestnut, males averaging brighter than females. Upperparts are coarsely patterned, and there is a strong breast band (quite unlike Dunlin). Head rather plain and finely streaked. Spring birds in very fresh plumage have thick grey edgings to feathers which, before they wear off, obscure the golden or chestnut below. Such individuals thus rather spangled

grey, brown and black, while some may look distinctly two-toned: predominantly grey on head, mantle and scapulars but chestnut on wings. There is, however, considerable individual variation. *Juvenile* Quite unlike adult summer and winter. Whole of upperparts black, with thick whitish feather edgings that produce beautifully neat, spangled appearance. Crown black, but face and underparts predominantly white, lacking summer adult's breast band (a small area of shading and streaking is restricted to breast sides).

Reference Identification of stints, including the rarer species, is very thoroughly dealt with by Grant & Jonsson (1984).

Dunlin, Curlew Sandpiper, Broad-billed Sandpiper and Knot

Where and When Dunlin is our commonest small shorebird, often abundant on estuaries in winter, and large numbers of migrants pass through in spring and autumn, when may be numerous also inland (usually when water levels low); small numbers breed in upland areas, mainly in northern England and Scotland. Curlew Sandpiper is a migrant from Siberia: adults pass through, mainly in eastern areas, in late spring and early autumn, and larger but variable numbers of juveniles are more widespread from August to October; very rare in winter. Broad-billed Sandpiper is a very rare but increasing spring (May–June) and autumn (July–September) migrant, mainly to east coast of England. Knot is a winter visitor to selected estuaries, principally in northwestern England and the Wash, where may occur in huge concentrations; more widespread on migration, when small numbers may turn up inland, mainly juveniles in August–September.

Dunlin *Calidris alpina*

General Features This abundant small wader should act as a yardstick when identifying all similar species, and observers should familiarise themselves with its various plumages. A small, hunched, rather dumpy bird with medium to long gently-curved bill. Bill length varies: individuals of race *arctica* (from northeast Greenland), common on migration, have shorter bills than *schinzii* (southeast Greenland, Iceland, Britain and southern Scandinavia) and the longer-billed *alpina* (northern Scandinavia and northwest USSR) that is common in winter. Feed in large flocks on mudflats, picking and probing with bill held downwards, not bunching as tightly as Knot.

Flight Identification Forms tight flocks like Starlings *Sturnus vulgaris*, flashing grey and white as they twist and turn over estuary. Closer views reveal rather plain pattern: narrow white wingbar and dark line down centre of rump.

Call A distinctive, drawn-out, rasping *treeeeep*.

Plumage *Adult summer* Easily identified by strong buff- or chestnut-patterned upperparts and large black belly patch. *Winter* Rather nondescript, with grey head and upperparts and grey suffusion on breast; slight supercilium. *Juvenile* Rather like a dulled version of adult summer. Upperpart feathering thickly edged buff or chestnut, and buffish breast lightly streaked brown. Importantly, belly lightly streaked blackish, forming messy patch. Generally looks neat and immaculate compared with contemporary summer adults, which often look patchy (in moult into winter plumage).

Curlew Sandpiper *Calidris ferruginea*

General Features Slightly larger, taller, more elegant and more gangly than Dunlin. Legs and bill longer, but differences in bill length and curvature subtle and should not be relied on for identification. Tends to feed in deep water, immersing bill and head below surface. Dunlin also feeds like this, but not quite so persistently.

Flight Identification Easily separated from Dunlin by striking *white rump.*

Call Flight calls similar in quality to Dunlin, but slightly softer and markedly disyllabic: a rolling *chirr-up*, very distinctive once learnt.

Plumage *Adult summer* Easily identified by reddish underparts. Size and structural differences separate it from summer Knot. *Winter* Full winter plumage not common in this country, as most spring and autumn adults show traces of summer plumage (noticeable red blotching on underparts). Winter plumage very similar to Dunlin, surprisingly difficult to pick out at any distance: slightly stronger thin white supercilium, extending well behind eye, and slightly whiter breast (although this variable on Dunlin). Perhaps best located by subtle structural differences outlined

above. *Juvenile* From mid August onwards, vast majority are juveniles. For separation from Dunlin, concentrate on underparts. Curlew Sandpiper has smooth, clean underparts with noticeable peachy tint to breast. (Often associates with juvenile Dunlins, which show blackish belly streaking, markings never shown by juvenile Curlew Sandpiper). Upperparts brownish-grey, evenly and neatly patterned with narrow black and buff feather edgings (juvenile Dunlin has thicker, coarser patterning). Has better-defined supercilium. Perhaps more likely to be confused with winter adult Dunlin, but latter uniformly pale grey above, with grey shading across breast.

Broad-billed Sandpiper *Limicola falcinellus*

General Features Structurally similar to Dunlin, but noticeably smaller and slightly shorter-legged. Thick-based bill not always obvious, but tip usually looks distinctly down-kinked. Despite statements to contrary, is not particularly lethargic.

Flight Identification Summer adults and juveniles look very dark, blackish, and show obvious breast band and narrow white wingbar.

Call A distinctive dry, hard trilling *pprrrrrrk*.

Plumage *Adult summer* Most occurring here are summer-plumaged adults and easily identified. At distance, look very dark, blackish, with dark, buffy-brown breast band and messy dark mottling down flanks. At closer range, upperpart feathers neatly edged chestnut and whitish, forming two sets of mantle and scapular lines recalling Snipe *Gallinago gallinago*. Most distinctive is stripy head pattern: thick white supercilium forks before eye, and 'upper supercilium' consists of narrow lateral crown-stripe (may be difficult to detect at distance). Prominence of 'split supercilium' highlighted by very dark

Juvenile Dunlin. Grey 'winter' feathers gradually replace juvenile feathers during the autumn.

Juvenile Dunlins are scalloped buff above, usually with dark spots on belly.

Winter Dunlin. Greyish above, white below, gently curved bill.

Moulting adult Dunlin may be confused with juveniles

Winter Curlew Sandpiper. Similar to Dunlin but whiter below, stronger supercilium, longer bill and legs

Juvenile Curlew Sandpiper. Note distinctive white rump.

Moulting adult Curlew Sandpipers show red blotching on underparts

Juvenile Curlew Sandpipers are neatly scalloped above, with peachy tint to breast. More elegant than Dunlin.

77

crown and eye-stripe, which broadens into thick patch on ear-coverts. Overall appearance recalls Jack Snipe *Lymnocryptes minimus*. Some fresh spring migrants show frosty grey feathering about head and breast (this gradually wears off); autumn adults lose much of pale upperpart edging through abrasion appearing rather uniformly blackish above. **Winter** Full winter plumage unlikely in this country. Predominantly blackish summer feathering replaced with grey, but characteristic head pattern retained (subdued). Darker leading lesser coverts form dark patch at bend of wing. **Juvenile** Similar to summer adult, but neat and immaculate. Breast sides finely and evenly streaked, and upperparts show well-defined white feather edgings and mantle and scapular stripes at time when summer adults are messy and abraded.

Knot *Calidris canutus*

General Features Although quite different from preceding three species, Knot is frequently confused with Dunlin by the inexperienced. At rest, best identified by size and structure. A medium-sized wader, much longer than Dunlin. Bill relatively short, as are legs (greenish or greyish, not black). Rather bulky, with short neck and long body. Unlike Dunlin, has attenuated rear end and primaries project well beyond tertials (exposed primary length approximately equal to tertial length). A rather slow, methodical feeder; on mudflats, often forms large tightly packed flocks.

Flight Identification Easily distinguished by combination of pale, greyish-white rump and tail, and obvious thick white wingbar.

Call An unobtrusive *knut knut*.

Plumage *Adult summer* Easily identified by brick-red underparts. Moulting adults patchy. Structure and bill length separate it from Curlew Sandpiper. *Winter* Rather nondescript, lacking strong facial pattern. Plain pale grey above; breast lightly mottled grey. *Juvenile* Similar to winter, but upperpart feathers have narrow pale edgings. Peachy tint to breast wears off as autumn progresses. Noticeable white supercilium curves down and then up behind eye. Plumage usually looks smooth and immaculate.

Ruff, Buff-breasted Sandpiper and Pectoral Sandpiper

Where and When Ruff is a very rare breeding bird but far more numerous as a migrant, mainly in freshwater habitats; variable numbers winter, most in southern half of Britain, tending to occur in fields, often with Lapwings *Vanellus vanellus* and Golden Plovers *Pluvialis apricaria*. Buff-breasted Sandpiper is a North American visitor, mainly to western Britain and Ireland, most in September (records in spring and late summer, often from English east coast, probably relate to birds that have arrived in previous years): between 1981 and 1990, there was an annual average of 21; small parties sometimes occur (as many as 16 have been seen together on the Isles of Scilly). Pectoral Sandpiper is another North American wader which, during 1981–90, occurred at a rate of about 80 a year, mostly in September–October in Ireland and southwest England; records in spring and late summer, often in eastern England, no doubt relate to individuals from eastern Siberia (where also breeds) or to birds that have crossed Atlantic in previous years.

Ruff *Philomachus pugnax*

General Features In many ways, a rather nondescript wader, varying in both plumage and size. Four basic plumage types: adult male summer, adult female summer, juvenile and winter (see below). Males are about size of Redshank *Tringa*

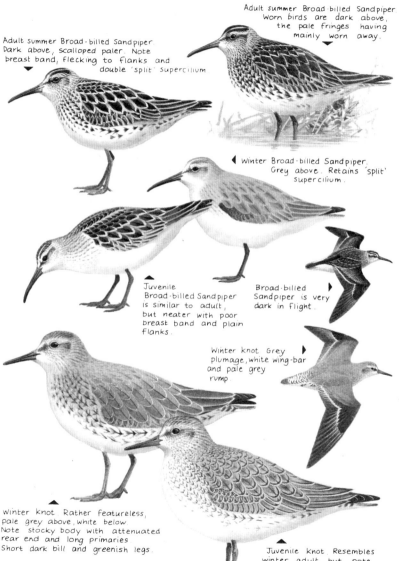

Adult summer Broad-billed Sandpiper. Worn birds are dark above, the pale fringes having mainly worn away.

Adult summer Broad-billed Sandpiper. Dark above, scalloped paler. Note breast band, flecking to flanks and double 'split' supercilium

Winter Broad-billed Sandpiper. Grey above. Retains 'split' supercilium.

Juvenile Broad-billed Sandpiper is similar to adult, but neater with poor breast band and plain flanks.

Broad-billed Sandpiper is very dark in flight.

Winter knot Grey plumage, white wing-bar and pale grey rump

Winter knot Rather featureless, pale grey above, white below. Note stocky body with attenuated rear end and long primaries. Short dark bill and greenish legs.

Juvenile knot. Resembles winter adult but note delicate upperpart patterning and peachy tint to breast.

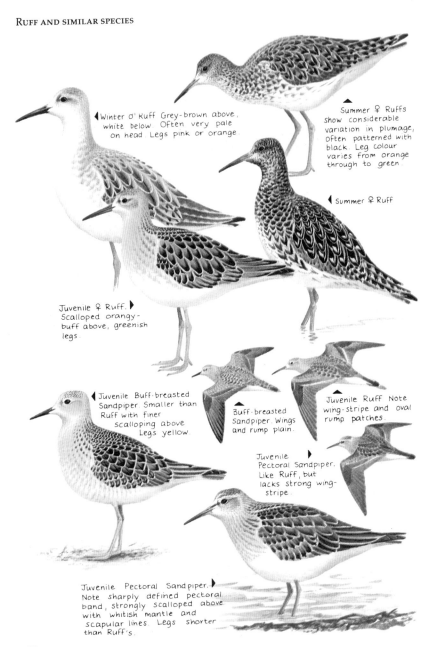

◀ Winter ♂ Ruff Grey-brown above, white below. Often very pale on head. Legs pink or orange.

Summer ♀ Ruffs show considerable variation in plumage, often patterned with black. Leg colour varies from orange through to green.

◀ Summer ♀ Ruff

Juvenile ♀ Ruff. ▶ Scalloped orangy-buff above, greenish legs.

◀ Juvenile Buff-breasted Sandpiper. Smaller than Ruff with finer scalloping above. Legs yellow.

Buff-breasted Sandpiper. Wings and rump plain.

Juvenile Ruff Note wing-stripe and oval rump patches.

Juvenile Pectoral Sandpiper. Like Ruff, but lacks strong wing-stripe.

Juvenile Pectoral Sandpiper. ▶ Note sharply defined pectoral band, strongly scalloped above with whitish mantle and scapular lines. Legs shorter than Ruff's.

totanus, females are about 25% smaller. Rather a gangly, small-headed, short-billed, bulky-bodied bird that strides around in purposeful manner. Will also wade into water to feed, immersing both head and bill below surface. Distant individuals can be confused with Redshank, which has similar walk. Redshank is, however, longer- and straighter-billed and darker below. Adult Redshank has red legs, but juvenile's are dull orange, a colour often shown by Ruffs. If in doubt, wait until bird flies (Redshank's white secondaries and rump should be conspicuous).

Plumage *Adult summer* Males readily identified by ornamental head plumes, which vary from white, black-and-white, through black and brown to ginger. Passage males often retain traces of this feathering. Adult females also variable: essentially brown, variably and irregularly patterned with coarse black-and-white markings. Some very heavily patterned, while others (no doubt mainly first-summers) are plainer and browner. Bill either dark or dark with pink base, while legs vary from pinky-orange to green (latter no doubt also first-summers). *Juvenile* Most August–October migrants are juveniles, easily separated from adults. Underparts a distinct orangy-buff, while upperparts very neatly patterned with pale feather edgings, producing attractively scalloped appearance. Bill dark (never showing pink base); legs dull, usually greenish. *Winter* Ruffs are more distinctive in winter. Essentially pale grey above (with paler feather edgings) and white below; often show noticeable white patch on forehead. Some, nearly always males, have white on sides of neck and on breast, while others are completely white-headed. Bill often has pink base; legs bright pink or orange, although first-winters show duller, greenish legs.

Flight Identification Shows prominent white wingstripe and white patches on sides of rump and uppertail-coverts; some virtually lack dark central dividing bar, creating white crescent-shaped rump patch. Long-winged, with effortless, languid flight action.

Voice Very silent, but rarely gives low, hoarse grunt.

Buff-breasted Sandpiper
Tryngites subruficollis

Size and Shape Superficially similar to a small juvenile female Ruff, but easily identified. Male larger than female, but basically a *small* wader, only slightly taller than Dunlin *Calidris alpina*. Shape resembles Ruff, but is less gangly, proportionately longer-bodied and squarer-headed.

Plumage Whole of underparts uniformly pale buff, less intense in tone and less orangy than juvenile Ruff. Some juveniles, however, much whiter on belly and a few show abrupt demarcation between the buff and the white. Large dark eye and pale eye-ring stand out strongly on bland, plain-looking face, and streaked crown can give slight capped effect. Like Ruff, upperpart feathers are edged buff, but edgings are narrower and therefore upperparts appear much less coarsely patterned. Legs ochre-yellow (greenish on juvenile Ruff). Ageing not easy, but summer adults have less well-defined, thicker buff edgings to upperparts, lacking dark submarginal crescents of juvenile. Autumn adults may show varying amounts of plainer, greyer winter upperpart feathering.

Flight Identification Always looks small and rather plover-like, lacking Ruff's easy, languid flight action. Pattern completely different from Ruff, lacking prominent wingstripe and with plain rump and uppertail-coverts. Underwings very white, with thick dark crescent across under primary coverts. In flight, feet do not project beyond tail (unlike Ruff).

Voice Like Ruff, a very silent wader, but occasionally utters a low, gruff *chu*.

Habitat and Behaviour Frequents short-grass habitats, e.g. golf courses, airfields, but will also associate with other small waders in more typical freshwater environments. An active feeder, walking quickly and daintily, picking every two or three steps, but actions rather erratic, with frequent changes of direction (lacks Ruff's smoother, more confident walk and slower, more deliberate picking action). Does not wade into water to feed. Often very tame, crouching low and freezing when approached or, alternatively, running off before observer, with neck extended.

Pectoral Sandpiper *Calidris melanotos*

Size and Shape In flight, superficially similar to Ruff, but quite different at rest. Male larger than female, but much smaller than Ruff, intermediate in size between Dunlin and Green Sandpiper *Tringa ochropus*. A less upright, more horizontal bird than Ruff, with rather long body and attenuated rear end. Legs rather short.

Plumage Easily identified by underpart pattern. Has clear-cut, well-defined, neatly streaked buff breast band, clearly demarcated from white belly. Like juvenile Ruff, has thick pale feather edgings on upperparts, but pale edgings to mantle feathers produce noticeable pale back V. Legs yellowish, but sometimes greenish, brownish or even orangy. Summer adults and juveniles similar, but adults are less neatly patterned and slightly messier than juveniles, with coarser head streaking and plainer, greyer-edged median coverts which contrast more with pale-edged scapulars. Summer males rather mottled on breast compared with females. Winter individuals plainer and greyer above, with diffuse feather edgings, and lack white mantle Vs. This plumage, however, unlikely to be seen in this country (post-breeding moult takes place mainly in winter quarters), but early-spring migrants may show greater proportion of winter feathering.

Flight Identification Resembles Ruff in having two oval white patches on sides of rump and uppertail-coverts, but lacks obvious wingstripe. Also lacks Ruff's languid flight action.

Voice Calls frequently in flight: a croaky *t-reep*, *kreep* or *chrupp*, recalling low, subdued Curlew Sandpiper *C. ferruginea*.

Behaviour Less mobile than Ruff, feeding on flexed legs with head down, and with rapid vertical picking motion.

Reference For separation of Pectoral from similar Sharp-tailed Sandpiper *C. acuminata*, see Britton (1973).

Snipe and Jack Snipe

Where and When Snipe *Gallinago gallinago* is a widespread and locally common resident, with numbers inflated by Continental immigrants in autumn and winter. Jack Snipe *Lymnocryptes minimus* is a rather localised winter visitor, occurring mainly from late September to April.

Habitat Jack Snipe is a peculiarly secretive bird, rarely straying from well-vegetated soggy places. Edges of reed-beds, overgrown ditches and coastal *Spartina* marshes are favoured habitats. Unlike Snipe, it avoids open mud at all costs and does not wade out into open water to feed. Generally speaking, the only chance of seeing it on the ground is from the seclusion of a well-situated hide.

Flight Identification Unlike Snipe, Jack Snipe waits until almost underfoot before taking flight, often startling the observer as it does so. Once airborne, it tends to fly low and straight, often rising rather half-heartedly and quickly dropping back into cover with half-closed wings although, like Snipe, may fly some distance. Can sometimes be repeatedly flushed. In contrast, Snipe's panicking escape flight is towering and zigzagging, often disappearing high into distance before resettling. Whereas Snipe takes to the air with a characteristic squelching call, Jack Snipe is usually silent, uttering at best a low, barely audible, rather desultory call, similar to Snipe's but weaker. Beware, however, occasional tight-sitting Snipe which may fly off without calling and without zigzagging. In flight, Jack Snipe is easily separated by its small size, short bill, prominent golden back stripes and shorter, more rounded wings.

Behaviour On the ground, Jack Snipe is decidedly crake-like in behaviour, feeding furtively on edge of reeds or among low vegetation. It uses its short bill to pick at the surface of mud, probing less than Snipe, and has a peculiar habit of rhythmically bobbing body up and down, like some sort of bizarre clockwork toy. Feeding Snipe, on the other hand, has more vigorous 'sewing machine' probing action which enables distant recognition simply by the rhythm of its head movements.

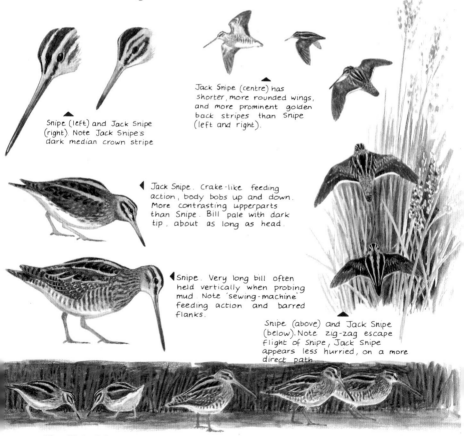

Snipe (left) and Jack Snipe (right). Note Jack Snipe's dark median crown stripe

Jack Snipe (centre) has shorter, more rounded wings, and more prominent golden back stripes than Snipe (left and right).

Jack Snipe. Crake-like feeding action, body bobs up and down. More contrasting upperparts than Snipe. Bill pale with dark tip, about as long as head.

Snipe. Very long bill often held vertically when probing mud. Note 'sewing-machine' feeding action and barred flanks.

Snipe (above) and Jack Snipe (below). Note zig-zag escape flight of Snipe, Jack Snipe appears less hurried, on a more direct path.

Two Jack Snipes

Three Snipes

Plumage Head pattern of Jack Snipe diagnostic: crown dark, lacking buff central crown-stripe of Snipe; instead shows narrow buff lateral crown-stripe (or 'upper supercilium'), producing distinctive head pattern reminiscent of Broad-billed Sandpiper *Limicola falcinellus*. In addition, dark eye-stripe curves strongly around lower edge of ear-coverts. Golden back stripes stand out more strongly than Snipe's, while underparts lack Snipe's flank barring. Bill short (about equal to head length) and has a pale base, while squat body and rather truncated rear end somehow complement Jack Snipe's furtive feeding behaviour.

Godwits

Where and When Two races of Black-tailed Godwit occur in Britain and Ireland: nominate race breeds in small numbers, mainly in eastern England, but is scarce on passage and in winter; Icelandic race *islandica* breeds in small numbers in northern Scotland, but is much more numerous in winter and on passage, with concentrations in southern Ireland, northwest, south and southeast England. Bar-tailed Godwit breeds in arctic Scandinavia and USSR (some summer here), and is widely distributed around coast in winter; a large passage up English Channel in April and May involves birds that have wintered in West Africa. Both species occur inland in small numbers, mainly on autumn passage.

Black-tailed Godwit *Limosa limosa*

Structure Distant godwits can be difficult to identify, but concentrate on structure. Black-tailed is tall, elegant, with a long, relatively straight bill, long neck and long legs. Note in particular that tibia is longer than Bar-tailed's.

Plumage *Adult summer* Chestnut down to lower throat, with white belly variably barred dark (summer male Bar-tailed reddish right down to undertail-coverts); chestnut very intense on Icelandic race, more cinnamon-orange on nominate. Upperpart pattern differs from Bar-tailed: wing-coverts rather uniformly grey, while mantle and scapulars have plain grey feathering mixed with variable amounts of chequered black and chestnut. Pale super-cilium peters out behind eye. Base of bill pink on both species, but rather more extensive on Black-tailed, becoming bright orangy-yellow when breeding. *Winter* Whole plumage *uniformly* grey, with whiter belly; whitish supercilium up to eye but not beyond. Bar-tailed is browner, and upperpart patterning recalls Curlew *Numenius arquata*. *Juvenile* Icelandic race orange on throat and breast, and so bright that often taken for summer adult by less experienced observers; is, however, very smooth, immaculate and uniform below, lacking sharp contrast between breast and belly and lacking any barring. Nominate race paler, less intensely coloured. Upperparts on Icelandic differ from adult summer Black-tailed and from all plumages of Bar-tailed: brownish-black, neatly and evenly patterned with thick orange feather edgings which produce attractive tortoiseshell pattern (nominate race has paler and narrower feather edgings); on both races orange fades as autumn progresses. Supercilium prominent only before eye.

Flight Identification Very easily identified by huge white wingstripe, black tail and square white rump, combining to produce striking pattern. Underwing pure white, contrasting with black tips to primaries and secondaries. Legs project much further beyond tail than on Bar-tailed, which, together with longer neck and bill, produces more attenuated look.

Voice When breeding, has rhythmic *wick-a-wicka-a-wicka* call; otherwise rather silent, occasionally monosyllabic *tuk* or *kik*.

Black-tailed Godwit

Winter Black-tailed Godwit ▶

Winter Bar-tailed Godwit ▶

Easily separated by wing, rump and tail patterns.

Summer Black-tailed Godwit. Orange confined to upper breast. Belly whiter, scalloped black. Note longer bill and legs than Bar-tailed Godwit ▶

◀ Summer ♂ Bar-tailed Godwit. Solidly brick-red below.

Winter Bar-tailed Godwit. Note patterned upperparts and brownish breast. The bill is upcurved, and shorter than Black-tailed Godwit. ▼

Summer ♀ Bar-tailed ◀ Godwit. Most lack red below.

Winter Black-tailed Godwit. Long bill and legs. Plain grey breast and upperparts. ▼

Juvenile Bar-tailed Godwit. Curlew-like upperparts, buffish breast,

▲ Juvenile Black-tailed Godwit. Poor supercilium, patterned back, orangy breast.

▲ Juvenile Black-tailed Godwit of the race 'islandica'. Brighter orange to head and breast, strongly barred above.

85

Bar-tailed Godwit *Limosa lapponica*

Structure Looks decidedly short-legged and rather stocky compared with Black-tailed, and shows slightly steeper forehead. Bill generally slightly shorter, but females have longer bill than males (no overlap in measurements); bill slightly but noticeably upcurved.

Plumage *Adult summer* Obvious sexual dimorphism. Males uniformly orange-chestnut on whole of underparts, lacking white belly and barring. Females usually gain some chestnut or cinnamon but lack colour intensity of male; some retain winter-like plumage throughout summer. Entire upperparts browner than Black-tailed, strongly patterned with chestnut, brown and black, producing more variegated pattern. Supercilium broader and extends further beyond eye, but on breeding males is rather concolorous with rest of head. *Winter* Again, far more variegated above than Black-tailed. Upperpart feathers brownish-grey with paler sides and blacker centres, producing pattern reminiscent of Curlew, quite unlike plain grey of Black-tailed. Underparts whiter than Black-tailed, but lightly streaked browner across breast. Supercilium is more obvious behind eye. *Juvenile* Unlike Black-tailed and winter Bar-tailed, underparts are evenly shaded with buff. Also shows a variegated, Curlew-like pattern to upperparts, quite unlike tortoiseshell scalloping of juvenile Black-tailed. Each feather shows a dark brown centre and broad, slightly notched buff sides, neater, more regular and more contrasting than winter adult. Supercilium differences as adult.

Flight Identification Completely different from Black-tailed: plain brown wings, barred tail, and white rump extending up back in a V, overall pattern reminiscent of Curlew. Underwing duller than Black-tailed's, and primary and secondary tips greyish and less contrasting. Legs do not project so far beyond tail, producing more truncated rear end. If bill not visible, distant Bar-tailed can be difficult to separate from Whimbrel *N. phaeopus* (see page 87).

Voice Quite vocal in flight, giving mellow, rhythmic *er-ik, ik-ik* or quicker *ik-ik-ik-ik*.

Curlew and Whimbrel

Where and When Curlew *Numenius arquata* is widespread as a breeding bird, mainly on damp upland moors in the north and west; Whimbrel *N. phaeopus* breeds only in Shetland, Orkney, the Hebrides and northern Scotland. Outside breeding season, Curlew is common right around the coast and also inland in some areas. Whimbrel is a fairly common spring (April–May) and autumn (July–October) passage migrant. Large concentrations (sometimes over 1000) have occurred in spring in Bridgwater Bay, Somerset; very small numbers winter in southern Britain and Ireland.

Size and Structure Whimbrel appears smaller, stockier than Curlew, with short neck and short legs; bill looks relatively straight, but markedly downcurved towards tip. Curlew has longer, more evenly curved bill (males have shorter bills than females); juveniles are slightly straighter-billed than adults.

Plumage Whimbrel's pale crown-stripe, dark lateral crown-stripes and dark eye-stripe should be obvious, but some Curlews show hint of crown-stripe. Juveniles of both have fresher, buffer plumage.

Flight Identification Curlew has relatively pale, mottled plumage with

Note more contrasting wing pattern of Curlew.

Winter Bar-tailed Godwit ▶ in flight. Similar to Whimbrel, note straight or upturned bill.

◀ Whimbrel   ◀ Curlew

Whimbrel. Smaller than Curlew, with shorter, straighter bill, curved at tip. Note strong supercilium and crown-stripes. ▼

Curlew. Large size, long curved bill, plainer appearance to head. ▲

contrasting dark outer primaries and primary coverts. On Whimbrel, wings are darker and more uniform. Whimbrel's shorter, rather more triangular wings produce quicker wingbeats than Curlew, whose longer wings produce slower, more languid, gull-like flight. Distant Whimbrels are difficult to separate from Bar-tailed Godwit *Limosa lapponica*. This problem is particularly acute in spring when large numbers of Bar-tailed move up English Channel, often well out to sea. In such circumstances, godwits often form large, purposeful flocks, whereas Whimbrels tend to form smaller, straggly lines. Whereas Whimbrel tends to give a head-up, crop-out impression in flight, Bar-tailed Godwit has long, almost drooping neck. When seen together, Bar-tailed is noticeably smaller and slimmer-winged.
Calls The easiest way to separate Curlew

and Whimbrel is by call. Curlew has a loud, mournful *cur-lew*, *cur-loo* or variations thereof (sometimes drawn into a bubbling call); also gives an alarm note: a rapid *kvi-kvi-kvi-kvi*. Whimbrel has a very distinctive, easily imitated seven-note whistle. Just to confuse matters, however, Whimbrel *rarely* gives a rather Curlew-like *cur-ew*, although this may be tagged on to the conventional call. Curlew has a well-known, haunting, bubbling song. Whimbrel's song is a liquid rippling, similar to the call but longer and more liquid and interspersed with a shriller *oo-eeep*.
'Hudsonian Whimbrel' There are four British records (1955–80) of North American race of Whimbrel *hudsonicus* or 'Hudsonian Whimbrel'. Separated by its brown lower back and rump; underwing browner, upperparts greyer, chest mottled and plumage more immaculate (*BWP*).

Large Tringa: Redshank, Spotted Redshank, Greenshank, Marsh Sandpiper and Lesser and Greater Yellowlegs

Where and When Redshank is common on coastal marshes and estuaries, but also occurs inland on migration and in winter; it breeds on coastal and inland marshes. Greenshank breeds in northern Scotland, but both it and Spotted Redshank occur more widely on passage (inland and on coast); both species winter in small numbers, mainly in milder coastal regions. Marsh Sandpiper currently averages about four records a year, April–June and July–October, mainly in freshwater marshes in eastern England. Lesser Yellowlegs is a rare North American vagrant, with widely scattered occurrences in spring, autumn and winter (averages about six a year). Greater Yellowlegs is an extreme rarity (29 records up to 1987), also from North America.

Redshank Tringa totanus

General Features A lively, noisy and excitable bird, typically seen flying off noisily when flushed from a saltmarsh creek; loose flocks form on open mudflats, packing together when roosting. At rest, a rather dumpy, featureless medium-sized wader, uniformly grey-brown from distance. At close range, bright red legs and bill base obvious on adults (duller on juveniles: see below). Feeds with brisk walk, stopping every few steps to probe or pick.

Plumage *Adult summer* Grey-brown to cinnamon, with variable amounts of black mottling and barring. *Winter* Plain grey-brown, lacking obvious markings at rest. *Juvenile* Potentially more confusing. Browner than adult, upperparts with neat, delicate buff spotting on feather edges. Legs and bill base dull orange (though latter may be grey). Can be confused with other species, notably Wood Sandpiper *T. glareola*, but darker, more uniform overall and plain-faced apart from pale eye-ring. If in doubt, wait until it flies.

Flight Identification Striking; easily identified by conspicuous white secondaries and white rump.

Calls Extremely noisy: calls loudly and excitably when flushed, *pit-u pit-u pit-u*; normal flight call more subdued, melancholy *tew* or *pit-ew*, mellower and less incisive than corresponding call of Greenshank. Other calls include mellow *tew du du*, *tew du* or more abrupt *tyip tyip tyip tyip*.

Spotted Redshank Tringa erythropus

General Features Superficially similar to Redshank, but much more elegant, with long fine bill and longer legs. More lively in pursuit of prey, and typically wades up to belly. Small parties usually feed in shallow water, are particularly fond of estuarine creeks and channels.

Plumage *Adult summer* Easily identified by black head and underparts and white-spotted black upperparts. Females duller and less evenly coloured. Moulting adults patchy and blotchy. *Winter* Very pale, readily separated from uniformly darker grey-brown Redshank. Upperparts pale grey, underparts white. Conspicuous white supercilium curves up and over eye, peters out behind. Bright red legs, but, unlike Redshank, bill base red only on lower mandible. *Juvenile* Quite different from adults, but juvenile plumage quickly lost during autumn. A dusky, smoky-brown wader, evenly coloured on underparts, but with delicate diffuse barring visible at close range. Neat pale feather edgings and spotting on upperparts. White supercilium contrasts even more markedly with dusky plumage.

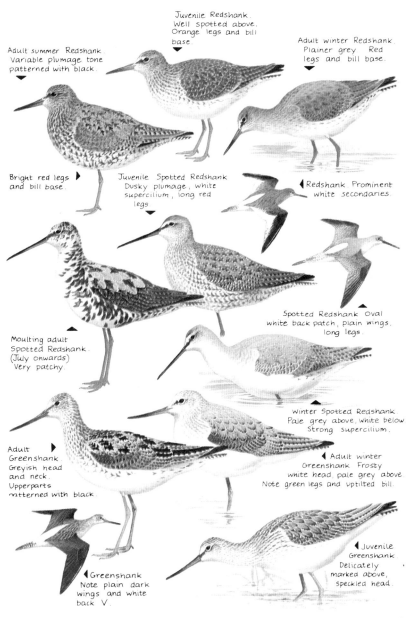

Adult summer Redshank. Variable plumage tone patterned with black.

Juvenile Redshank. Well spotted above. Orange legs and bill base.

Adult winter Redshank. Plainer grey. Red legs and bill base.

Bright red legs and bill base.

Juvenile Spotted Redshank. Dusky plumage, white supercilium, long red legs.

Redshank. Prominent white secondaries.

Spotted Redshank. Oval white back patch, plain wings, long legs.

Moulting adult Spotted Redshank. (July onwards) Very patchy.

Winter Spotted Redshank. Pale grey above, white below. Strong supercilium.

Adult Greenshank. Greyish head and neck. Upperparts patterned with black.

Adult winter Greenshank. Frosty white head, pale grey above. Note green legs and uptilted bill.

Greenshank. Note plain dark wings and white back V.

Juvenile Greenshank. Delicately marked above, speckled head.

89

Flight Identification More attenuated than Redshank, with long bill, and long legs projecting noticeably beyond tail. Easily identified by oval white patch on back (unlike Greenshank's white V). Rump and tail appear greyish; lacks Redshank's prominent white secondaries.
Call Diagnostic: a loud, disyllabic *tchoo-ik*. When flushed, may also occasionally give a softer *chu-chu*.

Greenshank *Tringa nebularia*

General Features Easily separated from both redshanks. From distance generally looks very pale, with frosty greyish-white head, pale grey upperparts and white underparts. Legs and bill base greenish (but former occasionally yellowish), bill slightly but distinctly upcurved (straighter on juveniles). Impetuous, energetic, noisy; often seen walking briskly along shoreline of a lake or reservoir or chasing small fish through estuarine shallows with lolloping gait and erratic changes in direction.
Plumage *Adult summer* Upperparts, particularly scapulars, show irregular black mottling. Head and breast greyer than in winter, and coarsely streaked. *Winter* Becomes very pale, with whitish head, evenly pale grey upperparts and very white underparts. *Juvenile* Similar to winter, but head greyer, not so white. Upperparts pale grey but neatly patterned, each feather edged paler. Sides of breast neatly streaked with grey. Looks smooth, immaculate and evenly patterned compared with late-summer adults, which retain some black upperpart feathering and look rather messy and coarsely streaked.
Flight Identification Distinctive: dark grey wings, pale tail and sharp white V extending up back.
Call Wary, flying off with penetrating *tew tew tew* which, when bird really spooked, becomes hoarse and angry. Also gives excited *chip*.

Marsh Sandpiper *Tringa stagnatilis*

General Features In many ways recalls miniature Greenshank. A small, delicate, dainty wader, about half size of Greenshank (body size smaller than Green Sandpiper *T. ochropus*), but with long fine bill and very long legs. Feeds on soft mud or in shallow water, with dainty walk and rather deliberate downward dabbing movement of bill. Legs greenish (may be yellowish or orangy on breeding adults). Bill very fine, completely dark.
Plumage *Adult summer* Rather nondescript. Head, breast and upperparts brownish, with profuse but delicate black streaking and mottling. *Winter* Moults into winter plumage shortly after breeding, so late-summer adults essentially pale grey above and very white below. Head very pale, with white forehead extending back to form noticeable wedge-shaped white supercilium; slightly darker patch behind eye. May recall winter Wilson's Phalarope *Phalaropus tricolor*, though latter has shorter yellow legs, an uptilted 'gravy boat' shape and *square* white rump (hardly contrasting with pale grey tail). *Juvenile* Plumage very similar to juvenile Greenshank. Upperparts dark grey with even narrow white feather edgings; neat grey streaking on sides of breast. Head not so pale as winter adult, but has same clearcut supercilium and darker ear-coverts.
Flight Identification Very much recalls miniature long-legged Greenshank. Upperparts greyish or brownish, with very pale tail and sharply pointed white V extending up back. Legs project well beyond tail, producing very attenuated appearance. Tips of secondaries may appear slightly paler.
Call A thin, abrupt, slightly subdued *teur* or *tiur*, can recall a rather 'full' Little Ringed Plover *Charadrius dubius*. At other times becomes a rather more 'chipping' *tyip tyip*.

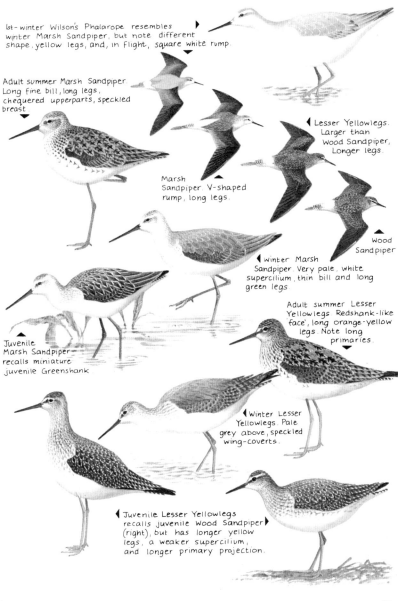

1st-winter Wilson's Phalarope resembles winter Marsh Sandpiper, but note different shape, yellow legs, and, in flight, square white rump.

Adult summer Marsh Sandpiper. Long fine bill, long legs, chequered upperparts, speckled breast.

Lesser Yellowlegs. Larger than Wood Sandpiper, longer legs.

Marsh Sandpiper. V-shaped rump, long legs.

Wood Sandpiper

Winter Marsh Sandpiper. Very pale, white supercilium, thin bill and long green legs.

Adult summer Lesser Yellowlegs Redshank-like 'face', long orange-yellow legs. Note long primaries.

Juvenile Marsh Sandpiper recalls miniature juvenile Greenshank

Winter Lesser Yellowlegs. Pale grey above, speckled wing-coverts.

Juvenile Lesser Yellowlegs recalls juvenile Wood Sandpiper (right), but has longer yellow legs, a weaker supercilium, and longer primary projection.

Lesser Yellowlegs *Tringa flavipes*

General Features Similar size to Redshank but slimmer and more elegant, with small head, longish neck and attenuated rear end (primaries extend 1–2cm beyond tail). Bill relatively short, but legs long and project well beyond tail in flight. Easily identified by bright ochre-yellow legs (note: Greenshank occasionally shows yellowish legs). Feeds with rapid, erratic side-to-side head movements.

Plumage *Adult summer* Head and breast streaked blackish, former plainer than winter and juvenile, with pale greyish supercilium. Upperparts dull brownish with irregular black markings, particularly on scapulars, but little white spotting. Pale yellow at base of bill. *Winter* Rather grey above, with light speckling on wing-coverts. Head and breast greyish; has white supercilium, petering out behind eye, and white eye-ring. *Juvenile* Resembles oversized juvenile Wood Sandpiper, with prominent white supercilium, petering out behind eye, white eye-ring, heavy white chequering on upperparts, and neat streaking on breast (forms band), but easily separated by larger size, long yellow legs, long primary projection and call.

Flight Identification Easily identified by *squared-off* white rump. Overall appearance recalls giant Wood Sandpiper, but note that legs protrude more conspicuously beyond tail. Rather easy flight action recalls Ruff *Philomachus pugnax*.

Call A rather quiet, abrupt *tu tu* or *tu tu tu*, like subdued Greenshank, but lacking 'ringing' quality. When alarmed, may give more anxious *ti ti tur tur tur*.

Greater Yellowlegs *Tringa melanoleuca*

Resembles Lesser Yellowlegs, but is larger than Greenshank and has long, gently upcurved bill. In summer plumage has heavier black underpart spotting than adult Lesser.

Green and Wood Sandpipers

Where and When Green Sandpiper *Tringa ochropus* is a fairly common autumn passage migrant from mid June, with peak in August; small numbers winter and there is a small spring passage, with a few present into May. Very small numbers of Wood Sandpipers *T. glareola* breed in Scotland, but otherwise it is strictly a spring and autumn migrant, mainly in May and mid July to September; highest numbers tend to occur in eastern counties. Both species occur almost exclusively in freshwater habitats.

Structure and Behaviour Although superficially similar in plumage pattern, Green and Wood Sandpipers are easily separated. Green is a rather hunched, short-legged, dumpy wader whose structure tends to recall a giant Common Sandpiper *Actitis hypoleucos*. Wood is slim, long-necked, small-headed and rather long-legged, its overall appearance vaguely suggesting miniature Redshank *T. totanus*. Wood is likely to be seen striding along an open shoreline, rather than feeding secretively on a small pool or muddy stream like Green.

Plumage Green is a *very dark* wader with *prominent breast band* and pale eye-ring, but, although it has white before eye, *it lacks a prominent supercilium*. The upperpart spotting is quite small, but beware of misidentifying a more coarsely patterned summer adult as Wood Sandpiper. Latter is much paler, browner, with *striking white supercilium*, white underparts with delicately streaked breast, and *heavily spotted or chequered upperparts*; its legs are paler than Green Sandpiper's.

Flight Identification Easily separated. Although both have plain wings and square white rump, Green is a very contrasting, black-and-white bird, whose overall appearance recalls a giant House Martin *Delichon urbica*; as well as contrasting white rump, note in particular its *blackish underwings*. Even in flight, Green looks a rather stocky wader and the legs do not noticeably project beyond tail; it tends to tower when flushed, calling noisily (see below). Wood Sandpiper looks much browner in flight, and slightly smaller white rump contrasts less with the browner plumage; key feature is *the pale whitish underwing*. Wood looks slimmer in flight, with feet projecting well beyond tail; it thus has a slim-winged, elongated appearance.

Calls Totally different. Green is a noisy, excitable bird and, when flushed, typically gives loud, ringing, *too-leet* or *too-leet . . . too-leet too-leet* (or variations thereof). Wood has a quick, shrill, high-pitched *chiff-if* or *chiff-if-if*.

Ageing Autumn juveniles of both species are neatly and delicately patterned, while contemporary late-summer adults are scruffier and more coarsely patterned. Some adult Green have a suspended wing

moult during autumn migration, so late-summer adults often have gaps in their inner primaries.

Other Confusion Species

Common Sandpiper At rest, distant Green can be confused with Common Sandpiper (see page 94 and page 95). Latter is smaller and browner, and tail protrudes well beyond wingtips; in addition, brown on breast tends to be confined to patches, while a small strip of white protrudes up around bend of wing. Differences in flight should be obvious (Common has a wingbar and a dark rump, and flies low with bowed wings and flicking flight).

Redshank Wood can be confused with juvenile Redshank at rest (page 88 and page 89). Latter has very *small* upperpart spotting, lacks supercilium, has darker breast and orange legs, and in flight shows white secondaries and white, V-shaped rump.

Lesser Yellowlegs Wood has similar plumage to Lesser Yellowlegs, particularly when juvenile. (See page 91 and page 92.)

Common and Spotted Sandpipers

Where and When Common Sandpiper *Actitis hypoleucos* is common summer visitor, mainly in upland areas of Scotland, northern England, Wales and Ireland. More widespread on migration, frequenting mainly freshwater habitats, but also occurs on coast. Small numbers winter, mainly in southern areas. Spotted Sandpiper *A. macularia*, its North American counterpart, is a very rare vagrant, mainly in autumn, but also occurs in spring and several have overwintered; currently about four records a year (a pair nested in Scotland in 1975).

Structure Structural differences are perhaps most likely to attract initial attention. Spotted is rather pot-bellied, flat-backed and square-headed compared

with Common. Most important is tail length: Spotted has short tail which usually protrudes only just beyond closed wings, while some have tail length equal to wing length so that wings completely cloak tail. Common has longer tail which projects well beyond wingtips. Spotted's shorter tail thus produces more truncated rear end, but beware of occasional shorter-tailed Common (perhaps mainly juveniles which have not fully grown their tail feathers).

Plumage *Juvenile* Most autumn Spotted are juveniles and are unlikely to occur before late August. Very detailed field notes are essential to ensure acceptance by *British Birds* Rarities Committee. Close

Juvenile Wood Sandpiper. Note browner plumage with strongly chequered upperparts and prominent supercilium

Juvenile Green Sandpiper. Plumper and shorter-legged, darker above and lightly spotted with a strong breast band. Note short supercilium.

Wood Sandpipers. Slimmer and slighter with legs projecting beyond tail. Note pale underwings, less contrasting rump and brown upperparts.

Green Sandpipers. Very black-and-white, legs short, not projecting far beyond tail. Note blackish underwings.

Adult Wood Sandpipers. Note slimmer shape, recalling a small 'shank'. Upperparts well chequered, streaked breast band and strong supercilium.

Wood Sandpiper. Note longer tibia than Green Sandpiper, legs typically paler and yellower.

Adult Green Sandpipers. Spotting stronger than on juvenile. Note stockier shape than Wood Sandpiper, recalling large Common Sandpiper.

Juvenile Spotted Sandpiper. Note short tail, well-patterned wing-coverts, stronger supercilium, two-toned bill and, usually, yellower legs.

Juvenile Common Sandpiper. Note long tail, less contrasting wing-coverts, duller bill and legs. Less clean-looking.

Winter Spotted Sandpiper Wing-coverts duller than juvenile. Bill, supercilium and leg differences as for juvenile. Primaries often completely cloak tail. Looks pot-bellied.

Winter Common Sandpiper. Note long tail.

Spotted Sandpiper (left) and Common Sandpiper (right). Spotted Sandpiper has more black on inner secondaries and a strongly barred tail.

Note difference in tertial pattern. Common Sandpiper (top) has notched edges, Spotted Sandpiper's are plain.

inspection should reveal following differences (in rough order of significance): **1 TERTIALS** Differences diagnostic. On Common, edges of tertials have buff notching; on Spotted, they are *plain*, with barring confined to tip. **2 WING-COVERTS** Prominently barred pale buff, black and brown on Spotted, forming large barred patch at distance; juvenile Common is also barred, but bars are closer in colour and, therefore, not so striking. (Note that this area can be obscured by breast and scapular feathers.) **3 BILL** Spotted's bill is usually flesh-coloured with dark tip; Common's is greyer and plainer. Some Spotted, however, have plain bill with inconspicuous horn-coloured base to lower mandible. **4 SUPERCILIUM AND EYE-RING** Eye-ring distinctly whiter and more obvious on Spotted and supercilium often also better defined, producing 'sharper' facial expression. **5 LEGS** Usually much yellower, often strikingly so, on Spotted, but some have much duller greener or greyer legs with little yellow apparent, and therefore more similar to Common (which usually have dull greeny-yellow legs). **6 PLUMAGE TONE** Spotted is generally slightly greyer than

95

Common, especially on head, neck and breast sides. **7 BREAST PATCHES** Smaller, neater, plainer and less extensive on Spotted. **8 OPEN WING** Wingbar is narrower towards base on Spotted and darker inner secondaries highlight white trailing edge; on Common, wingbar and trailing edge virtually converge on inner secondaries. **9 OUTER TAIL FEATHERS** More extensive barring on Spotted, making tail look barred to edge. Note that summer-plumaged Common has upperparts delicately patterned with black, so is readily distinguishable from juvenile Spotted *Adult* Adult Spotted may start to moult during autumn migration, but moult is not completed until arrival in winter quarters and many reach there still in full breeding plumage. This means that autumn adults in this country should retain much of their summer plumage and are, therefore, easily identifiable. Winter plumage is usually acquired in late October or early November. Adult winter and first-winter very similar, appear very plain above, with only buffish tips to wing-coverts; these feathers are, therefore, much plainer than on juvenile and do not stand out as a paler, barred patch. Winter Spotted Sandpipers are best identified by structure, bare-part coloration and facial pattern, but at least some seem to show traces of spotting on rear flanks and undertail-coverts throughout winter.

Calls Spotted's calls are generally quieter and less ringing than Common's, but there is some overlap. Note that some Commons utter softer calls, reminiscent of Spotted. Some of Spotted's calls recall Green Sandpiper *Tringa ochropus*. Single migrants often rather silent, sometimes uttering only single, quiet *pit* (Oddie 1980). *References* Oddie (1980), Wallace (1970).

Phalaropes

Where and When Grey Phalarope breeds in the Arctic and winters off western coasts of Africa. Autumn migrants passing down Atlantic are sometimes hit by westerly gales, and large numbers are occasionally seen off southwest England (particularly Cornwall); smaller numbers occur elsewhere, even inland. The peak month is September, but there are occasional records in both winter and spring. Small numbers of Red-necked Phalaropes breed in the northern isles, but virtually all European breeders migrate southeast in autumn to the Caspian and Black Seas and to the Persian Gulf, so species does not usually occur in western areas after gales; it is more likely to be seen in eastern counties in spring and early autumn (peak in August, much earlier than Grey), but occurrences are not necessarily associated with adverse weather. Wilson's Phalarope breeds in North America and is a vagrant, currently averaging about 10 records a year, mostly of young birds in September; there are, however, also records of adults in spring and late summer, often on the English east coast.

Grey *Phalaropus fulicarius* and Red-necked Phalaropes *P. lobatus*

General Features The two commoner species are easily told from other waders by their persistent swimming and by the prominent black patch through eye. In Britain and Ireland, Grey Phalarope is markedly pelagic, but storm-driven migrants occur in all types of saline and freshwater environments. Most Red-necked occur in coastal marshes or freshwater habitats.

Structure Grey is a slightly larger, bulkier bird, but concentrate in particular on the bill: on Red-necked it is very fine and needle-like, but on Grey it is thicker and blunter. As both are invariably tame, this is not difficult to evaluate, but note that differences are not so apparent at a distance.

Juvenile Red-necked Phalarope. Dark, with white wing-stripe.

Juvenile Red-necked Phalarope. Smaller than Grey Phalarope, fine bill. Dark above with buffish lines on mantle and scapulars. White patch at bend of wing.

Juvenile Grey Phalarope also looks dark in flight, note acquisition of grey 1st-winter feathering on scapulars.

Winter Red-necked Phalarope. Grey above with darker feather centres. Note fine bill.

Juvenile Grey Phalarope. Dark above like Red-necked Phalarope but lacks strong buff 'V's and usually shows grey patches on back and scapulars. Note larger size and thicker bill.

Advanced juvenile Grey Phalarope with extensive grey 1st-winter feathering.

Winter Grey Phalarope. Plain pale grey above. Note thick bill.

Juvenile Wilson's Phalarope, moulting to 1st-winter. Larger than other phalaropes, more terrestrial. Note yellow legs, white rump and plain wings in flight.

Plumage *Summer adults* The two species are totally different in summer: Red-necked has red confined to neck; Grey has entire underparts red, except for a white face, and yellow base to bill. In both species, the female is brighter than the male. *Juveniles and first-winters* Most autumn phalaropes seen in this country are in juvenile/first-winter plumage. In full juvenile plumage the two species are similar, so it is essential to concentrate on structure (see above). Grey Phalarope is dark blackish-brown above, with buff feather edgings and ill-defined Vs down sides of mantle; it also shows a strong pinkish-buff wash to breast. Red-necked is similar, but shows better-defined golden mantle and scapular Vs, which are usually prominent; it also shows a small white patch at bend of wing. Grey Phalarope has a square ear-patch that extends back horizontally from eye; on Red-necked, the ear-patch tends to curve down behind eye and ends in more of a point. By the time juvenile phalaropes migrate, they have usually lost most of the dark shading on the breast, but Greys usually retain a faint peachy tint. Migrant juvenile Red-necked do not usually show signs of obvious upperpart moult, presumably as most come through early. By contrast, juvenile Greys quickly acquire pale grey first-winter feathering and, even by early September, usually show a distinctly patchy two-toned appearance to upperparts; initially, scapulars stand out as a pale grey patch, but eventually most of juvenile mantle feathering is also lost so that, by late autumn, only wing-coverts and tertials remain dark brown (note that winter adults are wholly pale grey above, including tertials). *Winter* Best identified by structural differences as both are entirely pale grey above, but Red-necked is slightly darker and shows more noticeable pale feather edgings to many of upperpart feathers. Differences in shape of eye-patch may also be useful (see

above). Winter adult Red-necked are very rare in this country, whereas small numbers of adult Greys occur fairly regularly.

Flight Identification Difficult to separate, but Red-necked is shorter-winged than Grey. As vast majority of phalaropes seen on seawatches are Grey, it would be very unwise to claim a fly-by Red-necked. Grey is similar to Sanderling *Calidris alba* in flight, appearing pale grey with a prominent wingbar, but Grey Phalarope is longer-winged and has a rather long, full tail and distinctive side-to-side jinking flight action.

Calls Both give a monosyllabic *chip* call, that of Red-necked apparently being lower-pitched.

Wilson's Phalarope *Phalaropus tricolor*

General Features Completely different from Grey and Red-necked. A freshwater species that is much more at home on land, where confusion with Wood Sandpiper *Tringa glareola*, Lesser Yellowlegs *T. flavipes* and Marsh Sandpiper *T. stagnatilis* is more likely (see pages 90–94). Although Wilson's often swims, it does not generally do so persistently. Conversely, it should also be remembered that some common waders, such as Spotted Redshank *T. erythropus* and Greenshank *T. nebularia*, will also swim on occasion. Wilson's has a distinctive shape, with fine black bill, small head and long neck. The whole bird often looks tipped forward when feeding, rather like an uptilted gravy boat. Feeding action may be quick and erratic, or slow and methodical, sometimes stalking flies with head and bill stretched out parallel to ground.

Plumage *Adult summer* Female easily identified by grey, black and chestnut stripes on neck and grey and chestnut upperparts, but males are markedly duller, with brown and orange-brown replacing bright colours of female. *Juvenile, first-winter and winter adult* Juvenile and winter-plumaged Wilson's usually look very pale. Underparts are very white and there is a dark line through eye that extends obscurely down sides of neck. Juvenile brown above, with pale feather edgings, but most vagrants arriving in Europe have already started to acquire pale grey first-winter plumage on back and scapulars. Winter adults are com- pletely pale grey above and lack autumn juvenile/first-winter's dark brown wing-coverts and tertials. Unlike other phalaropes, the legs are yellow in autumn. In flight, shows plain wings, square white rump, and pale grey tail that hardly con-trasts with rump.

Call Generally silent, but occasionally gives unremarkable, soft, nasal *chu* or *yup*.

Arctic, Pomarine and Long-tailed Skuas

Where and When Arctic Skua breeds in northern and western Scotland and is a widespread coastal migrant, mainly in April–May and August–October. Pomarine Skua is an uncommon migrant, mainly in late April–May and August–October but, unlike the other two species, small num-bers sometimes occur until mid winter; it tends to be most numerous in North Sea, but there is a regular spring passage moves up English Channel and off Outer Hebrides and northwest Ireland. Long-tailed is by far the rarest skua (in 1981–90, about 370 records a year); like Pomarine, it is com-monest in North Sea, but there is also a large spring passage off Outer Hebrides. All three species may, however, turn up almost anywhere and small numbers even appear inland after gales or, more usually, during gloomy anticyclonic weather.

The three smaller skuas are notoriously difficult to identify. Individual variation is considerable, and the problem can be compounded by effects of bleaching and wear. Also, little is known about their immature plumages, which are unfamiliar in the northern hemisphere as skuas usu-ally remain in winter quarters during their first summer. A more general northerly return takes place in second summer, but skuas do not reach maturity until about three to five years old. In view of com-plexities of identifying winter adults and immatures, only summer adults and juveniles are dealt with in depth; other plumages are outlined on page 104.

Arctic Skua *Stercorarius parasiticus*

Structure Size intermediate between Pomarine and Long-tailed (similar in size to Common Gull *Larus canus*, but much sturdier), with pointed tail projection. Structural differences from Pomarine and Long-tailed are dealt with under those species.

Plumage *Adult summer* Dark-phase adults (commonest) appear completely dark fulvous-brown, usually with yellow-ish or olive cheeks and ear-coverts. Pale-phase adults have diffuse brownish cap and are mainly white below, usually with yellowish face; often have breast band, of variable width and extent. Three or four white primary shafts on upperwing (cf. Long-tailed), showing as pale crescent on underwing. Upperparts brown, showing little or no contrast between trailing edge (secondaries) and wing-coverts (again, cf. Long-tailed). Intermediate-phase adults vary between dark and light phases. *Juvenile* Juvenile skuas can usually be recognised by the barred underwing-coverts and axillaries, blue-grey to pinkish-grey bill base and blue-grey to whitish legs. Plumage tone varies, and Arctic is more variable than Pomarine; underparts vary from uniformly blackish through brown to greyish-white, barred brownish. Differences from Pomarine and Long-tailed are outlined under those species, but following are main charac-teristics of Arctic. 1 FEATHER EDGINGS

Adult summer Long-tailed Skua. Note upperwing contrast not shown in Arctic Skua.

Adult summer Arctic Skua Pale phase.

Adult summer Long-tailed Skua. Little white in wing, dark belly, long tail.

Adult summer Arctic Skua. Pale phase.

Adult summer Pomarine Skua. Pale phase.

Compare keel shapes, wing proportions and tail lengths and shapes.

Juvenile Long-tailed Skua. Note cold plumage tones, dark pectoral band, pale nape and elongated, rounded central tail feathers.

Adult summer Arctic Skua Dark phase.

Juvenile Arctic Skuas. Note warm plumage tones, pale nape, streaked upper-breast, pale tipped primaries and pointed central tail feathers. Dark birds (behind) more uniform.

Adult summer Pomarine Skua Dark phase.

Adult winter Pomarine Skua. Large and bulky. Barred uppertail-coverts. Short 'spoons' (may be lost when moulting).

Juvenile Pomarine Skua. Note large two-toned bill, greyish tone to head, which is more uniform and barred rather than streaked. Evenly barred breast and underparts. Usually lacks pale primary tips.

Juvenile Long-tailed Skua Note dark secondary bar, lacks white in primaries.

Juvenile Long-tailed Skua, pale phase.

Juvenile Long-tailed Skua, dark phase. Note blunt tail projection. Size of Kittiwake.

Juvenile Long-tailed Skua Cold, greyish tones. Neat, even barring to underwing, tail-coverts and rump. Dark breast, pale belly.

Juvenile Arctic Skua Note pointed tail projection, white primary bases, warm plumage tones, less distinct barring on rump and undertail-coverts.

Juvenile Arctic Skua, pale phase Note gingery plumage tones, indistinct barring beneath.

Juvenile Arctic Skua, dark phase. Bill looks uniform, undertail-coverts may appear plain.

Adult Great Skua Short tail, large white wing flashes. Large size, heavy body, black bill.

Juvenile Pomarine Skua Note double white wing patch on underwing. Heavy chest, broad-winged.

Juvenile Pomarine Skua Note size and bulk. Two-toned bill, heavily barred rump and undertail-coverts. Tail projection, if present, blunt.

101

Compared with Long-tailed, pale feather edgings are warmer in tone (buff or chestnut) and do not contrast against richer brown plumage. 2 UNDERTAIL-COVERTS Often barred; many juvenile Arctics, however, have uniformly dark undertail-coverts (always barred on Long-tailed), but such birds are usually solidly blackish-brown, without barring on belly and flanks. 3 UPPER PRIMARY PATCH First three or four primary shafts are white (only two on Long-tailed). 4 UNDER PRIMARY PATCH Does not generally show a narrow pale crescent in front of pale patch at base of primaries (unlike Pomarine). 5 TAIL PROJECTIONS *Short and pointed* (always blunt and often long on Long-tailed and Pomarine). 6 HINDNECK Most have contrasting pale hindneck (unlike Pomarine).

Pomarine Skua *Stercorarius pomarinus*

Structure and Flight Adults most easily identified by blunt, twisted central tail feathers, which look like spoons or legs/feet trailing out behind. Juveniles lack the 'spoons'; they do have a short, blunt projection, but this difficult to see at a distance (may even be absent). Winter adults show short projection that is hardly twisted, while some apparently bite it off! With Pomarines lacking 'spoons', it is essential to concentrate on overall size and structure. Pomarine is a large skua, approaching Lesser Black-backed Gull *L. fuscus* in size, but is a hefty, thickset, powerful bird with large head and heavy, hooked bill. Most importantly, the wings are broad-based and it has a barrel-chested appearance recalling Gyrfalcon *Falco rusticolus* (Arctic Skua is slimmer and flatter-chested); deep-chested appearance may be emphasised by a thick breast band. Juveniles or dark-phase adults can be confused with Bonxie *S. skua*, a mistake unlikely when identifying Arctic. Has slower, steadier, more purposeful flight than Arctic. It tends to chase larger birds,

such as Herring *L. argentatus* and Lesser Black-backed Gulls, and may even force them into sea. Like Bonxie, often feeds on scraps.

Plumage *Adult summer* About 90% of adults are pale phase. Apart from tail 'spoons' no single plumage character separates Pomarine from Arctic, though former is *generally* darker, has more ragged appearance to vent, more prominent breast band, greater incidence of flank barring and larger wing patches (*BWP*), but beware of superficial similarity between adult Pomarine and 'sub-adult' Arctic. *Juvenile* Main differences from Arctic are as follows. 1 PLUMAGE TONE Generally rather dark, and is fairly consistent in plumage tone. Typically gives a grey-brown impression with barred underparts and cinnamon or buff tips to upperparts, latter being generally better defined than on Arctic. 2 UNDERWING CRESCENT Best way to distinguish juvenile Pomarine is by prominent whitish crescent in front of large pale patch at base of under primaries; crescent is formed by pale bases of greater under primary coverts and, in good light, is visible at long range. Arctic may show faint, diffuse crescent in front of primary patch, but this hardly visible in the field. 3 TAIL-COVERT BARRING Has strong, pale barring on upper- and undertail-coverts, vent, lower belly and, sometimes, flanks. Arctic has narrower, more diffuse barring on vent and lower belly, giving contrast with undertail-coverts which Pomarine lacks. Note that dark Arctic may lack undertail-covert barring. 4 BILL Longer and heavier than Arctic, with more prominent gonydeal angle. Basal two-thirds pale bluish, olive or sandy, contrasting with dark tip, recalling first-winter Glaucous Gull *L. hyperboreus*; pale base may 'flash' paler at distance. Arctic's bill base is less prominent because (a) it is usually slightly darker, (b) the bill is smaller and (c) the adjacent feathers are lighter and so do not contrast with the base. **5** HEAD Drab grey-brown, rarely showing contrasting pale hindneck (usually shows a lighter grey wash). Wholly brown–headed birds with barred underparts are almost certainly Pomarine. The few Arctics that *lack* contrasting light hindneck are usually solidly blackish-brown, unbarred on belly, flanks and tail-coverts. Dark streaking on head is typical of Arctic and is never present on Pomarine, which instead is lightly barred. **6** TAIL PROJECTIONS Short and rounded (always short and pointed on Arctic); some Pomarines lack projections altogether. **7** LEG COLOUR There is overlap in leg colour, and all three species may show whitish legs.

Long-tailed Skua *Stercorarius longicaudus*

Structure and Flight Although there is a size overlap, Long-tailed is as different from Arctic as Arctic is from Pomarine. A small skua, *similar in size to Kittiwake Rissa tridactyla*. Adults readily identified by incredibly long central tail feathers which quiver in flight: can have streamers up to 18cm (7in) in length. Note, however, overlap with Arctic, which can have projections up to 14cm (5½in), but Arctic's tail appears thick and tapered. Juvenile Long-tailed has a short to medium *blunt* projection (see below). Has smaller bill than Arctic with less of a gonydeal angle, and smaller, more rounded head (producing 'gentle' appearance recalling Common Gull *Larus canus*). Slimmer body with shallower breast, and narrower wings, especially at base. Whole effect is more tern-like than Arctic Skua, and it tends to have a more continuously flapping flight.

Plumage *Adult summer* Do not rely solely on tail length, but concentrate on structure and plumage. Long-tailed are more consistent in appearance than Arctic and even Pomarine: dark-phased birds are rare and intermediates virtually unknown. Typical adults differ from Arctic in following respects. **1** CAP Neat, clear-cut and black. **2** UNDERPARTS White, lacking breast band, but vent and lower belly usually dusky, contrasting with white throat and upper breast (sometimes dusky area includes lower breast). Some, however (mainly from North American/east Siberian populations), are much whiter-bellied. **3** UPPERPARTS Cold slate-grey, contrasting with black primaries and secondaries, latter forming dark trailing edge to wing (Arctics are plain brown above). **4** UPPER PRIMARY PATCHES Little or no white in upperwing, usually just two white primary shafts (Arctic has three or four, forming definite patch). Under primaries of Long-tailed also dark. **Juvenile** Exhibits variety of plumage tones, but separated from Arctic by following differences. **1** PLUMAGE TONE Generally a colder, greyer-looking bird than Arctic. **2** UPPERPART BARRING Upperparts show clearly defined cream or whitish barring contrasting with grey-brown background colour, producing rather scaly effect at distance (Arctic has buffer barring which contrasts less with browner plumage). **3** TAIL PROJECTIONS *Blunt-tipped*; length varies from short to medium. Always short and pointed on Arctic, so those Long-tailed which show longer projections are quite distinctive, although can be difficult to make out at a distance. **4** PRIMARY PATCHES Only one or two primary shafts are pure white (on Arctic, three or four are white). Consequently, shows little white on upperwing, but a larger patch on underwing. **5** UNDERPARTS Typically greyish, with finely barred flanks; many show darker breast with white area immediately below. Upper- and undertail-coverts noticeably barred, former often forming paler horseshoe above tail (some Arctics have plain undertail-coverts, never found on Long-tailed). **6** HEAD A pale greyish area on sides of head and nape shows to greater or lesser degree. Some pale individuals strikingly white-headed. **7** UNDERWING-COVERTS Heavily barred, especially on axillaries (some darker Arctics have uniform underwing-coverts, never found on Long-tailed). **8** BILL Generally more black at tip (40–50% of bill is black, compared with 25–30% on Arctic), and the black usually extends back past gonydeal angle and frequently tapers along cutting edges about half way back towards base. **9** PRIMARIES Unlike Arctic, lacks buff edgings to tips of closed primaries.

Other Plumages

Owing to complexities of identifying winter adults and immatures, it must be stressed that following details are generalised. *Adult winter* On failed breeders winter plumage starts to appear from July onwards and may be complete by August, but for most moult starts late August and is completed in winter quarters. Unlike most juveniles, winter adults lack underwing-covert and axillary barring and have black bill and legs. On pale-phased birds, cap becomes less distinct and throat and neck duskier; upperpart feathers show pale edgings and tail-coverts are barred, as on juveniles. Dark-phased individuals more similar to summer adult, but may acquire indistinct barring on tail-coverts. All adults have shorter tail projections in winter, while moulting individuals may temporarily lose them altogether. *Immatures* Owing to our incomplete knowledge, the notes below give only an outline and it should be stressed that immature skuas are notoriously variable, a problem exacerbated by wear and bleaching. Following details relate to Arctic Skua (from *BWP*), but the *sequence* appears similar for all species, although Pomarine

seems to take a year longer to reach maturity. Juvenile plumage is moulted in mid winter and 'first-winter' plumage is characterised by mixture of adult winter (including slightly longer tail projection) and juvenile characters (such as pale legs and, on pale-phased birds, barred underwing-coverts and axillaries). Dark-phased 'first-winters' more similar to juveniles, but on average less heavily barred. 'First-winter' plumage is retained until late summer, when replaced directly by second-winter, so *no first-summer plumage in between*. Second-winter similar to winter adult, but pale-phased birds again retain some barred juvenile-type feathers, while darker individuals more similar to winter adult dark-phased, but with paler, grey-blue legs and, in second-summer, less uniform upperparts (caused by mixture of old and new feathers). In their second summer, some arrive in breeding colonies with variable amounts of adult-like summer plumage mixed in with second-winter plumage. From then on, moults gradually produce more adult-like plumage until maturity, and traces of winter plumage no longer retained in summer. Some fully mature adults, however, may also retain traces of winter plumage on arriving on breeding grounds, while some immatures mature before others, so ageing very difficult once juvenile characters (such as pale legs and partially barred underwing-coverts and axillaries) lost.

References Broome (1987), Davenport (1987), Jonsson (1984), Mather (1981), Olsen & Christensen (1984), Ullman (1984).

Mediterranean Gull

Where and When Small numbers of
Mediterranean Gulls *Larus melanocephalus*
now occur throughout much of England,
Wales and southeastern Ireland, more
numerously towards south and east
(largest concentration at Folkestone,
Kent). A few pairs have bred recently in
southern England, but most are visitors.
Adults appear from July onwards and
leave in March or April. Juveniles appear
later, generally in August, and in some
areas there is a pronounced spring
passage of first-years, some of which
remain for summer. Patient and persistent
scrutiny of local gull roosts, both inland
and coastal, should reveal their presence.
Size, Structure and Behaviour Slightly
larger, distinctly heavier, chunkier and
squarer-headed than Black-headed Gull
L. ridibundus. On the water looks rather
neckless, flat-backed and somewhat less
attenuated, while thick, rather blunt bill is
apparent at surprisingly long distances. In
flight looks bull-necked and deep-chested
with stiffer, less pointed wings, latter
effect perhaps emphasised on adults by
their lack of a white primary wedge. Has
rather a smooth, high-stepping, plover-
like gait and is often markedly aggressive
to other small gulls. Has distinctive low,
soft, but rather loud and far-carrying *er-r*
call, rising and falling slightly, rhythm
vaguely suggesting call of male Wigeon
Anas penelope.

Plumage *Adult* At rest, easily separated
from Black-headed Gull by prominently
white primaries and (in winter plumage)
by large black, wedge-shaped ear-covert
patch which often extends as narrow grey
shawl over back of head; head pattern,
however, variable, some showing less
extensive markings, while small minority
look peculiarly white-headed, lacking
obvious head markings. In summer plumage (usually attained in March), hood is
black (brown on Black-headed) with

prominent broken white eye-ring, and
extends further down nape than on Black-
headed (but this varies according to posture). Thick, blunt bill is bright red at all
times, and close view usually reveals black
subterminal band and small yellow tip. In
flight, a stunningly beautiful, ghostly
bird. Unlike Black-headed Gull, underwings are pure white, while upperwings
shade from pearly grey on mantle and
wing-coverts to pure white on primaries,
lacking both white primary wedge and
black primary tips of Black-headed. The
only real pitfall is albino Black-headed
Gull, Common Gull *L. canus* or Kittiwake
Rissa tridactyla: such freaks not unusual,
but their extreme whiteness, particularly
across mantle and wing-coverts, instantly
separates them from Mediterranean;
structural differences and bare-part
coloration also facilitate identification.
Second-year As adult, but with varying
amounts of black on primaries. Most have
relatively small subterminal markings,
often showing as black arrowheads on
closed wing; others have large black primary wedges and are less easy to pick out at
rest, but, unlike Black-headed Gull, usually show prominent white spots within
the black. When identifying second-years,
always bear in mind remote possibility of
hybrid Black-headed x Mediterranean
Gull, which shows characters intermediate between the two and may be
confusable on a cursory glance: note
particularly hybrid's slimmer bill and
slighter build, as well as traces of Black-
headed Gull plumage (such as hint of
white primary wedge and black tips to
trailing edge of primaries). Another
potential pitfall is late-summer adult
Kittiwakes: when still growing their outer
primaries, such birds have shorter, more
rounded wings than usual, and amount
of black at tip is severely reduced. *First-
year* At rest, does not always stand out

Adult winter Black-headed Gull

2nd-winter Mediterranean Gulls Similar to adult (right), but variable amount of black on primaries. Bill variable.

Adult winter Mediterranean Gull. White primaries, heavy bill and, usually, dark wedge behind eye.

1st-summer Mediterranean Gull moulting into 2nd-winter plumage.

2nd-winter Mediterranean Gull

1st-winter Black-headed Gull

1st-winter Mediterranean Gull. Note heavy bill, black face mask, pale mantle.

Juvenile Common Gull. Weak bill, pale legs. Browner and less contrasting, lacking strong greater covert panel of Mediterranean Gull.

Juvenile Mediterranean Gull. Very dark, strongly scalloped upperparts, pale greater covert panel, whitish head, dark bill and legs.

Juvenile Black-headed Gull

Adult winter Black-headed Gull. White primary wedges, black tips.

Adult winter Mediterranean Gull shows striking white underwing.

Black-headed Gull has dark under primaries.

Adult winter Mediterranean Gull shows white primaries.

2nd-winter Mediterranean Gulls show variable amounts of black in wingtip.

1st-winter Mediterranean Gull. Note pale 'saddle', dark eye patch and contrasting wings.

Moulting adult kittiwake may show very little black in wingtips.

1st-winter Common Gull shows less contrasting pattern, note dark 'saddle'.

1st-winter Common Gull. Underwing is less 'clean'.

1st-winter Mediterranean Gull

107

from Black-headed Gulls, but look for combination of black ear-covert wedge and heavy blunt bill. Bill is black at first, gradually acquiring pinkish, orangy or reddish base as winter progresses. Compared with first-winter Black-headed, closed wing shows browner median coverts, solidly dark tertials (only narrowly edged white) and solidly dark primaries; these plumage differences, combined with structural ones, produce unique 'jizz' that is very distinctive once learnt. In first summer, may gain at least a partial black hood and gradually lose dark-centred wing-coverts and tertials. In flight, has similar pattern to first-year Common Gull and, when seen with that species, can be surprisingly difficult to pick out, but again look for black ear-covert patch. Wings are, however, cleaner-looking and more contrasty than on Common, primary wedge and secondary bar are blacker, and mid-wing panel (greater coverts and inner primaries) is a clean grey; also, lacks Common Gull's obvious dark grey 'saddle' (back and scapulars), mantle being a pale pearly grey. Unlike Common, underwings lack brown markings and are cleanly white, the only real dark being at under-primary tips. Structural differences, particularly bull neck and shorter, stiffer wings, are also useful. *Juvenile* Even for observers familiar with first-winter Mediterranean Gull, their first juvenile may come as a surprise. Quite unique, being closest to juvenile Common Gull at rest, as well as in flight. Whole of upperparts, including lower nape, dark chocolate-brown, each feather neatly and cleanly edged white to produce attractively scalloped appearance. Greater coverts, however, plain grey, stand out as thick, pale unmarked strip along bottom of closed wing. Breast has brown mottling, concentrated mainly on sides. Unlike first-winter, head is relatively unmarked, with no real wedge and only a faint grey suffusion behind eye and over rear crown. Thick black bill stands out prominently from featureless head, while legs also noticeably dark, reddish-black. Flight pattern contrasty and similar to first-winter, except that mantle is blackish, not grey. In comparison, juvenile Common is browner and less contrasted: lacks pale greater-covert panel, has extensive brown underpart mottling, weak bill (with at least some pale at base), round head, gentle expression and, most important, pale greyish or flesh-coloured legs.

Immature Kittiwake and Little and Sabine's Gulls

Where and When Kittiwake is a common coastal species, seen at any time of year, but rarer in winter; also migrates overland, and small numbers (occasionally large flocks) may appear on inland reservoirs, mainly in March–April and September–October. Little Gull is a scarce passage migrant, mainly in March–May and August–October, but smaller numbers encountered throughout year; more likely to be seen inland than Kittiwake, but largest numbers occur at selected coastal sites, notably in Merseyside, Co. Durham and Firth of Forth. Sabine's Gull is a rare autumn passage migrant, mainly in September–October, with occasional spring occurrences from March to June; extremely rare in winter. Most records come from west coast, particularly Cornwall, but has occurred in most coastal counties and even inland on occasion; numbers depend on prevalence of westerly gales (in September 1983, several hundred Sabine's Gulls were seen in southwest England following a severe Atlantic depression; while at least 200 were recorded in southeast England, many inland, after the October 1987 'hurricane', apparently pushed in from the Bay of Biscay).

Kittiwake *Rissa tridactyla*

Flight Identification Juvenile and first-winter superficially similar to those of Little Gull as both species have large black W across wings. Kittiwake is much larger than Little and slightly larger than Black-headed Gull *L. ridibundus*. Grey mantle and leading wing-coverts are *quite dark and highlight extreme whiteness of inner primaries and secondaries*, and black W is better defined, particularly on primaries: this combination produces smarter, more contrasting 'grey-black-white' pattern than on first-winter Little Gull. Juvenile and first-winter Kittiwakes are similar, but juvenile has prominent black collar across nape, usually lost in first-winter plumage. Thick black bill contrasts strongly with white head, which shows black spot or smudge behind eye. Underwing snowy white, with dark tips to under primaries. First-summer (of both species) may become severely bleached and abraded.

Identification at Rest Looks equally smart and contrasting. Can be identified by thick black bill, predominantly white head, black collar (when present), rather dark mantle, and large black patch across wing-coverts.

Little Gull *Larus minutus*

Flight Identification A tiny gull, about two-thirds size of Kittiwake; size usually obvious even without other species for comparison. Feeding behaviour remarkably tern-like, flying back and forth and dipping down to water like Black Tern *Chlidonias niger* (Kittiwake more typically 'gull-like'). Juvenile easily separated from Kittiwake as *mantle completely blackish* (the feathers edged pale) and this coloration extends onto nape and sides of neck; crown and ear-coverts also black, quite unlike Kittiwake. As autumn progresses, moults into first-winter plumage and black feathering on mantle and scapulars is replaced by grey, while nape becomes

white; at certain stages of moult, can show effect of a dark collar, suggesting Kittiwake, but this rarely as clear-cut. First-winter *retains distinctive dark crown and ear-coverts* which Kittiwake lacks; in flight, looks less contrasty than Kittiwake as greys contrast less with whites, while black on primaries is less clear-cut (underwing too is a less pure white). First-summer may acquire a partial black hood.

Identification at Rest Juvenile easily identified by predominantly black upperparts and black crown and ear-coverts; attractive black-and-white plumage suggests large juvenile phalarope *Phalaropus*. First-winter more like Kittiwake, but again easily separated by black crown and ear-coverts, less contrasty upperparts and small, delicate bill.

Call Has quick, throaty, tern-like *ar – akar akar akar akar*, recalling squeaky toy (first-year Kittiwakes relatively silent).

Black-winged Little Gulls There are records of atypical first-year Little Gulls with whole upperwing black (with paler feather edgings), leaving prominent white trailing edge; in first winter, these show grey mantle and scapulars which stand out as 'saddle'. The illustration on page 110 is based on one such bird seen in Somerset in February 1987.

Sabine's Gull *Larus sabini*

Flight Identification A very distinctive gull, easily identified if seen well. Despite this, many claimed Sabine's, particularly distant individuals on seawatches, are misidentified Kittiwakes. Caution is, therefore, advisable. In early autumn (August–early September) most Sabine's passing offshore are adults and most retain a full black hood (by late autumn, reduced to a large black smudge across nape). *Combination* of hood, black primaries, dark grey mantle/wing-coverts and huge white triangle on inner primaries/secondaries allows instant recognition. Underwings pure white, with

Juvenile kittiwake. Note
clean, contrasting plumage.

Juvenile
Little Gull

1st-winter Little Gull.
Note small size and
dark cap.

1st-winter Little
Gull. Rare plumage
variant with all-
dark wings.

Juvenile Sabine's Gull.
Note brown head, mantle
and wing-coverts.
White triangle on rear
of wing.

1st-winter Sabine's
Gull. Similar to
juvenile but grey
mantle and black
rear crown.

Adult Sabine's Gull,
moulting from summer
plumage. Note
combination of black
head and striking
wing pattern.

Juvenile Little
Gull. Very dark above.

1st-winter
Little Gull. Very
small, note dark
cap.

Juvenile Sabine's
Gull. Note brown
head, nape and mantle.

Juvenile kittiwake. Note
black line on wing and black
collar.

1st-winter Sabine's Gull. Grey
mantle and scapulars. Black
area on rear of crown. This
plumage acquired on
wintering grounds, thus
very rare in northern
hemisphere.

dark tips to primaries. Sabine's is noticeably smaller than Black-headed Gull *L. ridibundus*, and has long, thin, pointed wings; forked tail is difficult to see at any distance. Juvenile (does not moult until winter quarters) has dark brown wing-coverts, mantle, nape and breast sides, latter two areas producing dark front to bird in flight; these brown areas, along with black primaries, contrast strongly with white triangle on rear of wing. Juvenile Sabine's therefore lacks black W, grey mantle, black collar and predominantly white head of juvenile/first-winter Kittiwake.

Winter Adults and First-summers Sabine's Gull does not normally occur in northern hemisphere in winter, so observers should not claim a winter Sabine's unless seen exceptionally well. First-years usually remain in winter quarters during their first summer, but occasional individual moves north in spring. First-winters resemble juveniles, but have grey back and scapulars (forming grey 'saddle') and dark smudging on nape. First-summers resemble adults but do not acquire full black hood.

Ring-billed Gull

Where and When A North American gull, unrecorded in Britain and Ireland before 1973, but currently averaging about 85 records a year, mainly in Ireland, South Wales and southwest England. Many are permanently ensconced on this side of Atlantic, migrating north and south along European coastline. First-years appear mainly from November to February, often remaining to summer (note that first-years are very rare before November); adults and second-years mostly between July and April. All age groups show marked spring passage, with peak in March and April. Ring-billed Gull *Larus delawarensis* is difficult to identify, especially in first-year plumages; most are found by experienced observers who habitually scrutinise their local gull flocks. A thorough understanding of all plumages of Common Gull *L. canus* and Herring Gull *L. argentatus*, including their abnormalities and idiosyncrasies, is essential. The following details outline its separation from similar Common Gull; differences from Herring are summarised at the end.

Size, Structure and Behaviour Ring-billed is always conspicuously smaller than majority of Herring Gulls, and basically resembles a big Common Gull. Size of all three species varies, however, and some male Ring-billed are noticeably larger than most Common Gulls, while small females are about same size: comparisons should always be made with *several* individuals of the commoner species. Ring-billed is slightly different structurally, looking bulkier, stockier and deeper-chested, while on the water it looks flat-backed, sleek and attenuated compared with Common. Most obvious structural difference is the bill, which looks longer, noticeably thicker and more 'parallel': this effect is apparent even at distance, when black band (or tip) makes bill appear rather blunt. Head is slightly more angular, less rounded than Common, but this has been over-emphasised and head shape depends largely on attitude; when relaxed, Ring-billed can look quite round-headed. Size difference may be more obvious in flight, when Ring-billed looks distinctly longer- and broader-winged than Common. Wingtips are more pointed than those of Common (on adults and second-years emphasised by differences in wingtip pattern: see below). Legs often noticeably longer than on Common, resulting in a strutting walk (may recall Mediterranean Gull *L. melanocephalus*). Ring-billed Gulls are often attracted to man, may become very tame.

111

Plumage *Adults* Always remember that winter adult and second-year Common Gulls, and also second-year and third-year Herring Gulls, often show a prominent, clear-cut ring on bill. The best way to pick out an adult or a second-year Ring-billed at rest is by a combination of mantle colour and tertial and wingtip patterns. Mantle is noticeably paler than that of Common, being closer in shade to that of Black-headed Gull *L. ridibundus*, while tertials look rather square and lack Common's conspicuous broad white crescent. At close range, tertial tips on Ring-billed *are* whiter, but are narrow and do not contrast with paler mantle. Closed primaries look uniformly black, with three inconspicuous white primary tips which decrease in size towards wingtips (unlike Common, the large white mirrors on outer primaries are not readily apparent at rest). Pale mantle and black primaries, unrelieved by obvious white tertial crescent, produce pattern quite distinct from adult Common and in fact quite similar to adult Black-headed. Two pitfalls need to be considered: **1** unusually pale Common Gulls do exist, and **2** second-year Commons often show a narrow tertial crescent and little white in primaries. Make sure that your 'adult Ring-billed' is not a second-year Common.

To avoid such pitfalls, it is absolutely essential for identification to be confirmed by other features. Structural differences, outlined above, are especially important, and pay particular attention to bill: the black band should stand out clearly and cleanly and contrast with pale base, even in winter. Eye colour is diagnostic: Ring-billed has pale irides (as well as narrow orange orbital ring), but pale eye is difficult to detect at any distance. Usually shows a squint-eyed expression, in contrast to dark-eyed, open-faced look of Common. Ring-billed tends to have paler, mottled head streaking (but this so variable on Common as to render it of limited value in the field) and yellower legs.

If a suspected Ring-billed flies or wing-flaps, concentrate on wingtip pattern: Common has two large, conspicuous white mirrors right across wingtip, but on Ring-billed mirrors are small, relatively inconspicuous and often confined to just one mirror on inner web of outer primary (relative lack of white emphasises more pointed wing shape). Pale mantle and wings contrast strongly with black primary wedges so that, in flight, Ring-billed's pattern looks surprisingly similar to that of Herring Gull; very white underwings reinforce this impression. *Second years* Similar to adult, but easily aged by presence of dark feathering on primary coverts. Most show vestigial black markings on tail and, sometimes, secondaries, though many lack these markings, while, conversely, some second-year Commons also show them. Ring-billed shows only small white mirror on inner web of outer primary (often difficult to see); second-year Common shows one or two obvious white mirrors. The age at which Ring-billed develops adult bare-part colouring varies: most attain complete black bill band and yellow base by first summer, although some still retain black tip and/or greenish base a year later; and some remain dark-eyed into second summer. *First-years* The most difficult to identify, as many of the subtle differences are inconsistent. First-year Ring-billed have distinctive 'jizz' *once learnt*, but should always be identified by a combination of minor differences. Close views and detailed notes essential, and observer should always bear in mind possible occurrence of odd Common Gulls (for example, unusually pale individuals). All following features (in rough order of significance) should be checked. **1** BILL The best character, being heavy, thick, 'parallel' and blunt-ended (Common's bill looks slender, pointed and weedy). Usually pale orangy-pink with prominent black tip, reminiscent of bill of first-winter Glaucous Gull *L. hyperboreus* (some

Adult winter Common Gull. Note thin bill, dark eye, dark grey upperparts and thick white tertial crescent.

Adult winter Ring-billed Gull has thick bill and pale eye. Best picked out by pale upperparts and thin white tertial crescent.

1st-winter Common Gull. Thin bill, lightly spotted head and nape, dark back and scapulars, wide pale edges to tertials.

1st-winters; upper two Common Gulls, lower one Ring-billed Gull. Both show great variation in upperpart moult and wear.

Note median-covert pattern in fresh plumage. The dark centres are spade-shaped on Common, arrow-shaped on Ring-billed Gull.

1st-summer Ring-billed Gull. Concolorous upperparts.

1st-winter Ring-billed Gull. Heavy bill, usually heavy spotting on head, neck and breast. Pale back and scapulars, pale greater coverts and narrow pale edges to tertials.

2nd-winter Herring Gull. Note barred greater coverts and tertials, heavier build. Often shows a pale eye. Note short primary projection and often a pronounced 'tertial step'.

1st-summer Common Gull. Note dark 'saddle'.

113

Adult winter Ring-billed Gull. Pale grey above, note small white mirrors.

2nd-winter Ring-billed Gull. Contrasting wing pattern, one small mirror. Most but not all show traces of tail band.

Adult winter Common Gull. Dark grey above, large white mirrors.

2nd-winter Common Gull. Darker upperparts, larger white mirrors.

1st-winter Ring-billed Gull. Pale mantle, obvious pale greater covert panel, ill-defined tail band.

1st-winter Common Gull. Dark grey 'saddle', less contrasting wing and (usually) clear-cut tail band.

1st-summer Common Gull (above) shows dark 'saddle'. 1st-summer Ring-billed Gull has paler 'saddle' which does not contrast with wing-coverts.

Commons have similar bill colour, but many have a duller, grey or greenish base). **2** TERTIALS Solidly dark brown, *narrowly* edged white (on Common, paler brown, with thick white edgings, but beware effects of abrasion). **3** MANTLE AND SCAPULARS Pale grey, lacking dark 'saddle' effect of Common. Whitish tips to many of the scapulars and retention of some dark juvenile feathering may create more variegated pattern than on Common, but dark feathers are moulted and pale tips wear off as winter progresses. **4** GREATER COVERTS Usually appear pale grey, sometimes barred on inners (unlike Common), and produce pale strip along bottom of closed wing and noticeable pale mid-wing panel in flight. **5** HEAD AND UNDERPARTS Usually well mottled and spotted about head and breast and more heavily marked below, often with heavy dark barring or spotting on upper- and undertail-coverts, which Common usually lacks. Both species, however, variable. **6** TAIL Dark of tail band usually extends up outer web of each tail feather to intrude into tail base, which usually shows delicate greyish mottling or shading; tail therefore looks messy compared with clear-cut band and white base shown by most Commons. On some Commons, however, dark also intrudes into the white, while minority also show grey mottling at base, so differences not absolute. Ring-billed has dark mottling or barring on outer web of outer tail feather, which Common seems to lack. **7** MEDIAN COVERTS In fresh plumage, brown centres to median coverts are pointed on Ring-billed, rounded on Common, but this distinction breaks down with wear and fading and is of little use in worn plumage. **8** LEGS Sometimes quite pink on first-year Ring-billed.

In their first summer, both species fade and bleach and eventually replace wing-coverts and tertials with grey second-winter plumage. First-summer Commons look washed out and pale, their outer primaries and secondaries fading to brown and rest of wing becoming creamy and worn, contrasting conspicuously with dark grey 'saddle', particularly in flight. Ring-billed also fades, but, because it lacks dark 'saddle', the mantle and wing-coverts look uniformly pale grey and concolorous. Unlike Common, first-year Ring-billed soon gains pale bill tip and, by first summer, bill is usually similar to that of adult. *Juveniles* Similar to first-winter, but mantle and scapulars brown, edged white, and head and underparts also heavily marked. Full juvenile has never been recorded in Britain and Ireland.

The Herring Gull Problem

First-year and second-year Ring-billed may be confused with second-year and third-year Herring Gulls respectively, both of which can show prominent bill band. Herring should, however, always appear large, bulky, angular-headed, heavy-billed and meaner-looking. If in doubt, check wing-coverts: second-year Herring shows noticeable brown *barring* across wing-coverts (including greater coverts), which first-year Ring-billed lacks; in addition, second-year Herring shows rather mottled tertials and, usually, a pale eye. In flight, second-year Herring shows fairly uniform grey inner primaries, producing pale grey 'window' extending to tips of feathers; first-year Ring-billed has dark subterminal marks on these feathers. Third-year Herring is also easily separated as it retains traces of dark mottling on wing-coverts, vestiges of immaturity that second-year Ring-billed would never exhibit (although *small* amounts of brown may be retained on leading lesser coverts); third-year Herring also has pinkish legs, whereas second-year Ring-billed would show greenish or yellowish legs.

Great Black-backed, Lesser Black-backed, Herring and Yellow-legged Gulls

Where and When Great Black-backed Gull breeds fairly commonly, mainly on rocky coastlines, right around British Isles except British east coast south of Firth of Forth; more widespread in winter, when Norwegian immigrants are common in the east, often penetrating some way inland, though in many western areas distinctly unusual inland. Lesser Black-backed Gull has similar breeding distribution, but often nests inland on buildings, and in winter has rather a southerly distribution with most inland, often on farmland; darker Scandinavian Lesser Black-backs (races *intermedius* and *fuscus*) also occur mainly in winter. Herring Gull is a common and familiar breeding bird around much of coast and also inland on buildings; it, too, is more widespread in winter, when Scandinavian immigrants of nominate race *argentatus* are numerous in some northern and eastern areas. Yellow-legged Gull* is a migrant, mainly from Mediterranean, which occurs most frequently in southern counties, most numerously in July–September, with a smaller wintering population remaining until February (by spring and early summer, only a few immatures generally remain); can often be found by searching flocks of Lesser Black-backed Gulls, with which it often associates.

Great Black-backed Gull *Larus marinus*

Size and Structure A huge, bulky brute of a gull, with large head, deep chest, pronounced tertial step and rather 'stumpy' rear end. Although variable, most are about 25% larger than Lesser

Black-back, which in comparison is rather slender with long primaries that usually produce very tapered look to rear end. Deep, powerful bill shows prominent gonydeal angle, is always conspicuously larger than that of Lesser Black-backed and Herring Gulls. In flight, is slow, lumbering and pregnant-looking, with rather rounded wings, whereas Lesser Black-back's are long, narrow and pointed (despite its 1.5m wingspan, wings look *proportionately* shorter than those of Lesser Black-back).

Calls Adult's calls deep and powerful.

Plumage *Adult* If seen well, separation from Lesser Black-back not difficult, but, if accurate size assessment not possible, confusion is surprisingly easy, especially if poor light affects mantle coloration. Great Black-back is virtually black on mantle, readily separating it from British race *graellsii* of Lesser Black-back. Scandinavian Lesser Black-backs, however, are much darker above, nominate *fuscus* being similar in shade to Great Black-back. When in doubt, concentrate on size, structure and leg colour. Great Black-back has flesh-coloured legs, whereas Lesser's are yellow (but duller in winter and the yellow can be difficult to make out in weak light). Great Black-back retains a white head in winter, whereas race *graellsii* of Lesser Black-back has heavily streaked head until at least January (nominate *fuscus*, however, is whiter-headed in winter). Great Black-back has a thicker tertial crescent. In flight, Great Black-back has *large white tips to outer two primaries* forming diagnostic white spot at wingtip, which Lesser Black-back does not show to same extent (Lesser

*The taxonomy of the Herring Gull group is both complex and controversial. We have decided to follow the recent Continental trend of treating the southern yellow-legged 'Herring' Gulls as a separate species in anticipation that this approach will eventually gain official acceptance in Britain and Ireland.

usually has only one *subterminal* mirror confined to inner web of outer primary, so this is less conspicuous). *Juvenile and first-year* Most likely to be confused with similarly aged Herring Gulls, so correct size evaluation essential. Pay particular attention to large black bill, which usually contrasts strongly with predominantly whitish head and underparts (which become even whiter after post-juvenile moult). Appears *barred* or *chequered* grey-brown and whitish above (Herring is browner, with a less contrasting, duller ground colour, but some paler individuals can look more similar to Great Black-back). Bill remains black throughout first winter, but often attains pale tip and base in first summer (Herring usually acquires paler base during first winter). Usually shows ill-defined tail band, made up of a series of narrow lines. *Second-year* Becomes even whiter on head and underparts and gradually acquires blackish feathering on back and scapulars. Bill becomes paler, with black only at tip, and eye gradually turns pale. *Third-year* More similar to adult, but still retains traces of immaturity, such as dark in tail, some brownish upper-part feathering and dark subterminal bill marks; also lacks white primary spots at rest. Adult plumage is attained by fourth winter, but probably even at this age some still retain a few traces of immaturity.

Lesser Black-backed Gull *Larus fuscus*

For differences from Great Black-back, see that species (page 116).

Size and Structure Similar in size to Herring Gull, but generally distinctly smaller and slighter, with smaller bill. At rest, proportionately longer primaries produce tapering rear end. These subtle structural differences are particularly useful in flight, especially when identifying first-years or birds high overhead: compared with Herring, Lesser Black-back then looks slim, with proportionately longer, narrower and more pointed wings.

Calls Adult's calls are deeper than those of Herring Gull.

Plumage *Adult* British race *graellsii* is dark grey above, intermediate between Herring and Great Black-backed Gulls. Bill brighter than Herring, eye-ring red (usually orange or orange-yellow on Herring), and legs bright yellow in summer and dull creamy-yellow in winter. In winter, head and neck show heavy grey streaking. Seen from below, is dusky grey across inner primaries and secondaries (Herring is white across this area). Lesser Black-backs become darker towards the north and east. In Netherlands, Denmark and southern Norway, *intermedius* occurs, which is, as name suggests, intermediate in shade between *graellsii* and nominate *fuscus* (northern Norway east to the western USSR): its upperparts are black, similar in shade to Great Black-back, and, consequently, it lacks *graellsii*'s contrast between grey of wings and black of wing-tips; it is also smaller, relatively longer-winged, slimmer-bodied and shorter-legged than *graellsii*, and has a whiter head in winter, with lighter grey streaking confined to crown and hindneck. Whereas *graellsii* and *intermedius* have a complete post-breeding moult from mid May to December, *fuscus* moults much later, from October to April. Great caution must be taken when identifying Scandinavian Lesser Black-backs in Britain, and effects of light must be carefully considered, particularly when watching gulls at evening roost: in certain lights, even *graellsii* can look very dark. *Juvenile and first-winter* Similar to Herring Gull, but generally darker (although head and underparts gradually whiten with age). Note in particular that tertials tend to be fringed and tipped with white, rather than notched and barred like Herring, so centre of tertials appears more solidly brown. Most significantly, in flight Lesser Black-

3rd-winter Herring Gull of British race 'argenteus'

Adult winter Herring Gull of northern race 'argentatus'. Note darker mantle, large white wing 'mirrors', pale bill. Size may approach Great Black-backed Gull.

Adult winter Herring Gull of British race 'argenteus'.

Adult winter Yellow-legged Gull. Mantle dark (similar to Common Gull), very little head streaking. Yellow legs, red orbital ring.

Adult summer Yellow-legged Gull. Domed head, sleek and immaculate. Bright yellow bill.

Adult winter Lesser Black-backed Gull of Scandinavian race 'fuscus'. Very dark above. Small white primary tips.

3rd-winter Lesser Black-backed Gull of British race 'graellsii'.

Adult winter Lesser Black-backed Gull of British race 'graellsii'.

3rd-winter Great Black-backed Gull. Note large size, pinkish legs and small white primary tips.

Adult winter Great Black-backed Gull. Note large size, heavy bill, black mantle. Large white primary tips, legs pinkish. Head white in winter.

Adult Herring Gull of British race 'argenteus'

Adult Herring Gull of northern race 'argentatus'. Dark mantle, reduced black in wingtips.

Adult Lesser Black-backed Gull. Note underwing pattern.

Adult Yellow-legged Gull. Dark mantle, squared-off black wingtips with little white.

Adult Lesser Black-backed Gull of British race 'graellsii'.

Adult Yellow-legged Gull. Compare underwing with Herring Gull.

Adult Herring Gull

Adult Lesser Black-backed Gull of Scandinavian race 'fuscus'.

Adult Great Black-backed Gull. Massive, note extensive white in wingtips.

Adult Great Black-backed Gull. Huge, deep chested large bill.

back is uniformly dark across inner primaries so that *it lacks pale inner primary 'window' of Herring Gull*; greater coverts (especially outer ones) are also predominantly dark (mainly pale on Herring) and form a second dark band in front of dark secondary bar, so whole wing looks darker and more uniform in flight. Tail band is better defined than on Herring and contrasts more strongly with white rump. *Second-year* Head and body become whiter, and dark grey feathering gradually appears on back and scapulars. Eye gradually turns pale, and bill also becomes paler. In second summer, mantle and scapulars predominantly dark grey, forming 'saddle'. *Third-year* Similar to adult,

but retains traces of immaturity, such as dark in tail, remnants of brown in wings and dark subterminal bill markings; also lacks adult's white spots on closed primaries. Fourth-winter resembles adult, but some still retain traces of immaturity, such as dark subterminal bill marks and flesh-coloured legs.

Herring Gull *Larus argentatus*

Size and Structure The familiar 'seagull' of seaside towns. Generally slightly larger and bulkier than Lesser Black-back, with shorter, less attenuated rear end and, in flight, proportionately shorter, broader, rounder wings.

Plumage *Adult* Easily identified by pale grey mantle, black-tipped wings and pale pink legs. Beware confusion with Common Gull *L. canus* (see page 113). Herring Gulls breeding in Britain and Ireland are of race *argenteus*. In Scandinavia, nominate race *argentatus* takes over, becoming larger, darker and with less black in primaries as one moves north. In many parts of northern and eastern Britain, most winter Herring are of Scandinavian origin: while many are not safely separable in the field from *argenteus*, the more extreme examples are markedly different (see pages 118 and 119 and page 124; also below, under Yellow-legged Gull). *Juvenile and first-year* For differences from similarly aged Lesser Black-back, see that species (page 117). *Second-year* Gradually acquires pale eye, extensively pale base to bill and, eventually, pale grey back and scapulars. *Third-year* Resembles adult, but retains traces of immaturity such as dark primary coverts, dark in tail, dark subterminal bill markings and, sometimes, variable brown markings on wing-coverts; lacks adult's white primary spots at rest. Fourth-winter resembles adult, but note that some adult Herring Gulls have blackish markings on their greater primary coverts, regardless of how old they are.

Yellow-legged Gull *Larus cachinnans*

Superficially similar to Herring Gull, but apparently more closely related to Lesser Black-back; for identification purposes, it is perhaps more helpful to think of this species as a Lesser Black-back with pale mantle, rather than as a Herring with yellow legs. Those that occur in Britain seem to be of western Mediterranean race *michahellis*, which is generally slightly larger and bulkier than race *argenteus* of Herring Gull, although some, no doubt females, are no bigger than Lesser Black-back.

Plumage *Adult* It is not necessary to see the yellow legs to identify Yellow-legged Gull. When separating adults, the following should be looked for (in rough order of significance): **1** MANTLE Darker grey, intermediate between *graellsii* Lesser Black-back and *argenteus* Herring (similar, in fact, to Common Gull). **2** LEGS Yellow: bright in summer, but paler and washed out in winter (when colour can be difficult to determine). **3** HEAD SHAPE Looks bulbous and neck thick (although crown feathers can be flattened). **4** HEAD STREAKING Lacks heavy head streaking in winter and looks very white-headed, but this feature valid only until about January (when *argenteus* Herring can acquire white head); shows faint grey streaking over eye in autumn and early winter. **5** BILL Brightly coloured; may acquire black band in winter. **6** EYE-RING Red, like Lesser Black-back (orangy-yellow or orange on Herring), producing beady-eyed effect at distance. **7** UPPERWING In flight, black wingtips cut off squarely across wing, show little white at tip (just one subterminal mirror on outer primary). **8** UNDERWING Shows dusky grey across under secondaries and inner primaries (although this not so dark as on Lesser Black-back, Herring is white across this region). **9** MOULT Moults earlier than Herring, so shows practically full-grown primaries in September (when local race *argenteus* of Herring usually has short, partially grown primaries which produce stumpy rear end). **10** SHAPE Somehow always looks sleek and immaculate. **11** CALLS Like Lesser Black-back, calls are deeper than those of Herring Gull.

When identifying adult Yellow-legged Gulls, several pitfalls need to be considered. Race *argenteus* of Herring can look dark in certain lights, a problem particularly acute at evening gull roosts. Greatest confusion, however, is likely to occur with Scandinavian Herring Gulls *argentatus*: many of latter have a darker mantle,

Juvenile Herring Gull. Paler than Lesser Black-backed Gull. Note notched tertials and greater covert pattern. ▼

1st-winter Herring Gull. Note tertial and greater covert barring. Head pale brown, bill black becoming pale at base.

2nd-winter Herring Gull gradually acquires grey mantle. Tertials and greater coverts finely patterned. Eye becomes pale.

Juvenile/1st-winter Yellow-legged Gull. All black bill, whitish head and breast, tertials barred only at tips. Recalls Great Black-backed Gull.

2nd-winter Herring Gull. ▼

1st-summer Herring Gull. Some very pale due to fading and wear. Bill usually with pale base.

2nd-winter Lesser Black-backed Gull. Note dark grey feathers in mantle. ▶

Juvenile Lesser Black-backed Gull. Dark, with unbarred tertials and outer greater coverts.

1st-winter Lesser Black-backed Gull. Tertials and greater coverts as juvenile. Bill all black. Pale forehead often gives 'hooded' effect to head.

1st-winter Great Black-backed Gull. Heavy black bill. Whitish head and underparts. Chequered upperparts. Obvious tertial step.

Juvenile Great Black-backed Gull. Boldly patterned plumage, heavy black bill, long legs. ▲

2nd-winter Great Black-backed Gull. Black appearing on mantle, whitish head and underparts.

121

1st-winter Herring Gull. Paler inner primaries form 'window'. Greater coverts barred and do not contrast with rest of wing.

1st-winter Lesser Black-backed Gull. Primaries completely dark, dark outer greater coverts, contrast between rump and tail.

1st-summer Herring Gull. Very faded.

1st-winter Great Black-backed Gull. Coarsely marked upperparts, diffuse barred tail band.

1st-winter Yellow-legged Gull. Inner primaries only slightly paler, outer greater coverts form dark panel, whitish head and rump, neat black tail band.

2nd-winter Yellow-legged Gull. Dark 'saddle', well defined tail band. Plumage suggests 1st-winter Common Gull.

2nd-winter Lesser Black-backed Gull

2nd-winter Herring Gull

3rd-winter Lesser Black-backed Gull of race 'graellsii'

3rd-winter Herring Gull

3rd-winter Yellow-legged Gull. Note dark mantle and large bright yellow bill.

though it tends to be a colder shade of grey, but such birds generally show *reduced black in wingtip, large white tips to outer two primaries, larger white primary spots at rest and thicker white tertial crescent* (see page 125); in flight, dark *argentatus* are *predominantly white on underwing and often show little black even on under primaries.* All this is in marked contrast to Yellow-legged's extensive black wingtips (which show little white), black under primaries and dusky grey shading across under secondaries and inner primaries. In addition, *argentatus* shows very heavy head and neck streaking in winter and tends to show a large, pale, washed-out bill, a very angular head and, consequently, a particularly 'mean' expression; it is also bulkier, has a pronounced tertial step, less attenuated primaries and is altogether less sleek than Yellow-legged. Finally, *argentatus* has flesh-coloured legs and a yellowish eye-ring. *Juvenile and first-year* Differences in immature plumages are still not fully known. First-year Yellow-legged, however, shows very white head and underparts and contrasting black bill,

a combination recalling first-year Great Black-back. In flight, dark primaries and secondaries contrast strongly with rest of upperparts, and dark tail band is well defined. Juveniles have pale *fringe* to tertials (similar to Lesser Black-back; Herring has variable pale mottling and notching). For detailed discussion of juveniles, see Dubois & Yésou (1984). *Second-year* Becomes easier to identify with age, and second-years, once they have acquired adult-like dark grey back and scapulars, are more straightforward. Such birds show dark 'saddle' in flight, contrasting dark primaries and secondaries, and fairly clear-cut tail band, whole effect recalling giant first-winter Common Gull. Wing-coverts seem to be mainly *fringed* with white, rather than barred with brown and white like Herring. May also show red eye-ring, and yellow tint to legs. *Third-year* Similar to adult, but shows usual third-year traces of immaturity on wings and tail.

References Dubois & Yésou (1984); for detailed discussion of gull plumages, see Grant (1986).

Glaucous and Iceland Gulls

Where and When Both are scarce winter visitors, mainly October–May, but numbers vary considerably from year to year. They are liable to occur anywhere that attracts large gulls. Most of our Glaucous Gulls *Larus hyperboreus* originate from eastern Greenland and arctic Europe, so tend to occur most in the northwest, the north, and down east coast. Iceland Gulls *L. glaucoides* originate from Greenland, so have more of a northwesterly distribution. Both are separated from Herring Gull *L. argentatus*[†] by their white primaries, but, to differentiate between them, concentrate on size, structure, head and bill shape and, on first-winters, bill colour.

Size and Structure Size varies sexually, males averaging larger than females, but Glaucous is usually much larger than Herring, approaching Great Black-backed Gull *L. marinus* in size; Iceland is similar to or slightly smaller than Herring. Glaucous is a large, powerful, mean-looking brute, with prominent tertial step and relatively short, blunt primary projection. Iceland is a rather stocky, gentler-looking, less powerful gull, often lacking tertial step and with long, tapered primaries that produce attenuated rear end. A useful way of evaluating difference in primary projection is that on Glaucous projection beyond tail is same as, or shorter than, bill length,

† All references to Herring Gull are to British race *argenteus*, unless otherwise stated.

whereas on Iceland it is longer than bill. In autumn this distinction must be used with caution, since moulting individuals may have shorter primaries (although this would not apply to juveniles/first-winters, which do not moult primaries in first autumn).

Head and Bill Although overall size and shape may be first clue to identification, pay particular attention to head and bill shape. Glaucous has a long, thick, heavy, rather 'parallel' bill, longer and thicker than Herring's, but (unlike Great Black-back) lacking prominent gonydeal angle; its prominence is complemented by a low forehead, flat crown and peaked rear crown, all of which reinforce general impression of severity. Iceland's bill is shorter, slimmer, stubbier and more pointed, similar to, or slightly shorter than, that of Herring; its steeper forehead and rounded head create gentler expression reminiscent of Common Gull *L. canus*. (Head-shape differences require cautious evaluation: both species can vary according to attitude.)

Flight Identification Glaucous is a large, heavy, lumbering gull, with broad wings and a lazy flight that recalls Great Black-back. Iceland is smaller, but has rather stocky body and proportionately longer, narrower wings (although tips rather rounded); its tail appears slightly, but distinctly shorter than Herring's and slightly more wedge-shaped, and its flight is more energetic than that of Glaucous.

Plumage *First-years* Both are essentially pale, biscuit-brown, intricately and delicately mottled and barred, but with whiter primaries. Plumage tone varies individually, but most become paler through bleaching and abrasion. Bill colour is diagnostic: Glaucous has pink bill with prominent, clear-cut 'dipped-in-ink' black tip; Iceland's is usually black with small, inconspicuous pale area at base (pale becomes more extensive as winter progresses, but black tip not clear-cut and

extends back along cutting edge so that, at any distance, tip appears to merge with pale base). *Second-years* Usually paler and less well patterned than first-years, may look very creamy when worn. Some attain grey feathering on mantle. Again, plumage tone varies individually, so concentrate on bill and eye coloration for accurate ageing. Most significantly, both species acquire pale irides during second year. On Iceland, bill base turns creamy and black tip becomes sharply defined so is more similar to first-winter Glaucous, but (unlike Glaucous) black tends to protrude back along cutting edge so that tip less clear-cut. Second-year Glaucous usually acquires pale tip to bill and, sometimes, yellowy tint to base. *Third-years* Both gain grey mantle and scapulars, but retain traces of immaturity on otherwise white wings and tail. Show dark terminal or subterminal markings on yellow bill, but Iceland may acquire greenish or greyish tint to base. *Adults* Both are similar. Fourth-years may retain hints of immaturity, including small dark markings on bill.

Pitfalls

Before claiming either species, the following pitfalls should be considered.
Glaucous x Herring hybrids In some Icelandic Glaucous Gull colonies, as many as two-thirds of gulls show evidence of hybridisation with Herring Gull. Icelandic 'Glaucous Gulls' are largely resident, but hybrids do turn up in Britain and Ireland. Such birds may show characters intermediate between the two species, but others may be very similar to Glaucous, revealing their true identity by traces of black in primary tips (adults) or traces of dark brown on outer primaries, secondaries and tail (immatures).
Northern Herring Gulls Dark Scandinavian Herring Gulls of nominate race *argentatus* are common winter visitors to northern and eastern Britain. Some, probably from extreme north of range, are large

1st-winter Glaucous Gull.
Large bill, pink with black
tip, angular head shape,
short primary projection,
obvious 'tertial step'

1st-winter Iceland Gull.
Small dark bill, rounded
head, long primary
projection.

2nd-winters closely
resemble 1st-winters.
Eyes become pale,
Iceland Gull (above)
loses dark base to
bill.

Both species gradually attain grey
upperpart feathering. This is
3rd-winter Glaucous Gull.

Adult winter
Iceland Gull

Adult winter Glaucous
Gull. Note differences
in structure.

Iceland Gull of race 'kumlieni'
resembles nominate race,
but shows grey primary tips.

Hybrids between Herring and
Glaucous Gulls are not uncommon,
and show intermediate
characteristics.

Herring Gulls of the race
'argentatus' are very large
and can show very little
black in wingtip. 1st-winters
can appear very pale.

1st-winter Iceland Gull. Long slim wings, light build. Bill usually all-dark.

1st-winter Glaucous Gull. Big and heavy deep chested. Long thick bill which melts into head. Broad, rounded wings.

1st-winter Iceland Gull

1st-winter Glaucous Gull

Some 1st-winter Herring Gulls may appear very pale with 'washed-out' tail and primaries. Note darkish tail band and secondary bar.

Both Glaucous and Iceland Gulls share this sequence of plumages to maturity. 1st and 2nd-year birds are often very similar in plumage, so check eye colour and bill pattern when ageing

2nd-winter Iceland Gull

3rd-winter Iceland Gull

Adult winter Iceland Gull

Iceland Gull of the race 'kumlieni'. Slightly darker than the nominate with grey marks on the primary tips. Do not confuse with 'argentatus' Herring Gull. Has typical Iceland Gull structure.

Adult winter Glaucous Gull

Some Herring Gulls of the race 'argentatus' are very large with little black in the primaries, and white under-primaries. The upperparts are much darker grey than Glaucous Gull.

126

and dark and show little black in wingtips. In flight, the black may be very difficult to detect at any distance, while underwings are almost entirely white, often with faint grey shading only at primary tips. As they can approach Great Black-back in size, such birds can be misidentified as Glaucous at distance; they are, however, much darker above (similar to or even darker than Common Gull), while on the water they show pronounced tertial step, thick white tertial crescent, and black primaries with very large white mirrors and primary tips.

It seems increasingly likely that the large, pale, 'Glaucous-like' immature Herring Gulls that occur from time to time in northern and eastern areas are these birds' offspring. It may be difficult, however, to decide what is a Glaucous x Herring hybrid and what is an immature Northern Herring, but unless an immature gull shows obvious pro-Glaucous characters, such as a Glaucous-like bill, consider possibility of Northern Herring Gull (see page 125). First-years seem to be fairly consistent in appearance: large (sometimes approaching Great Black-back), heavy-billed, shape typical of *argentatus* Herring Gull (see page 125), but they are very pale brown on a whitish background; the primaries are brown (much paler than first-winter *argenteus*), with white feather edgings and pale submarginal markings, and bill has pronounced gonys and is mainly black. In flight, they resemble very pale and severely washed-out *argenteus* Herring Gulls.

Albinos Older field guides may state that second-year Glaucous and Iceland Gulls are completely white. This is not so: even heavily abraded second-years retain a creamy look, and close inspection will reveal traces of delicate patterning on wings and tail. A pure white gull will almost certainly be aberrant, and structure and bare-part colour provide best clues to identity. (Note: albino Lesser Black-back closer to Iceland in shape than albino Herring.) Third-summer Glaucous and Iceland may look very white at distance, but closer views should reveal grey 'saddle' (mantle and scapulars) and other features outlined above.

Moulting Herring Gulls In autumn, moulting adult Herring may show severely reduced areas of black in wingtips, which appear noticeably rounded as result of partially grown outer primaries. In flight or at distance such birds may suggest Glaucous or Iceland. Fortunately, with local *argenteus* this phenomenon occurs prior to main arrival of Glaucous and Iceland Gulls (but *argentatus* moults later, finishing in November–January).

'Kumlien's Gull' There have been a number of recent records of northeast Canadian race of Iceland Gull *kumlieni*, or 'Kumlien's Gull' (possibly overlooked in past). Before identifying this race, first establish beyond doubt that bird concerned is an Iceland Gull, mainly by structural characteristics outlined above; note also that adult Iceland has a red orbital ring (yellowish on Glaucous and Herring). Adult Kumlien's shows dark grey in outer primaries, usually along outer web and subterminally across tip; although fairly obvious at rest, this may be difficult to see in flight. There would seem no reason why Glaucous x Herring hybrids or 'Northern' Herring Gulls would ever show grey (as opposed to black) in wingtip. Immature Kumlien's are something of an unknown quantity, but may also show primary markings and slightly darker tail.

References Hume (1975, 1978).

Sandwich and Gull-billed Terns

Where and When Sandwich Tern *Sterna sandvicensis* is a common summer visitor, likely to be seen all around coast from March to October (and, rarely, in winter); small parties may appear briefly inland on migration. Gull-billed Tern *Gelochelidon nilotica* is a very rare migrant, currently averaging about four records a year; most occur in May, with fewer in summer and autumn, on south and east coasts of England (pair bred in Essex in 1950). In the ten-year period 1977–86, 44% of all Gull-billed Tern records submitted to the *British Birds* Rarities Committee were rejected (many were probably from inexperienced observers who, having obtained brief views of a fly-by tern, submitted a description which provided little detail other than a thick, gull-like bill). This high rejection rate, however, belies fact that Gull-billed is not actually difficult to identify. The similarly sized Sandwich Tern is the confusion species, but many observers do not appreciate that juvenile Sandwich has shorter, thicker-looking bill than adult, has rounder wings and also calls quite differently.

Structure and Flight An awareness of structural differences between the two species is essential first step to identification. Sandwich is large, similar in size to Kittiwake *Rissa tridactyla*, and it lacks long tail streamers of Common *S. hirundo*, Arctic *S. paradisaea* and Roseate Terns *S. dougallii*. Compared with Gull-billed, it is a *noticeably slim, rakish-looking bird* with long, narrow, often rather angled wings; head and neck protrude noticeably, and bill is long and slender with a yellow tip. Gull-billed is similar in size and also lacks long tail streamers. Compared with Sandwich, however, is sturdier and more thickset, with a relatively short, thick black bill and rather short, thick neck; wings are *broad-based* and long, but not so sharply pointed as Sandwich, and swept back rather than angled. Overall effect may recall a small gull, and slow, easy, graceful, rather languid flight suggests Common Tern (indeed, whole effect in flight may recall juvenile or winter-plumaged Common, rather than Sandwich).

At rest, Gull-billed again looks shorter-necked, has a rather more rounded breast, the closed primaries are deeper-based and, most significantly, it is long-legged (tarsus about 25% longer than that of Sandwich: *BWP*); looks round-headed when at ease, but head can look rather square when raised. Apart from bill, most significant difference on summer adult is lack of a crest (crest always obvious on adult summer Sandwich at rest). Net effect of these structural differences is that, on ground, Gull-billed again looks more gull-like; in winter and juvenile plumages (see below), it suggests elongated winter adult or second-winter Mediterranean Gull *Larus melanocephalus*.

Calls Calls of adults totally different: Sandwich has well-known shrill, guttural, rasping *kerr-ick*, whereas Gull-billed has a low, deep *ger-erk* or *ger-vik* (quite unmistakable). Confusion arises, however, with calls of juveniles (quite different from adults' calls): Sandwich has high-pitched, squeaky and rather throaty *pee-up, peep* or *pee-pee-pee-pee*, and Gull-billed a similar high, but soft *pee-eep* or a quick *pe-pe-eep*.

Plumage *Adult summer* Most significant difference is colour of rump and tail: on Sandwich both are white, but on Gull-billed are whitish-grey and, therefore, concolorous with mantle and wings. When assessing this character, however, the strength of the light has to be taken into account (strong light may make this area look whiter). Other significant difference is wingtip pattern: Gull-billed shows noticeable dark trailing edge to both upper and under primaries, that on underwing recalling Common Tern; Sandwich lacks dark trailing edge to upper primaries and, although it also has dark tips to under primaries, these are, in comparison, greyer, less clear-cut and less obvious.

Both species undergo a complete post-breeding moult, moult of primaries starting with inners in late summer, finishing with outers in early to mid winter (on reaching winter quarters); in late winter, inner primaries are moulted a second time, prior to spring migration. Result of this moult sequence is that, while in Europe, both species have old outer and new inner primaries. When new, primaries have pale grey bloom (radii) which is steadily lost with wear, revealing progressively more of blackish base colour (rami): this produces contrast between old dark outer primaries and new grey inners, so that both species often have noticeable dark outer primary 'wedges'. In Europe, wings will look most uniform in spring, but wedges will be most pronounced when outer primaries oldest (late summer and autumn). It seems, however, that *on average* Gull-billed wears less dark than Sandwich and usually shows less obvious primary wedges. Even as late as early September, some adults still look uniformly pale whitish-grey across entire upperwing: at distance, they look very concolorous and show little contrast between upperwing and underwing (according to *BWP*, however, about one-third of European Gull-billed do not change inner primaries a second time in late winter; presumably, they will look more uniform across whole primaries and account for at least some of these plain-winged individuals). Other plumage differences less significant: when head raised, the black extends right down nape on Gull-billed (on Sandwich, confined to a cap, and nape is white); when at ease, the black/white demarcation line on head/nape is rounded on Gull-billed (pointed on Sandwich). *Adult winter* Adult Sandwich starts to lose black on lores, forehead and crown from

mid June onwards, so by late August/ September has prominent white forehead and a black shawl from eye back over nape. Individuals in full winter plumage by late July are probably non-breeders (*BWP*). Adult Gull-billed starts moult later than Sandwich, from late July to mid August, although some still have full black crown in early September. Significant difference between moulting adults is that Gull-billed *does not gradually acquire a white forehead*; instead, whole cap is moulted at once so that transitional individuals have entire cap mottled with white. When moult completed, Gull-billed has completely different head pattern from Sandwich: instead of a black shawl across nape, it has a white head with discrete black patch immediately in front of and behind eye, strongly reminiscent of first-year Mediterranean Gull; some have very fine black streaking on crown and nape (difficult to see in field), while others have grey wash to rear crown, but Gull-billed apparently never shows a black shawl. When moulting back into summer plumage in late winter, Gull-billed shows black mottling right across crown. *Juvenile* Easily separated. Juvenile Sandwich has completely black crown (including forecrown), but, owing to body moult soon after fledging, by autumn acquires white forecrown and black shawl (as winter adult); has upperparts strongly patterned with dark brown and white (note in particular that patterning occurs along leading wing-coverts: cf. Gull-billed Tern below). During late-summer post-juvenile moult, however, much of upperpart patterning is lost so that, by autumn, mantle and scapulars are plain grey and traces of immaturity are confined to wing-coverts, tertials and tail (latter is mainly black). Perhaps most important point is that bill of juvenile Sandwich is often markedly shorter than adult's and lacks yellow tip, thus looks stubbier and, to the inexperienced, can suggest Gull-billed; attention to plumage

Adult summer Gull-billed Tern. Thick-set and gull-like. Note primary pattern, grey rump and tail, thick bill.

Adult summer Sandwich Tern. Note protruding head, slender, pointed wings. Usually shows dark primary wedges. White rump and tail.

Juvenile Gull-billed Tern. Black 'face' patch recalls Mediterranean Gull. Relatively plain above, buff mottling on back and wings.

Juvenile Sandwich Tern. Bill shorter than adult. All dark crown, strongly patterned back and wings. Tail marked black.

Moulting adult Sandwich Tern (late summer). White forehead, dark primary wedges.

1st-winter Sandwich Tern. Darkish carpal bar, secondaries and outer tail. Black 'shawl' over head.

1st-winter Gull-billed Tern. Plainer above, grey rump and tail. Head mainly white.

Adult summer Sandwich Tern. Greyish under primaries.

Moulting adult Gull-billed Tern (September). Black crown becomes peppered with white. May show darker primary wedges.

Adult summer Gull-billed Tern. Thick-set and neck-less. Dark trailing edge to under primaries.

detail therefore essential. Note also that juvenile terns can fly before outer primaries are fully grown, so that recently fledged individuals have noticeably shorter, more rounded wings than adults: on Sandwich this, combined with shorter bill, can suggest something unusual.

Juvenile Gull-billed is totally different from juvenile Sandwich. It lacks a black crown or shawl and instead shows small black ear-covert patch like winter adult (very close inspection may reveal brown shaft streaks on crown and nape feathers,

not readily apparent in the field); instead of being strongly patterned on upperparts, mantle and scapulars are relatively plain, usually appearing *uniformly ginger* in the field but, by September, this colour fades to cream and is soon replaced by grey first-winter feathering. Note in particular its fairly plain wing-coverts, lacking Sandwich Tern's dark feathering along leading coverts. Overall effect is that, from a distance, juvenile Gull-billed looks very plain above (in flight, can be difficult to separate from winter adult). Other differ-

Juvenile Roseate Tern. Superficially similar to juvenile Sandwich Tern.

Adult winter Forster's Tern. Head pattern suggests Gull-billed Tern. Bill shape, size and structure more similar to Common Tern. Note red legs.

Adult winter Gull-billed Tern. Thick bill, white head with variable black eye patch and long legs.

Juvenile Sandwich Tern. Chequered mantle and carpal bar. Black crown. Note bill is shorter than adult's.

1st-winter Sandwich Tern. Forehead white, chequered mantle replaced by grey feathers. Tertials retained.

1st-winter Gull-billed Tern. White head with black eye patch. Stubby bill. Plain grey above, poorly marked tertials.

Adult winter Sandwich Tern. Slender bill, black 'shawl' over head and spiky crest.

ences include tertials, which are ginger with a brown feather centre (juvenile Sandwich has tertials also strongly patterned with dark brown); tail feathers, which are grey with pale tip and dark subterminal patch (on Sandwich, black, thickly edged with white). Note that, like adult, juvenile Gull-billed shows a prominent dark trailing edge to under primaries. *First-year* In early winter, towards end of post-juvenile moult, both species resemble winter adult, but are easily aged by retained juvenile tertial and tail feathers. First-winter Sandwich also shows a dark secondary bar (absent on winter adult). By late winter, even these feathers are lost and both resemble winter adult. First-winter Sandwich begins to moult its juvenile inner primaries from early December to January, and the moult is completed by May to July, when the inner primaries start to moult again. First-winter Gull-billed starts its inner primary moult between December and late March, and it is often suspended in early summer and resumed from July to December; it then starts to replace its inner primaries again (*BWP*). In their first summer (when both species remain in winter quarters) they resemble winter adult, but some Gull-billed show broad black drops to feather centres of crown and nape (*BWP*). *Second-summer* Subsequently, resemble adult. Second-summer Sandwich, however, does not attain full summer plumage, but shows white flecking on forehead, lores and crown; second-summer Gull-billed may show narrow white fringes to black feathers of cap.

Habitat and Behaviour Gull-billed Tern is not a bird of the open sea, but occurs on coastal marshes, lagoons and estuaries and even hawks insects over dry land; also catches larger prey, such as frogs, and one Norfolk vagrant developed a liking for Little Tern *S. albifrons* chicks. Unlike Sandwich Tern, it does not habitually plunge-dive.

Other Confusion Species

Roseate Tern Note similarity between juvenile plumages of Roseate (page 137) and Sandwich Terns: Roseate is easily separated by size and shape, more similar to Common and Arctic Terns.

Forster's Tern Winter and juvenile Gull-billed may be confused with winter or juvenile Forster's Tern *S. forsteri*, which also shows black ear-covert patch. Forster's (virtually annual in Britain and Ireland since 1980, mainly in winter) is easily separated from Gull-billed by following features: 1 bill is long and thin, 2 it is much smaller (slightly larger than Common Tern), 3 structure is more similar to Common (in particular, it has a longer tail), and 4 it has pale legs (dull orange on first-winter, bright scarlet on adult). In addition, in first-winter plumage especially, Forster's Tern has whiter inner primaries than Gull-billed.

Winter and First-year Common Tern Beware also winter-plumaged (can occur from July onwards) and first-summer Common, which lack long tail streamers, show all-dark bill and have grey tint to rump and tail: are easily separated by size and shape, dark carpal bar and (when adult) red legs. First-year Common Terns are similar to winter adults, but often show great contrast between old, dark outer primaries and inner secondaries and new-grey inner primaries and outer secondaries; such individuals may be encountered throughout the summer.

Lesser Crested Tern Winter-plumaged Sandwich may be mistaken by the inexperienced observer for winter Lesser Crested Tern *S. bengalensis* (much rarer in Britain, where five recorded up to 1987). Latter, however, is slightly larger, has slightly darker upperparts and has stouter, dagger-like bull which is orange/yellow (duller on first-winters).

Common, Arctic and Roseate Terns

Where and When Common Tern is a widespread coastal and local inland breeding species, with a protracted spring and autumn migration; in summer, non-breeders may occur far from traditional nesting areas. Arctic Terns predominate in northern Britain, passing through southern areas mainly in late April and early May and again from August to October; more pelagic than Common, it is rather more susceptible to displacement by westerly gales. Roseate Tern is rare and declining, with largest colonies in the Irish Sea, eastern Scotland and northeast England; rare elsewhere, and extremely rare inland.

Common *Sterna hirundo* and Arctic Terns *S. paradisaea*

Approach to Identification Because of identification difficulties, many observers lump Common and Arctic as 'Commic' Terns but, with exception of spring adults, the two species are readily separable, even at distance. There is no excuse for a continuation of the 'Commic' Tern tradition, but it must be stressed that thorough practice is essential.

Structure Common is slightly but distinctly larger and sturdier than Arctic, with longer bill, neck and legs; in flight, adult is distinctly longer-winged and proportionately shorter-tailed. Arctic is more delicate, shorter-legged and more reminiscent of a marsh tern *Chlidonias*. In flight, adult Arctic has a shorter 'arm', but narrower, more pointed primaries, and a strikingly long tail reminiscent of Swallow *Hirundo rustica* (but beware Arctic with worn or broken tail streamers); wings often form inverted W shape, with 'arm' pushed further forward and primaries angled back more than on Common. Although lacking long tail streamers, juvenile Arctic also has longer tail and rather shorter, narrower wings than more

evenly proportioned juvenile Common; as they can fly before outer primaries fully grown, young juveniles of both have shorter, more rounded wings than adults.

Flight Common Tern's long wings produce easy, languid flight action. Arctic has slightly shallower, quicker wingbeats, but differences depend on conditions and must be used with caution.

Plumage *Adult summer* Pay particular attention to following features. **1** UPPER PRIMARIES Common moults inner primaries twice a year (in late summer and in late winter) but outers only once (in early winter), so that, when in Europe, there is always contrast between new inner primaries and old outers: when new, feathers have pale grey bloom (radii) which is steadily lost with wear, revealing progressively more of blackish base colour (rami), so older outer primaries are darker than newer inners; contrast is least obvious in spring, when may show only small, dark wedge on middle primaries, but, as summer progresses, outer primaries wear darker and, by late summer, are entirely dark, producing contrasting blackish wedge. Arctic Tern has *complete* wing moult once a year (in late winter, prior to spring migration), so primaries are all similarly aged and, therefore, appear uniformly grey throughout species' stay in northern hemisphere; never shows Common Tern's dark primary wedges. **2** UNDERWINGS Common has rather silvery-grey underwings with broad, diffuse dark grey trailing edge to under primaries; from below, only inner primaries appear translucent. Arctic has very white underwings (recalling Kittiwake *Rissa tridactyla*), with neat clear-cut black trailing edge to under primaries; whole of under primaries appear translucent viewed against light. **3** BILL Bright orange-red, black-tipped bill of summer Common may be visible at considerable distance; in contrast, Arctic has shorter, stubbier, blood-red bill. It must be stressed, however, that both have black bills in winter, and a small number of spring and autumn Common show black or dark red bill; second-summers may also show a black bill, as well as white forehead: any 'Commic' Tern with long, bright orange-red bill with clear-cut black tip is safely identifiable as a Common, but it is not safe to identify darker-billed individuals without reference to other characters. **4** UNDERPARTS Spring Arctic tends to have darker grey underparts than Common, but some Commons are also dark (individual variation and vagaries in lighting conditions make this a difficult field character). **5** HEAD On adult Common, black on head extends further down nape, whereas Arctic has more rounded black 'skull cap'. *Juveniles* Juveniles easily separated, even at distance. Note that structural and underwing differences are as for adults, but juveniles show shorter tail streamers, have blunter wingtips and may be slightly smaller. Following plumage differences are most significant. **1** UPPERWINGS Less delicate Common has thick, dark carpal bar, grey secondary bar (narrowly tipped white) and grey primaries. To observers familiar with juvenile Common, appearance of autumn's first delicate, neat, clean-cut, white-looking Arctic should prove something of a revelation: has essentially white secondaries and paler, whiter primaries than Common, in some lights whole rear wing looking strikingly white (this impression of whiteness is emphasised by 'Kittiwake-white' underwings); note also its lack of obvious carpal bar. **2** UPPERPARTS Common shows a distinct brown tint to upperparts; Arctic has clean grey upperparts, any buff being lost soon after fledging. Also, Common shows greyer rump. **3** BILL Common usually shows more orange at base of bill. *Adult winter* Certainly by August, and sometimes even in July, adult-type Common may show

signs of winter plumage; indeed, some will have attained full winter plumage by time they head south. Structural and underwing differences remain the same as in summer, but long tail streamers are lost. As well as attaining dark bill and white forehead, winter adults have dark carpal bar, traces of dark secondary bar, a grey tail and grey-washed rump. Moulting individuals often look rather tatty. Winter-plumaged Common may confuse beginners and often suggest marsh terns, particularly when they turn up on inland fresh water, where (like marsh terns) they tend to feed by surface-picking rather than plunge-diving. (Several erroneous claims of Whiskered Terns *C. hybridus* have proved to be winter adult, or even juvenile, Common.) Arctic may acquire black bill and white forehead before leaving our shores, but does not otherwise moult until winter quarters, so any Commic' Tern undergoing wing moult in autumn should be a Common. *First-summer* Vast majority of Common and Arctic Terns remain in winter quarters during their first summer, but a few head north with adults. Formerly thought to be a separate plumage morph, known as *'portlandica'* (after the first described specimen, at Portland in Dorset), this term is now redundant: it is simply a euphemism for 'first-summer', and its use should be discontinued. First-summer Common is similar to winter adult, but individuals undergoing active wing moult in our summer may have worn one-year-old dark outer primaries contrasting with fresh grey inners (see page 137). Unlike juvenile Common, juvenile Arctics have completed primary moult by their first spring so, by time any reach northern hemisphere, will have uniformly grey adult-like remiges and fresh rectrices (lacking long streamers); otherwise, similar to winter adult, with dark bill, white forehead and faint dark carpal bar (smaller and less obvious than on Common). They

Adult Common Tern. Early spring (and late autumn) migrants may show a dark bill.

Adult Common Tern shows dark mid-primary wedge in spring and summer. Outer primaries darken as summer progresses, producing large dark wedges.

Adult Common Tern. Note silvery-grey underwings with thick, diffuse dark trailing edge to outer primaries.

Common Tern has proportionately longer wings and shorter tail than Arctic Tern, producing a more languid flight action.

Adult winter Common Tern. Note dark carpal bar and secondaries, grey wash to rump and tail. Failed breeders may be in this plumage by July.

Adult Arctic Tern Snow-white underwing with narrow, clear cut black trailing edge to primaries.

Spring adult Arctic Tern. Completely plain grey across wings with no primary wedges.

Adult autumn Arctic Tern does not acquire dark primary wedges and shows no sign of wing moult, but gains white forehead.

Arctic Tern has proportionately shorter, narrower, more pointed wings and a longer tail than Common Tern, producing a quicker flight action.

Note differences in wing-shape and pattern of black. Common Tern (left) and Arctic Tern (right).

Adult Roseate Tern
Note protruding head,
narrow wings and very
long tail.

Adult Roseate Tern
No black on under
primary tips

Autumn adult Roseate
Tern. Outer two or three
primaries gradually
darken producing a
thin dark wedge.

lack, therefore, strongly variegated plumage of first-summer Common, look more uniform overall, and have a white rump.

Calls Calls of adult Common are fuller and throatier than those of Arctic and include characteristic, grumpy, *keeyar*. Juveniles have repeated *ki-ki-ki-ki* . . . begging call, often rapidly alternated with adult's answering *kip*.

Roseate Tern *Sterna dougallii*

Structure Smaller, more delicate than Common. Has extremely long tail streamers, even longer than Arctic's, which may quiver up and down in flight. Head and neck project slightly more than on other two species, and narrow wings appear rather more centrally placed, producing rather stiffer flight action.

Some adult Common Terns
show a blackish bill in
early spring or late summer

Adult summer Common Tern
Note shape of black cap, long
red bill with black tip.
Tail equals wing tip.

Adult winter Common Tern
develops white forehead
and dark bill.

Adult summer Arctic Tern.
Black 'skull cap'. Short blood
red bill. Small and dainty.
Short legs.

Adult winter Arctic Tern
also acquires white
forehead and dark bill
Head-shape and pattern
recalls a marsh tern.

Adult summer Roseate
Tern. Bill mainly black.
Very pale above.
Bright orange legs, very
long tail.

Juvenile Common Tern. Silvery-grey underwing. Thick diffuse dark trailing edge to primaries.

Juvenile Common Tern. Brownish mantle, grey secondaries, dark carpal bar.

1st-summer Common Tern. Note dark carpal bar, dark secondaries and contrasting dark, worn, outer primaries

Juvenile Arctic Tern. Very white underwings with clear-cut narrow black primary tips.

1st-summer Arctic Tern. Plain wings with only faint carpal bar.

Juvenile Arctic Tern. Very white primaries and secondaries. Faint carpal bar. Wings shorter and tail proportionately longer than Common Tern.

Juvenile Roseate Tern. Scalloped 'saddle' All-dark crown (until late autumn) Pale wings with white border.

Juvenile Roseate Tern. Note white underwing with only faint greyish primary tips.

Juvenile Common Tern. Pale base to bill, brownish mantle, dark carpal bar.

Juvenile Arctic Tern. Faint carpal bar, all dark bill. Grey upperparts.

Juvenile Roseate Tern. Scalloped 'saddle', dark crown, black legs.

Plumage *Adult summer* It is helpful to remember that Roseate shares many characters with larger, more distantly related Sandwich Tern *S. sandvicensis*. Like that species, upperparts are very white, but key feature is that *Roseate lacks dark border to under primaries*, showing at best only faint grey shading (difficult to see in field). Underparts show delicate rose-pink flush in summer. Like Common, acquires dark blackish primary wedges as summer advances and these contrast conspicuously with very pale upperwings. *Any very white 'Commic'-like tern that shows blackish primary wedges should prove to be Roseate* (but beware confusion with much larger Sandwich). Slender bill black (with variable amounts of red at base) but note that both Common and Arctic can show black bills, even in mid summer. Other differences include: **1** cap tends to go straight back from bill at rest (rather than curving up behind eye), and **2** feet and longer legs are extremely

bright orange (recalling Puffin *Fratercula arctica*). May acquire white forehead before migrating in autumn. *Juvenile* Easily separated from Common and Arctic. Bears uncanny resemblance to a miniature juvenile Sandwich Tern with a dark brown-scalloped 'saddle' (mantle and scapulars) and all-dark forehead (some start to acquire white forehead by late September). Wings predominantly whitish, lacking dark tips to under primaries of juvenile Common and Arctic. Unlike Common and Arctic, legs black.

Calls Adult has diagnostic, high-pitched, shrill *tch-wit* or *tchu-weet* call, in quality somewhere between Sandwich Tern and Spotted Redshank *Tringa erythropus*. Also an equally characteristic harsh, rasping 'zraaak'. Calls of juvenile squeakier.

References Scott & Grant (1969), Grant & Scott (1969), Grant *et al.* (1971), Hume & Grant (1974).

Marsh Terns

Where and When Black Tern is a spring and autumn passage migrant, commonest in southern England, occurring at lakes, reservoirs, gravel pits and on coast; large flocks sometimes appear during gloomy, anticyclonic weather. White-winged Black Tern is a very rare but annual spring and autumn migrant, currently averaging about 13 records a year; usually found among flocks of Black Terns. Whiskered Tern is a very rare vagrant, currently about three a year, usually in April–June and occasionally in autumn.

General Features Small, compact terns; compared with larger *Sterna* terns, are rather stiff-winged and lack prominent tail fork. Usually feed over fresh water: do not plunge for food (Whiskered may belly-plunge on occasion), but note that, on fresh water, Common *Sterna hirundo* and Arctic Terns *S. paradisaea* usually feed by surface-picking, just like marsh terns.

Black *Chlidonias niger* and White-winged Black Terns *C. leucopterus*

Structure White-winged Black is slightly shorter-billed than Black (recalling Little Gull *Larus minutus*), has slightly shorter and rounder wings and slightly stiffer wingbeats.

Plumage *Adult summer* Easily separated. Black Tern has black head and body, grey upper- and underwings and grey rump and tail. In comparison, White-winged Black is a stunning bird: head and body are black, but forewing is white and underwing-coverts black, contrasting with pale grey under primaries and secondaries, and rump and tail are strikingly white; on upperwing, outer primaries and inner secondaries are blackish, contrasting with rest of wing; has red legs (usually black on Black Tern). *Winter adult* Autumn adult White-winged Black nearly

Juvenile Black Tern.
Brown mantle, grey
wings, dark carpal
bar, grey rump.

Note that winter Black Tern (left) shows dark
shoulder patch, whereas White-winged Black Tern
does not.

Moulting adult Black
Tern

Adult White-winged
Black Tern often shows
black underwing late
into its moult.

Juvenile White-winged
Black Tern. Dark 'saddle',
pale wings, white rump.

Adult winter
Black Tern is
plain grey above.

Adult winter White-
winged Black Tern.
Pale grey wings with
contrasting dark
outer primaries and
secondaries.

Juvenile Whiskered Tern.
Brown 'saddle' soon
lost in late summer.
Chunky appearance.

Moulting adult
Whiskered Tern
becomes patchy
on belly.

Winter Common Tern.
Note whitish rump.

Adult winter Whiskered Tern.
Plain grey above. Note stubby
bill and white flecking
to black cap.

Note typical
marsh tern
shape-
compact with
shallow tail
fork.

Juvenile Common Tern.
Whiskered Terns are
more likely to be
confused with Common
Tern.

1st-winter
Whiskered Tern

always retains remnants of summer plumage, particularly white rump and tail, traces of black on underwing-coverts and white on upperwing-coverts: therefore, readily identifiable. Full winter-plumaged individuals very rare in this country, but may be distinguished from Black Tern by following features. 1 BREAST PATCHES Lacks Black Tern's dark breast patches (absence of this feature should be very carefully checked). 2 UPPERWING Paler than Black and, in autumn and early winter, shows contrasting blackish outer primaries and inner secondaries, a result of feather darkening caused by wear. 3 RUMP Noticeably whitish compared with Black. 4 HEAD Dark on head less extensive than on Black, producing rather white-headed appearance in comparison: black is confined to small patch behind eye and streaking over rear crown (black is more solid and more extensive on Black Tern). *Juvenile* Black is plain grey across whole upperparts, with browner mantle and scapulars and thick, dark carpal bar; from below, breast patches obvious. Juvenile White-winged Black easily separated by following features. 1 'SADDLE' Has dark brown 'saddle' (mantle and scapulars) contrasting sharply with pale grey wings (but see below). 2 RUMP 'Saddle' also contrasts strongly with white rump (particularly obvious when flying back-on). 3 WINGS Distinctly paler than juvenile Black. 4 CARPAL BAR Narrower and less conspicuous than on Black. 5 BREAST PATCHES Completely lacking. 6 HEAD PATTERN Like winter adult, black on head less extensive, confined to ear-coverts and rear crown. Overall, juvenile White-winged Black is a very contrasting bird: dark 'saddle', pale wings and white rump stand out even at distance. Note, however, that in late autumn dark 'saddle' may be less obvious owing to combination of fading and acquisition of first grey winter back feathering; conversely, juvenile Black can look quite contrasting in certain lights, so

essential to check all features before claiming identification. *First-summer* Both species remain in winter quarters during first summer, but occasional individual moves north with adults. Any Black or White-winged Black largely in winter plumage during summer months is likely to be first-summer, which often show strongly variegated plumage owing to contrast between new and old feathering. **Hybrids** Although hybrid Black x White-winged Blacks are rare, any White-winged Black should be checked for evidence of hybridisation. One such juvenile in Avon had white rump, pale wings and dark 'saddle' of White-winged Black, but breast patches and structure of Black (Vinicombe 1980).

Whiskered Tern *Chlidonias hybridus*

Structure Although obviously a marsh tern, larger and stockier than the other two, which, along with generally pale plumage, means that winter adults, juveniles and first-summers are far more likely to be confused with Common and Arctic Terns (see page 133). Has typical *Chlidonias* shape, rather neckless and short-tailed (with only shallow fork) with shorter, thicker, straighter wings than Common. Bill rather stubby, but varies sexually: males have longer bills than females (no overlap).

Plumage *Adult summer* Easily identified. Very uniformly pale grey across wings, rump and tail; black cap, white face and blackish or dark grey underparts contrast with white undertail-coverts; bill blood-red. Beware confusion with darker-bellied Common and Arctic, or even with oiled individuals. *Adult winter* Similar to adult summer, but white instead of dark underparts; black on head reduced to a line through eye and across nape. Transitional individuals may retain complete black crown while losing dark underparts.

Bill becomes black. *Juvenile/first-winter* Juvenile has dark brown 'saddle' (mantle and scapulars) with individual feathers edged white. Unlike the other two species, however, Whiskered starts to moult soon after fledging, so full juvenile plumage unlikely to occur in Britain and Ireland: by time they migrate, have lost or started to lose much of dark juvenile mantle and scapular feathering, so late-autumn juvenile/first-winters look rather plain grey above (often with some dark brown retained on scapulars). Juveniles have dark bill and legs, and small areas of black confined largely to ear-coverts and rear crown. *First-summer* Fairly similar to adult, although underparts mainly white with only few scattered dark feathers. (First-summer Whiskered seem to return north more regularly than other terns.) **Pitfalls** Although rather nondescript, Whiskered in non-breeding plumage easily identified by typical *Chlidonias* shape and pale grey upperparts. Winter adult, juvenile and first-summer Common Terns have longer tail with deeper fork and longer, narrower, more angled wings, producing more languid flight. Juvenile Common has brownish tinge to mantle and scapulars, dark carpal bar, orange base to bill and orange legs. Winter adult and first-summer Commons have darker outer primaries, dark carpal bar, white rump (although may be sullied grey) and grey tail; bill dark, but legs red. Arctic have narrower, more angled wings and longer tail: juveniles are very clean-looking, grey and white, with very white secondaries; adults in full winter plumage do not occur in this country, but first-summer is easily distinguished from Whiskered by structural differences, white rump and tail and black tips to under primaries.
Reference Vinicombe (1980).

Auks

Where and When Guillemot and Razorbill breed on most coasts of British Isles (mainly absent on English east coast from Northumberland to Isle of Wight), Guillemot much more numerous; both disperse widely in winter, can be encountered almost anywhere around coast, but largest numbers occur during periodic 'wrecks'. Puffin has more northerly breeding distribution (small numbers persist along south coast of England); in winter markedly pelagic, few being seen from shore except during wrecks. Little Auk is rare winter visitor, but large flights or wrecks occasionally reported in northern areas or in North Sea, when some may even be blown well inland. Brünnich's Guillemot is a very rare winter visitor, mainly to Shetland and northern Scotland, where one or two usually washed up dead each winter; regular occurrence of tideline corpses suggests that small numbers regularly winter in area.

Guillemot *Uria aalge* and Razorbill *Alca torda*

Bill When separating Guillemot and Razorbill, pay particular attention to bill. Slim and pointed on Guillemot and obvious at some distance, even in flight, when Guillemot has distinctly pointed head/bill profile. Razorbill's diagnostic oblong bill is readily apparent in flight, giving characteristic blunt-headed impression at distance; white lines on bill, particularly horizontal one, are noticeable in summer. **Size and Structure** Guillemot is slightly smaller and slimmer and, on water, shows more rounded head than Razorbill. Latter is a sturdier, larger-headed bird, with back of head rather more angular, and has noticeably long, pointed tail (may be obvious when diving); when at rest on sea, tail is cocked to give bird more of a banana-like shape compared with Guillemot, which has shorter tail and, consequently, more truncated rear end.

Plumage *Adults* Guillemots are very brown, whereas Razorbills look jet-black in the field, this easily separating them (providing light conditions good). Guillemot has dark streaking on flanks (lacking on Razorbill), in flight producing darker-looking 'arm pit'. In winter plumage, Razorbill has solidly black ear-coverts, with lobe of white extending up behind. Guillemot has less extensive black on head, curving up behind eye, with a dark furrow projecting into white, from eye back. *'Northern Guillemots'* Guillemots become slightly larger and darker towards the north of their range, so that the nominate northern race can look black in the field and thus more similar to Razorbill; may also show more heavily streaked flanks and, in winter, a partial or complete dark collar on lower throat. Incidence of 'bridled' Guillemots also increases towards north: in summer plumage these individuals have narrow white eye-ring and narrow white furrow running from eye back. (Note that 'bridled' Guillemots can be decidedly uncommon in south of range.) *Juvenile to first-summer* Juveniles leave nest sites before fully grown, are cared for at sea by adults. Guillemots at this age are small, short-billed and fluffier than adults and lack dark flank streaking; can usually be detected by persistent high-pitched begging calls. Juvenile Razorbills are similarly small, and have poorly developed stubby bills lacking adults' white markings. Juveniles of both vary, but Razorbills *tend* to be darker on chin and throat than Guillemots, and seem far less vocal. Both species resemble winter adults after post-juvenile moult, but bill remains less well developed; first-winter Guillemots have less streaked flanks than adults and may have bolder area of white on nape. First-summer birds develop summer plumage later than adults and may retain white feathering on chin and throat (as can older individuals); have faded brown wings.

Puffin *Fratercula arctica*

Distinctive and well known, but distant individuals in flight, winter adults and young birds may be less straightforward.
Size and Structure Small size (about three-quarters that of Guillemot and Razorbill) usually apparent. In summer, huge, triangular, brightly coloured bill and white face should be obvious; in winter, bill duller and face greyer. Juveniles have smaller, less deep, stubbier bill which is predominantly greyish. On water, looks stocky and large-headed, with truncated rear end with short tail projecting only about 1cm beyond wingtips. Fluorescent orange legs and feet obvious in summer, duller and yellower on juveniles and in winter.
Flight Identification Looks small, with short, rounded wings slightly angled back from carpal; shows more 'head and neck' than Razorbill or Guillemot, and short, square tail produces stubby rear end. Upperparts black (like Razorbill), but lacks white trailing edge to wing; broadly black across rump area (Razorbill and Guillemot have fairly narrow black line down rump). Underwing looks very dark, even black (although grey at close range). Flight action rapid, with frequent shifts in body angle.

Little Auk *Alle alle*

Size and Structure A tiny auk, only two-thirds size of Puffin and half size of Guillemot or Razorbill. On water, looks small, stubby, horizontal and neckless, with small, but thick, black bill (producing snub-nosed effect) and short, cocked tail.
Plumage Most distinctive features in winter are prominent white lobe extending from throat right up behind ear-coverts, and narrow black semi-collar around lower throat; white tips to secondaries may be noticeable, but particularly important are three or four short white lines across scapulars, usually visible at

Winter Razorbill. Heavy body with blunt head and pointed tail. Plain underwing.

Winter Puffin. Dark underwing, triangular head.

Winter Little Auk. Starling-sized, dark underwing, rapid wingbeats.

Winter Guillemot. Slimmer body, pointed bill.

Adult summer Puffin. All-dark rump, lacks white trailing edge to wing. White 'face'.

Little Auk in winter

Summer Razorbill. Black above. Note pointed tail.

Summer Guillemot. Southern birds are browner above than Razorbill.

Juvenile Guillemots and Razorbills go to sea when half grown, during July and August

Winter Little Auk. Tiny. Note head pattern and small bill. Little Auks do not arrive in British waters until late autumn.

Winter Guillemot. Note head pattern, short tail, streaked flanks.

Winter Razorbill. Note extent of white on cheeks, plain flanks, pointed tail.

Juvenile Razorbills tend to be darker on the throat than Guillemots.

Winter Brünnich's Guillemot. Note thick bill, extensive black on 'face', plain flanks.

1st-winter Puffin. Smaller bill than adult, dusky face and rear flanks.

some distance. In summer plumage, chin and throat black, and has narrow white half-circle over eye. First-winter duller and browner.

Flight Identification Looks very small, with rapid wingbeats and dark-looking underwings.

Brünnich's Guillemot *Uria lomvia*

Very rare vagrant; should not be identified unless all following differences clearly established.

Bill Pay particular attention to length and shape of bill. Distance between eye and foremost extension of feathering on bill is twice that from tip of feathering to tip of bill (on Guillemot, about equal). Bill therefore thicker and stubbier; upper mandible downcurved towards tip, while lower may show slight gonydeal angle half way along; shows narrow white stripe at base of upper mandible ('tomium stripe'), but this faint or lacking on some (some Guillemots may also show suggestion of this feature; beware also effects of

Guillemots carrying fish in bill, especially when observed from distance).

Size and Structure Slightly larger and stockier than Guillemot. Has steeper forehead, with stronger forehead peak; tail, although short like Guillemot, may be persistently cocked. Juvenile Guillemots and Razorbills have shorter bills, so particular care required in late summer and early autumn (when Brünnich's unlikely to occur.)

Plumage In winter, dark of head includes whole of ear-coverts, so black of head more extensive than on Guillemot or Razorbill. Moults into and out of winter plumage much later than Guillemot (so any dark-headed guillemot in late autumn/early winter or any pale-headed guillemot in spring is worth second look). Is blacker than most Guillemots, lacks extensive flank streaking and, in summer, white of breast protrudes into black of throat in a sharper point than on most Guillemots.

Reference Grant (1981).

Pigeons and Doves

Where and When Woodpigeon, Stock Dove, feral Rock Dove (or 'Feral Pigeon') and Collared Dove are common in much of British Isles. Wild Rock Doves are restricted to northern and western Scotland and northern, western and southern Ireland. Turtle Dove is a summer visitor (late April–October) to England and eastern Wales (rare Ireland and Scotland).

Woodpigeon *Columba palumbus*

A large pigeon, easily identified by conspicuous thick white line across middle of open wing, visible at bend of wing at rest; also has white patch on sides of neck (lacking on juveniles, which are browner than adults and have dark eye, like Stock Dove). In flight, easily identified by shape: small head, full breast, rather swept-back pointed wings and fairly long tail; from

below, underwings grey and tail crossed by thick pale band. When flushed, takes off with loud clatter of wings, often bursting violently from cover. In display, flies steeply upwards, claps wings and glides downwards. Song is well-known, lazy, *coo-COOO coo-coo coo*, peculiarly evocative of balmy summer days.

Stock Dove *Columba oenas*

In winter, often associates with Woodpigeon. In flight, easily identified (with practice) by shape alone: smaller than Woodpigeon and more evenly proportioned, being stocky and compact, with shorter, stiffer, more triangular wings and shorter tail; note also thick black border to end and rear of wing and dark grey underwing (cf. Rock Dove). Lacks white in plumage. On ground, note brightly

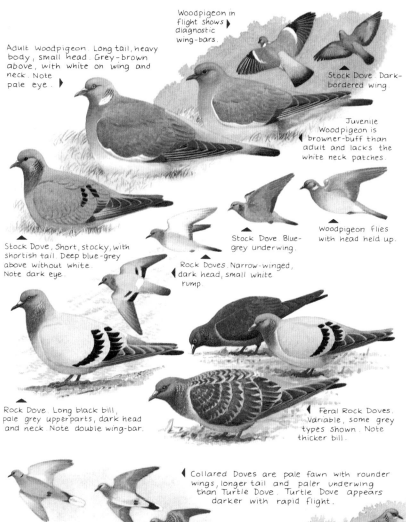

Woodpigeon in flight shows diagnostic wing-bars.

Adult Woodpigeon. Long tail, heavy body, small head. Grey-brown above, with white on wing and neck. Note pale eye.

Stock Dove. Dark-bordered wing.

Juvenile Woodpigeon is browner-buff than adult and lacks the white neck patches.

Stock Dove. Blue-grey underwing.

Woodpigeon flies with head held up.

Stock Dove. Short, stocky, with shortish tail. Deep blue-grey above without white. Note dark eye.

Rock Doves. Narrow-winged, dark head, small white rump.

Rock Dove. Long black bill, pale grey upperparts, dark head and neck. Note double wing-bar.

Feral Rock Doves. Variable, some grey types shown. Note thicker bill.

Collared Doves are pale fawn with rounder wings, longer tail and paler underwing than Turtle Dove. Turtle Dove appears darker with rapid flight.

Note undertail pattern. Collared Dove (left) shows more white.

Collared Dove has plain upperparts, Turtle Dove (left) is patterned.

Turtle Dove

Collared Dove

145

coloured bill and cere: red with yellow or whitish tip (cf. grey bill and whitish cere of Rock Dove; juvenile Stock, however, also has dull greyish or brownish bill). Note also emerald-green neck patch (lacking on juvenile), double black bar on inner greater coverts and tertials, and short tail compared with Woodpigeon. Eye dark (white on adult Woodpigeon). Male's display flight straight: slow, deep wingbeats, before clapping wings over back and then gliding with wings slightly above horizontal. Song a deep *ooo-ah*, sometimes given about ten times in accelerating sequence.

Rock Dove *Columba livia*

Wild Rock Doves are attractive: pale grey above with two thick black bars across tertials/greater coverts and median coverts, a white rump and darker grey head and underparts. In flight, latter contrast markedly with silvery-white underwings (grey on Stock Dove and Woodpigeon). Grey bill and whitish cere (cf. adult Stock). Feral Rock Doves are highly variable: many resemble their wild ancestors, many are chequered or irregularly patterned, and plumage varies from grey to blackish, white or brown. Adult's eye usually red or orange (dark on Stock Dove). Shape important when separating Rock from Woodpigeon or Stock Dove in flight: is intermediate between the two, and more pointed protruding head and swept-back wings easily separate it from stockier, more compact Stock Dove. Often glides on V-shaped wings. Display flight consists of exaggerated slow, deep wingbeats followed by loud wing claps and long glide on V-shaped wings. Song a moaning *oo-oo-oor*. Inhabits cliffs and buildings, usually ignores trees (though may use them as daytime roost).

Collared Dove *Streptopelia decaocto* and Turtle Dove *S. turtur*

Collared is a familiar pale, sandy dove with pale underwings and long tail, distal half of which is white; easily separated in flight from Turtle Dove by proportionately shorter, more rounded wings which produce lolloping flight. In flight, Turtle Dove has dark grey underwings, contrasting pale belly, and narrower white tip to tail; smaller, with shorter, more tapered tail than Collared Dove, its swept-back, fairly pointed wings produce whipping flight action. Differences at rest obvious, Turtle being easily identified by rufous tortoiseshell pattern of upperparts, grey head and vinous breast. Juvenile Turtle Dove much duller and drabber than adult, lacks richly rufous upperparts, grey crown, vinous breast and a noticeable neck patch. Juvenile Collared also duller than adult, lacks half-collar and has pale feather edgings on upperparts. Collared is generally associated with suburban gardens and farmyards; Turtle is most likely to be encountered in open, arable farmland or bushy places. Songs completely different: Collared gives familiar cooing *coo-oo oo*, Turtle gives soft, purring *turrrr turrrr*; Collared also gives harsh, nasal 'excitement' call. In display, both species fly up and glide down on spread wings.

Long-eared and Short-eared Owls

Where and When As a breeding bird, Long-eared Owl *Asio otus* is widespread but thinly distributed throughout Britain, inhabiting coniferous woodland; in Ireland, it is the commonest owl and, in absence of competition from Tawny Owl *Strix aluco*, is found more frequently in broadleaved woodland. Short-eared Owl *A. flammeus* breeds in open country, mainly in Scotland, Wales, and northern and eastern England. Both species are more widespread in winter, when Short-eared Owls move into lowland areas; variable numbers of Continental immigrants swell numbers of both species, October being best time to come across newly arrived migrants.

Habitat and Behaviour Habitat and behavioural differences are generally first clue to identification. Short-eared is frequently seen in broad daylight, particularly on winter afternoons, hunting over rough ground; usually roosts on ground among rough vegetation. Long-eared is more or less strictly nocturnal, not normally hunting in broad daylight; usually roosts in conifers or thick hedgerows or bushes, often at some height, and, when flushed, will fly off silently through trees and quickly disappear (often roosts communally in favoured areas). Biggest identification problem arises with migrants, which can appear at coastal migration spots at any time of day; in such circumstances, Long-eared will often settle on ground when trees or bushes unavailable.

Identification at Rest Long-eared is a slim, upright owl, usually found in a conifer or thick bush: easily identified by its long 'ear' tufts and thick vertical dark lines running down face from tufts to bill, a pale eye-brow and a rather orangy facial shield; eyes are brilliant orange (best seen when flashed open when startled), and underparts heavily streaked and barred

right down to belly (some are less heavily streaked on belly). Short-eared is generally paler and less upright, usually seen sitting on ground or on a fence post: it has short 'ear' tufts and yellow (or orangy-yellow) eyes which, unlike Long-eared, are surrounded by circular black patches; underpart streaking is confined mainly to upper breast.

Identification in Flight *General plumage tones* Both species are very variable, but Long-eared is typically darker and browner than the sandier, buffer Short-eared. Because of darker plumage tones, Long-eared generally appears a more uniform, less contrasting bird in the field. Some Short-eared are, however, darker than others, while some Long-eared are particularly pale, almost whitish-buff on underparts. *Upperwing* Upper primary patch on Long-eared is a rich, orangy-buff to rusty colour; on Short-eared, it is paler, sandy-buff to almost white, and therefore more obvious. Upperwing of Short-eared is generally paler and upperwing-coverts more blotched than streaked, giving less uniform and distinctly mottled appearance compared with Long-eared. Paler coloration of Short-eared means that dark carpal patches stand out more strongly than on Long-eared, while primary and secondary barring also appears stronger and more contrasting. On Short-eared, primary barring continues on to secondaries; on Long-eared, barred primaries give way to *finely* barred secondaries. Short-eared has a pale trailing edge to wing that Long-eared lacks (on particularly pale Short-eared, however, this can be surprisingly difficult to see). *Underwing* Both have pale underwings with dark carpal patch. Long-eared's primaries are crossed with three to five dark bars. On Short-eared, tips of outer primaries appear more solidly black and innermost secondaries form small dark patch. *Tail*

Long-eared Owl.
Broader, more rounded
wings, primary patch
orangier, upper parts
patterning less
distinct.

Short-eared Owl.
Generally paler and
sandier than Long-
eared Owl, with paler
primary patch. Note
white trailing edge
to wing (sometimes
inconspicuous), coarse
blotching on upperparts,
and strongly barred
tail. Wingtips less
rounded.

Underwing tip of
Long-eared Owl is
more finely barred.
The body is
usually heavily
streaked.

Short-eared Owl.
More solid dark
to primary tips.
Streaking mainly
confined to
upper breast.

Note black face stripes,
orange eyes.

Long-eared Owl usually
roosts in thick cover
above ground; newly
arrived migrants may
roost in more exposed
positions.

Short-eared Owl. Yellow eyes,
surrounded by black.
Usually roosts on ground.

On Long-eared, uppertail is generally more closely barred on a darker background, producing more uniform-looking tail than Short-eared, which has four or five prominent bars on a paler, sandier background. **Underparts** Underpart streaking is confined mainly to upper breast on Short-eared, but on Long-eared extends down belly, creating overall darker, more uniform impression (difference not, however, totally reliable, as on some Long-eared streaking fizzles out on belly). **Structure** Long-eared is shorter and broader in the wing than Short-eared, with tips broader and more rounded; is also proportionately shorter-tailed. Short-eared's wing is narrower and more tapered, this emphasised by fact that wing is held more forward than Long-eared's.

Calls Short-eared's most familiar call, given by both sexes, is a hoarse, high-pitched bark, heard mainly on breeding grounds. Displaying males have a wing-clapping display flight, as well as a hollow *boo-boo-boo-boo* advertising call (*BWP*). In early spring, male Long-eared gives slow, low, cooing *oo*, repeated at intervals of about 2.5 seconds (*BWP*), rather quiet, but audible for some distance; also gives variety of other calls in breeding season, including nasal, buzzing, wheezing and barking noises. Begging young have a very distinctive, far-carrying mournful *eee-oo* (like squeaking of a rusty hinge), heard from late May to July.

References Davis & Prytherch (1976), Kemp (1982), Robertson (1982).

Swift, Alpine Swift and Pallid Swift

Where and When Swift is a familiar and common summer visitor, mainly late April – late August, with stragglers into October or even November. Alpine Swift is a rare but annual vagrant, mainly in spring, currently averaging ten records a year. Pallid Swift is an extreme rarity (six records up to 1984), but there have been a number of further unsubstantiated claims, and it seems likely that identification difficulties are masking its true status here; of the six British records, two have been in May and four in November, so very late swifts are clearly worth checking carefully.

Aberrant Swifts *Apus apus*

Before identifying a vagrant swift, it is absolutely essential to eliminate the possibility of albinistic or leucistic 'Common' Swift, examples of which are not infrequent. Such birds may show a white rump (suggesting Little Swift *A. affinis*, White-rumped Swift *A. caffer* or Pacific Swift *A. pacificus*): it is, therefore, essential to take very detailed notes on any swift with a white rump, concentrating in particular on structure, and to look for evidence of albinism, such as traces of white feathering elsewhere on the body. The aberrant individual illustrated on page 150 is loosely based on one seen example seen in Dorset in 1983. Pale, sandy, leucistic Swifts have also been recorded, and these may suggest Pallid Swift.

Alpine Swift *Apus melba*

When faced with a vagrant Alpine Swift, check two things to eliminate an aberrant Swift: **1** be sure to evaluate size accurately (Alpine Swift is about 1½ times the size of a Swift), and **2** make sure that upperparts are pale (they should be similar in tone to those of a Sand Martin *Riparia riparia*). Plumage tone does, however, vary according to light, and Alpine Swifts can sometimes look surprisingly dark. White belly is always conspicuous, but white throat can be difficult to see. Long wings produce slow, deep wingbeats which create a rather languid flight action and, at times, fast, purposeful flight may even suggest Hobby *Falco subbuteo*.

Pallid Swift. Paler than Swift, pale fringes to underparts, darker primaries, large white throat patch and slightly blunter wing tips.

Partial albino Swift. Such individuals are not infrequent and can cause confusion with rarer species.

Swift

Swift

Pallid Swift. Note dark eye, darker 'saddle', darker primaries and front of wing, contrasting with paler greater coverts and secondaries.

Swift

Alpine Swift. Very large, white belly and throat (although latter can be hard to see). Pale brown above.

Pallid Swift *Apus pallidus*

Although difficult to pick out from Swift, Pallid Swift is not actually difficult to identify *if seen well*. Prolonged, close-range views in good light are, however, essential and *all* following differences should be carefully checked. **1** PLUMAGE TONE In good light, Pallid has distinctly paler, milkier plumage than Swift, but differences in plumage tone can be difficult to evaluate at distance or in poor or strong light. **2** WING PATTERN Note particularly that dark outer primaries and leading edge of underwing contrast with rest of underwing, which is paler. This effect is mirrored on upperwing, where greater coverts and secondaries can stand out as being quite noticeably paler. **3** BODY COLOUR Darker

body contrasts with paler underwings, while darker mantle produces effect of slightly darker 'saddle'. **4** FEATHER EDGINGS Pale edgings on underparts (particularly on flanks) may be obvious at close range. **5** HEAD Forehead and throat are noticeably pale, and latter area is larger than on Swift, so dark eye stands out more noticeably. **6** WINGTIP SHAPE On Swift, outer primary is longest, producing sharply pointed wing shape; on Pallid, outer primary and one next to it are same length, producing slightly blunter wing shape. This can be surprisingly obvious when looked for. **7** TAIL FORK Slightly shallower on Pallid. **8** CALL Pallid's is markedly disyllabic: *cheeu-eet* or *churr-ic*.

Reference Harvey (1981).

Skylark, Woodlark and Short-toed Lark

Where and When Skylark breeds commonly throughout Britain and Ireland, with general retreat from high ground and some southward withdrawal in winter. Woodlark breeds on heathland, mainly in East Anglia, Surrey, Hampshire, Dorset and Devon, some sites (particularly East Anglia and Devon) being deserted in winter, when may occur on nearby stubble, often with Skylarks; a few appear at south and east coast migration sites, particularly in March–April and October–November. Short-toed Lark is a regular vagrant (about 14 records a year), mainly in May and September–October; most occur at coastal migration sites, particularly in Shetland and Scilly.

Skylark *Alauda arvensis*

General Features A familiar bird of open ground. Largish, broad-beamed but rather nondescript lark, with short crest and thickish, pointed bill. Face rather plain (only faint eye-stripe behind eye), with slight, but noticeable, supercilium. General plumage tone varies considerably, but upperparts well streaked and breast shows finely streaked gorget. Juveniles noticeably scalloped on back and scapulars.

Flight Identification More distinctive: shows conspicuous whitish trailing edge to wing and white outer tail feathers; relatively slim-winged (for a lark), evenly proportioned. Flight flappy, with periodic wing closures. Overhead migrants look rather thrush-like. Over breeding grounds has distinctive fluttery flight, indulges in aerial chases, and hovers above long grass before alighting.

Voice Song, from stationary position high in sky, a familiar thin, continuous musical refrain, often containing strongly mimetic phrases. Call a hard, rippling *chirrup*; flocks also give soft, conversational *see-up* calls.

Leucistic Skylarks Occasional pale, leucistic Skylarks perplex the inexperienced.

Woodlark *Lullula arborea*

General Features Unlikely to be seen away from traditional southern heathland sites. Readily perches in trees (unlike Skylark), but feeds on ground. Distinctly smaller than Skylark, structural differences should instantly attract attention: a stocky lark, with short crest and noticeably short tail. When settled, most distinctive character is prominent, creamy-white supercilia which meet on nape in a V or a pale mottled area; facial pattern stronger than Skylark's, with noticeable dark brown stripe behind eye and rear border to ear-coverts. Upperparts strongly and richly streaked, while clear band of black streaking crosses breast. Buffy-white tips to black primary coverts may be noticeable at rest and in flight. Juveniles strongly scalloped above.

Flight Identification Short tail particularly obvious, and looks very round-winged compared with Skylark. Jerky, undulating flight strangely reminiscent of Lesser Spotted Woodpecker *Dendrocopos minor*. Lacks both white trailing edge to wings and white outer tail feathers (outer web of outer tail feather is sullied brownish-white); instead shows whitish tip to tail

Voice Beautiful mellow and rich song, delivered in shorter phrases than Skylark, contains characteristic *lu lu lu* phrases; often given in circular song flight. Call a melodic, liquid, soft *toolooeet*.

Short-toed Lark *Calandrella brachydactyla*

General Features A small, compact, pale sparrow-like lark; can appear rounded and dumpy or sleek and pipit-like. Moves in erratic bursts, with hesitant, jerky walk. Characteristic plumage

Juvenile Skylark
Heavily scalloped
with poor crest.

Adult Skylark.
Large lark with
crest and white outertail
feathers. Note heavy bill
and long hindclaw.

Skylark may have
crest raised or
flattened.

In flight, Skylark shows
white trailing edge
to wing.

Woodlark in
flight. Note short
tail and diagnostic
'wrist' patches.

In flight Short-toed
Lark shows no white
in wing.

Woodlark. Smaller
than Skylark with
short white-tipped
tail and black-and-
white wingpatch.

Short-toed Lark. Ground colour
varies, some show chestnut-
'capped' effect. Note long tertials
hide primary tips.

Short-toed Lark. Pale with
heavier bill than Woodlark.
'Plain-faced' with little
marking on underparts.
Black neck patch
sometimes obvious, as
is dark median-covert
bar.

pattern, but varies considerably in tone: most are pale sandy-brown above and whitish below, some are distinctly darker and very dingy, dark buffy or even browny below, others show reddish tints to head and, faintly, to tail. Typically looks uniformly whitish and unstreaked below, but close inspection usually reveals small dark patch at sides of breast (this may be invisible until bird stretches up); diffuse fine streaking may be present (even in spring) across upper breast and below dark side patches. Lacks strong crest and often appears rather round-headed; this, combined with thickish pale bill and dark eye-stripe behind eye, creates facial expression suggesting female House Sparrow *Passer domesticus*. Upperparts pale sandy, lightly streaked across back and scapulars (in autumn may retain scalloped, dark-centred juvenile scapulars). Dark centres to median coverts may pro-duce dark wing line reminiscent of Tawny Pipit *Anthus campestris*. Very long tertials more or less completely cloak primaries (a diagnostic difference from Lesser Short-toed Lark *C. rufescens*). Legs noticeably pale, orangy or pinky.

Flight Identification A slim, evenly proportioned lark, shape rather more pipit-like than most other larks. Flight fast and dashing, but maybe rather jerkier than Skylark. Lacks white trailing edge to wing, shows only inconspicuous white outer tail feathers; typically, looks pale and sandy.

Call Flight call usually a hard *t-trip trip, trrick trrick*, a more trilling *pirrrick* or a more clipped, sparrow-like *chip chip*, all vaguely suggesting a hard, sparrow-like Skylark. Softer calls include high-pitched *which . . . wick . . wick* and clear, drawn-out *tee-uu*.

Reference Dennis & Wallace (1975).

Tawny and Richard's Pipits

Where and When Tawny Pipit is a rare spring (mainly May) and autumn (late August–September) migrant, mostly to south and east coasts; occasional in summer, with stragglers into October. Richard's Pipit is a late-autumn visitor from Siberia, seen mostly at well-watched coastal migration sites from mid September to November; occasional winter and spring records. Any large pipit seen before middle of September is, therefore, most likely to be Tawny; after early October, Richard's is far more probable.

Structure and Behaviour Both are large, slim, rather wagtail-like pipits, with long, orangy legs, liable to be seen running around on short turf, feeding with start–stop action and frequently wagging tail. Richard's also likes longer grass and may hover with spread tail, rather like Skylark *Alauda arvensis*, before alighting (rarely, Tawny may do this). Flight of both is strong, undulating, rather wagtail-like.

Adult Tawny Pipit *Anthus campestris*

Easily identified. A pale, sandy pipit, lacking obvious back and breast streaking. Conspicuous pale supercilium, but best feature is median coverts, which stand out as a line of dark spots, contrasting with rest of plumage. Beware possibility of pale, leucistic Rock Pipits *A. petrosus*, which, however, easily separated by their blackish legs, *pseep* call and rocky habitat. Can also be confused with dull, buffish juvenile and first-winter Yellow Wagtails *Motacilla flava* or, conceivably, with summer-plumaged Water Pipits *A. spinoletta*, both of which can also be eliminated by their blackish legs and calls. All other pipits likely to be seen in Britain and Ireland are darker and (apart from Richard's) smaller than adult Tawny, although both Rock and Water Pipits are very nearly as big and often appear more bulky.

Richard's Pipit *Anthus novaeseelandiae* and Juvenile and First-winter Tawny Pipits

Richard's is easily separated from *adult* Tawny, being larger, darker and more heavily streaked. Juvenile Tawny, however, is much more similar to Richard's, and there has been considerable past confusion between the two. In reality, the problem of their separation should not often arise in this country, as young Tawny Pipits start to moult out of juvenile plumage in late July/August (well before arrival of first Richard's); after end of August, most young Tawny resemble adults, so adult-like Tawny in late autumn often not safely aged, though some retain traces of juvenile plumage (dark-centred scapular feathers, traces of back and breast streaking) well into autumn. When faced with a puzzling bird, following features separate Richard's from juvenile Tawny. **1 SIZE AND STRUCTURE** Richard's is a larger, bulkier bird, with rather hefty, almost thrush-like bill slightly angled up from horizontal. Tawny is slimmer, more wagtail-like, with smaller, slimmer bill. Richard's has a very long, curved hind claw; Tawny's is shorter and straighter. **2 HEAD PATTERN** Careful attention to head pattern essential. Richard's has prominent, thick supercilium (almost recalling autumn Whinchat *Saxicola rubetra*) which usually extends diffusely around rear of ear-coverts. Most important, concentrate on lores: *these are very pale and plain on Richard's* (but note that at certain angles, especially when front-on, Richard's can show hint of a dark line). Pale lores, a pale area around eye and a pale 'hollow' centre to ear-coverts all combine to give Richard's a pleasant 'open-faced' character; also has variable narrow moustachial stripe, and prominent dark malar stripe broadening into blotch on side of lower throat. Juvenile Tawny also shows prominent whitish supercilium (contrasting with

streaked crown), but it ends squarely above rear of ear-coverts. Most important, *Tawny shows dark line from bill to eye* and solidly dark ear-coverts, creating sharper facial pattern than Richard's; *narrow* moustachial and malar stripes. **3 MANTLE COLOUR** Richard's is brown above, thickly streaked darker, recalling Skylark. Juvenile Tawny is also heavily streaked, with black and buff lines down mantle, but pale edges to these feathers may produce slightly scalloped effect. Note, however, that some Richard's are less heavily streaked than others and, in bright light, their mantle can look surprisingly plain, prompting confusion with juvenile/first-winter Tawny: it is probably these fresh, plainer-backed Richard's that have been responsible for periodic late-autumn controversies. **4 MEDIAN COVERTS** Both species show a dark median-covert bar, but only on adult Tawny does it contrast strongly with pale plumage. **5 UNDERPARTS** On Richard's, strongly gingery-buff, especially on flanks, with diffuse, sparsely streaked breast band. Tawny is creamy-buff below, juveniles showing gorget of profuse fine blackish streaking. **6 OUTER TAIL FEATHERS** Sullied buff on Tawny. Conspicuously white on Richard's, recalling Reed Bunting *Emberiza schoeniclus*. **7 CALL** Typical calls diagnostic, but differentiation requires practice. Richard's has loud, rasping, sparrow-like *chreep* or *chreep chreep*. Tawny has softer, less explosive, sparrow-like *cheeup* or *treeup*, a softer *shleeup*, recalling Yellow Wagtail, and a musical, sparrow-like *chlip* or *schlup*. Note, however, that both species give abbreviated versions of these calls which are easily confused.

Other Confusion Species and Aberrant Plumages

Richard's could be confused with both Rock and winter-plumaged Water Pipits: note latter two species' dark legs and *pseep* calls (see page 159). Beware also confusing

Some autumn Richard's Pipits retain a few juvenile feathers. Lores may sometimes appear dark, depending on the angle of light.

Richard's Pipit. Large and robust, rather thrush-like. Note pale lores, wide malar stripe. Flanks are strong buff rather than creamy. Dark-streaked upperparts. Dark tail with white outer edges. Note long hind claw.

Tawny Pipit moulting from juvenile into 1st-winter plumage. Superficially like Richard's, but note strong 'face' pattern with dark lores. Thin malar stripe. Flanks creamy, and tail lighter than Richard's, with creamy outer edges.

Juvenile Tawny Pipit (rare here). Note spotting on flanks and scalloped back.

Adult Tawny Pipit. Pale, poorly marked back and plain breast. Rather wagtail-like. Note short hindclaw.

155

Richard's with Skylark: note in particular latter's crest and whitish trailing edge to wing. An unusually dark Tawny Pipit at Portland, Dorset, in 1983 had upperparts dark brown and underparts strongly sullied with orangy-brown: whether this was simply aberrant or was some obscure geographical variant is not known, but such individuals could cause further con-

fusion with Richard's.

(Note that Blyth's Pipit *A. godlewskii*, recorded perhaps a couple of times in Britain, is extremely similar to both Richard's and juvenile Tawny, and very difficult to distinguish from the former in the field: see Alström, 1988.)

References Williamson (1963), Grant (1972).

Small Pipits: Meadow, Tree, Red-throated and Olive-backed Pipits

Where and When   Meadow Pipit is an abundant breeding, passage and wintering species throughout much of Britain and Ireland. Tree Pipit is a summer visitor (early April–October) breeding on heathland, woodland edges and rough ground with scattered trees. Red-throated Pipit is a vagrant, averaging about seven records a year, mainly in May and September–October. Olive-backed Pipit currently averages about 10 autumn records a year (but a remarkable influx in October 1990 involved some 42 individuals); a few spring and one winter record. Both vagrants most frequently recorded at well-watched coastal migration sites.

Meadow *Anthus pratensis* and Tree Pipits *A. trivialis*

Similar. Separation complicated by seasonal and individual variation in plumage tone and patterning, but with practice not difficult, though many distinguishing features subtle or inconsistent.

Calls   The easiest distinction. Meadow has familiar *sip sip sip* (number of notes varies, as does power of delivery). Tree has short, incisive *zeep, spzeep* or a more scolding *speez* (overhead migrants easily detected by call); in flight, also a very soft, *barely audible*, single *sip*. On breeding grounds, both species utter variety of calls: Meadow gives dry *si-sip* or soft, nerv-

ous *sitip* anxiety note; Tree gives soft *sip* alarm call (particularly when carrying food) or high-pitched, ringing, *stick* (when young under threat).

Songs   Diagnostic. Meadow gives accelerating sequence of tinkling notes as it rises in song flight, succeeded by more musical notes and ending as trill as it descends. Tree gives similar sequence but louder and fuller, vaguely suggesting Chaffinch *Fringilla coelebs*, and ending with a characteristic loud far-carrying flourish: *seea seea seea*.

Structure   Subtle but definite differences. Tree is slightly bigger, longer and sleeker-looking, with longer, heftier and more wedge-shaped bill angled upwards from 'face'. Meadow is rounder-headed and less streamlined. Tree's longer wings readily apparent in flight, producing slightly stronger, more purposeful flight than Meadow (weaker, more hesitant). Length of hind claw diagnostic: short and arched on Tree, much longer and straighter on Meadow (difference difficult to see in field).

Behaviour   Tree is far more arboreal than Meadow, but Meadow readily perches on trees and bushes, particularly when flushed. When feeding, Meadow wanders rather aimlessly through vegetation; Tree is stealthier and more purposeful, though rather furtive.

Meadow Pipit in worn
plumage Dull brown above,
heavily streaked below,
where streaks often
merge into a breast
spot. Rump plain.

Meadow Pipit in
fresh autumn plumage.
Yellow-buff beneath
extending to flanks.
Lores often pale,
upperparts tinged
olive.

Tree Pipit in fresh
autumn plumage.
Often strong cream
flush to upper
breast.

Note heavy bill
and strong facial
pattern of Tree
Pipit.

Summer Tree Pipit Larger
than Meadow Pipit,
'cleaner' below with
thin flank streaks.

Olive-backed Pipit. Usually
shows distinctive 'face'
pattern Heavily marked
below but almost plain
olive above.

Greyish Meadow Pipits
occur. The strong
streaking prompts
confusion with
Red-throated Pipit.
Check the
rump.

Autumn Red-throated Pipit. Whitish
or creamy underparts with
heavy streaking, strong on
flanks. Pale lines down
back usually obvious
Note streaked rump.

Plumage Differences in plumage have to be evaluated sensibly, bearing in mind that adults show considerable wear by mid summer. In fresh autumn plumage, Meadow has greenish tint to upperparts and olive-buff wash to underparts. Spring adults are generally browner above and whiter below, showing little hint of green tones. Some particularly pale, cold, stripy Meadow Pipits (likely to be *A.p. theresae* from Iceland) pass through western areas in spring and autumn, may be confusable with Red-throated Pipit. In fresh plumage, Tree is better marked than Meadow, and following differences most useful.
1 FACIAL PATTERN Tree has, on average, better-marked supercilium from eye back and more prominent dark eye-stripe behind eye (and often across lores). On Meadow, supercilium and eye-stripe more subdued and lores usually plain (looks markedly plain-faced in comparison). **2 THROAT AND BREAST COLOUR** Tree has submoustachial stripe, throat and breast strongly tinged orangy-buff, contrasting with whitish belly. **3 BREAST AND FLANK STREAKING** Tree has gorget of neat, well-defined streaks across breast, giving way on flanks to faint pencil streaking (may be difficult to detect in field). On Meadow, breast streaking more random, and often streaks coalesce to form dark spot in centre of breast; unlike Tree, streaking extends quite strongly on to flanks. *Flank streaking perhaps best and most consistent individual plumage difference.* **4 UPPER-PARTS** Look more contrasty on Tree. Wingbars and tertial edgings generally more prominent, and dark centres to median coverts form blackish bar, this often highlighted by contrasting white feather edgings (equivalent to dark bar shown by Tawny Pipit *A. campestris*). In summer, Meadow is noticeably colder, greyer, plainer and often tattier than Tree, lacking strong greenish or buffy tones, but Tree also wear and fade by mid summer, becoming browner and plainer.

Red-throated Pipit *Anthus cervinus*

Call Most likely to be confused with a contrasty Meadow Pipit (see above), but identity best confirmed by call, usually the first indicator of Red-throated among a flock of Meadow. (Records of non-calling individuals are likely to be very critically scrutinised by *British Birds* Rarities Committee.) Call a very distinctive long, thin, piercing, metallic *pseeeeeee*, trailing off towards end. Also gives a low *chup*.
Plumage *Autumn* Looks colder and less buff than Meadow, and much more heavily streaked. Malar stripe ends in thick blotch on sides of neck, joining heavy, thick breast striping (note in particular that this extends in two long thick lines down flanks). Upperparts strongly striped, with two pale 'tramlines' down sides of mantle usually prominent (more so than on many Meadow Pipits). Wings also more strongly marked, dark feather centres contrasting with pale edgings. Unlike Meadow and Tree Pipits, rump is heavily streaked (often visible from side when tail depressed when feeding). Looks shorter-tailed than Meadow in flight. *Summer* Easily identified by brick-red 'face' and throat (winter adults may show at least a hint of this colouring). Spring migrants are usually in summer plumage, but some retain winter plumage (sometimes so worn that upperparts look rather plain and dark, lacking pale 'tramlines').

Olive-backed Pipit *Anthus hodgsoni*

Most like Tree Pipit and, similarly, often found in or around trees. Easily identified, following being the most significant characters. **1 FACIAL PATTERN** Prominent thick, creamy supercilium, highlighted by thin black lateral crown-stripe and thin dark eye-stripe, whole effect vaguely recalling Redwing *Turdus iliacus*. Has whitish spot at rear of ear-coverts (often termed the 'supercilium drop') and dark

ROCK AND WATER PIPITS

lower rear border to ear-coverts. **2** MANTLE On race occurring in Britain and Ireland (*yunnanensis*) mantle shows distinct green tint and is only faintly streaked, at distance looking uniformly olive-green or (duller individuals) greenish-brown. **3** BREAST Heavily streaked with thick black lines (extend more thinly onto flanks). **4** TAIL-WAGGING Wags or 'pumps' tail more persistently than Tree Pipit.
Call Basically similar to Tree Pipit: a shrill *zeep . . . zeep, tzzseep . . . tzzseep* or *psee . . . psee,* generally slightly shorter, shriller than Tree (with slight Redwing-like quality), but often with more of a consonant at end; usually given doubly. High-flying individuals may sound more abrupt: *ski . . . ski,* similar to Tree but throatier.
Pitfalls Not difficult to identify, but note that some Tree Pipits show faint 'super-cilium drop', while some are atypically plain on mantle.
Reference Mullarney (1987).

Rock and Water Pipits

Where and When Rock Pipit and Water Pipit have been traditionally regarded as conspecific, but were 'split' by the British Ornithologists' Union in 1986. Rock Pipit is a familiar resident of rocky coastlines, although largely absent as a breeding bird from much of English east coast between Humberside and Kent; it frequents a variety of coastal environments in winter, when numbers are swollen by visitors of Scandinavian race *littoralis* (these seem to occur mainly on east and south coasts of England). Rock Pipits may also occur inland in small numbers, mainly in September–October and again in March, but also occasionally betweentimes. British Water Pipits are thought to originate from the mountain chains of southern Europe and are widespread but local from October to April, mainly in southern England; found in a variety of freshwater habitats, such as cress beds, reservoirs, sewage farms and freshwater marshes, they generally avoid saline environments but may sometimes be seen in coastal marshes.

Rock Pipit *Anthus petrosus*

Habitat and Behaviour In many ways rather nondescript, but nevertheless easily identified when in its typical habitat: rocky coastlines. Although rarely found far from intertidal zone, wintering or passage individuals may occur in less typical surroundings, such as inland lakes and sewage farms; here they invariably select an area most like their normal habitat, such as a reservoir dam or a stretch of stony shoreline. Usually rather solitary, and often relatively tame.
Size and Structure Compared with Meadow Pipit *A. pratensis,* Rock is a larger, bulkier, more upright bird with longer legs and a noticeably longer, more dagger-like bill. In flight, longer-winged and longer-tailed and has more purposeful flight action than the weaker, rather more hesitant Meadow Pipit.
Plumage Its smoky-olive plumage is darker than Meadow Pipit's, and underparts are rather a dull yellowy-cream, with heavy brown streaking covering not only breast and flanks but also much of belly; has narrow but noticeable (usually broken) eye-ring, a subdued creamy supercilium (often indistinct) and dull creamy-buff wingbars. Two further features eliminate Meadow Pipit: outer tail feathers are creamy or pale brown (white on Meadow), and legs are dark, blackish at long range but dark pinky-red close-up (bright pinky-orange on Meadow).
Call A single, loud, shrill *pseep* or *feest.* Meadow Pipits usually give thinner, weaker *sip sip sip* and, although single calls are not infrequent, the difference in quality is distinctive once learnt.

159

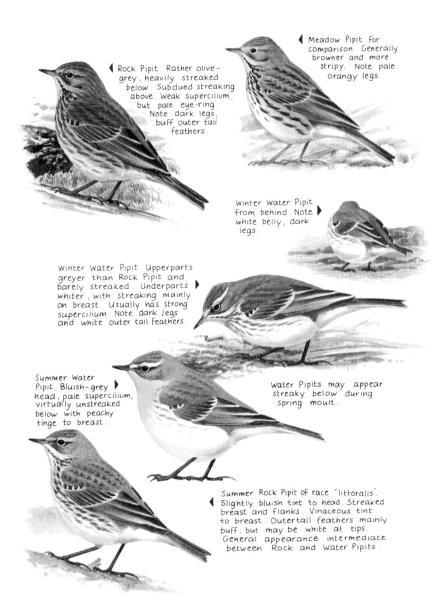

◀ Rock Pipit. Rather olive-grey, heavily streaked below. Subdued streaking above. Weak supercilium, but pale eye-ring. Note dark legs, buff outer tail feathers.

◀ Meadow Pipit for comparison. Generally browner and more stripy. Note pale orangy legs.

Winter Water Pipit from behind. Note white belly, dark legs. ▶

Winter Water Pipit. Upperparts greyer than Rock Pipit and barely streaked. Underparts whiter, with streaking mainly on breast. Usually has strong supercilium. Note dark legs and white outer tail feathers. ▶

Summer Water Pipit. Bluish-grey ▶ head, pale supercilium, virtually unstreaked below with peachy tinge to breast.

Water Pipits may appear streaky below during spring moult.

Summer Rock Pipit of race 'littoralis'. ◀ Slightly bluish tint to head. Streaked breast and flanks. Vinaceous tint to breast. Outertail feathers mainly buff, but may be white at tips. General appearance intermediate between Rock and Water Pipits.

Water Pipit *Anthus spinoletta*

Habitat and Behaviour From damp freshwater habitat a large, timid, streamlined pipit is flushed at some distance and rises high into air, giving a loud, shrill, strident *fist*: as it gains height, it swings back behind the observer and drops into similar habitat several hundred metres away; its flight is strong and direct, it is longer-winged and longer-tailed than a Meadow Pipit, and its underparts look contrastingly pale as it shoots overhead. Such is a typical encounter with a Water Pipit. In similar circumstances, Rock Pipit would probably have flushed at close range, flown low over water and resettled after a relatively short distance. Although such behavioural differences should not be relied upon too heavily, it is surprising how often they hold true. Water Pipits sometimes occur in small parties, often in company of Meadow Pipits. Unlike Rock, they readily perch in trees and bushes.

Plumage When seen well, superficially similar to Rock, but smarter and more contrasting, rather browner above (plainer than Meadow) and whiter below, with streaking largely confined to breast and flanks. What usually attracts attention is the supercilium, which typically extends from bill, over eye, and tapers towards nape (this feature varies and some individuals are less well endowed than others). Wingbars and tertial edgings are whiter than those of Rock, while outer tail feathers are *white*, not creamy or brownish. Unlike British Rock Pipits (race *petrosus*), acquires a distinct summer plumage (usually well advanced by time it leaves this country in late March and April), when becomes quite striking and rather wagtail-like: partial body moult produces a pale blue head (supercilium is retained), and off-white underparts are virtually plain with a beautiful pale pink flush across breast (some streaking may persist on breast and flanks).

Call Differences in quality of the two species' calls are subtle: whereas Rock gives a *pseep* or *feest*, Water Pipit gives a *fist*, slightly thinner and shorter than Rock, and suggesting something intermediate between Rock and Meadow. As with behaviour, difference should not be relied upon absolutely, but a good indicator once learnt.

'Scandinavian Rock Pipit'

Unlike British birds, which are similar throughout year, Scandinavian Rock Pipits (race *littoralis*) acquire a distinct summer plumage which enables them to be distinguished with some certainty before they depart in spring. There appears, however, to be something of a cline between Rock Pipits in northern Britain and those in southern Scandinavia and there is also individual variation, so not all will be certainly identifiable. 'Classic' examples acquire certain plumage characters in spring that are ordinarily associated with Water Pipit: a potential Water Pipit in atypical habitat or outside normal range should therefore be carefully checked to eliminate possibility of a *littoralis* Rock Pipit. Latter shows blue-grey tone to head, a distinctive creamy-white supercilium (at least from eye back) and rather whitish wingbars; the underparts take on a strong creamy-buff, yellowish or pinkish suffusion (off-white, suffused pink, on Water Pipit), overlain with variable amounts of brown streaking on flanks and breast (usually much heavier than on Water). Some individuals, however, are virtually plain on breast, so great care must be taken. Unlike Water Pipit, *littoralis* Rock has creamy or pale brown outer tail feathers, although on some outer tail feather is whiter towards tip. Note that, in summer, some British Rock Pipits acquire greyer plumage tones which may occasionally suggest *littoralis*.
References Johnson (1970), Knox (1988), Williamson (1965).

Grey, Yellow and Citrine Wagtails

Where and When Grey Wagtail is typically associated with upland streams, breeding throughout much of Britain and Ireland except in large swathe of eastern England from Humberside to Essex, where thin on the ground; in winter, when general retreat from high ground, a southward withdrawal and some emigration, is more widespread (often in city centres). Yellow Wagtail is a summer visitor late March – October (very rare in winter), breeding mainly in England, east Wales and southern Scotland (virtually absent from Ireland): of the Continental races, blue-headed *flava* is a scarce migrant and occasional breeder, grey-headed *thunbergi* a rare migrant, mainly on northern and eastern coasts in spring; birds showing characters of following races have occurred either as variants or as vagrants: black-headed *feldegg*, Spanish race *iberiae*, ashy-headed *cinereocapilla* and Far Eastern races *beema* and *simillima*. Citrine Wagtail is a rare autumn vagrant, with one or two in most years (August–October); one summer record.

Grey Wagtail *Motacilla cinerea*

Easily identified. Lively, restless; very long tail (much longer than Yellow Wagtail's) is energetically wagged, particularly when alighting. Unlike Yellow, head and mantle are grey (with very slight green tint) and has narrow white supercilium. Rump yellowish-green. On juveniles and winter females, underparts vary from pale yellow to washed-out peachy-yellow, the only intense yellow being on undertail-coverts. Males tend to be yellower on breast and, in summer, have black chin and throat (as may some summer females). Legs pinkish or pale brown (blackish on Yellow). In flight, a slim, streamlined wagtail with long, quivering tail and thick white wingbar. Call a loud, abrupt, hard, metal-

lic *tzip* or *tzizip*, sometimes drawn out into almost musical *tiss-is-is-is-is-is*. Generally rather solitary, frequenting streams, rivers, rocky shorelines, farmyards, areas of concrete and rooftops; occasionally in grassy fields, but does not habitually feed among cattle.

Yellow Wagtail *Motacilla flava*

A more evenly proportioned, shorter-tailed wagtail, green above and yellow below; habitually associates with cattle. Spring males yellow and green on head, females duller green with yellowish supercilium; have thin double white wingbar and narrow white tertial edgings. Juveniles duller and buffer (some, particularly females, very colourless, may even suggest Tawny Pipit *Anthus campestris*: see page 153); have messy blackish malar stripe and necklace across lower throat (lost after post-juvenile moult in late summer/early autumn). Call a very distinctive *swee-up*, very useful when picking up overhead migrants. Often occurs in small flocks and, in autumn, large numbers may roost in reedbeds.

The racial complexity of Yellow Wagtails is notorious. Apart from spring males, most birders do not bother to identify them racially. Many of so-called 'extra-limital' races seen in this country (e.g. 'Sykes's Wagtail' *beema*) may just be hybrids or local variations (have bred in groups in southeast England: Milne 1959). A rough guide to the various head patterns is shown below. Only race currently considered by the *British Birds* Rarities Committee is black-headed *feldegg*. Even this race is variable: some have extensions of black on to sides of neck, some are very bright above, others are duller and more olive, while some intermediate types show a black head with white supercilium. Call subtly different from that of British race *flavissima*, having

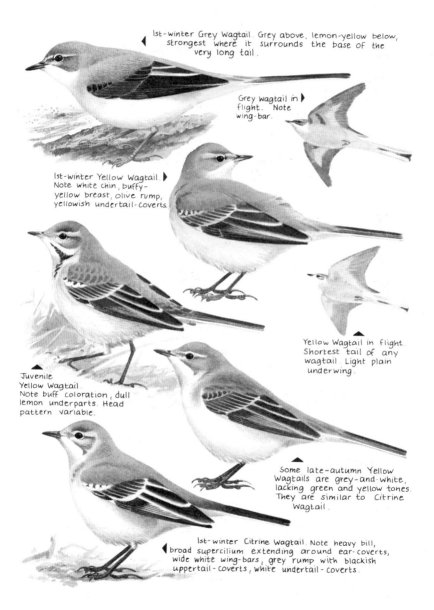

1st-winter Grey Wagtail. Grey above, lemon-yellow below, strongest where it surrounds the base of the very long tail.

Grey Wagtail in flight. Note wing-bar.

1st-winter Yellow Wagtail. Note white chin, buffy-yellow breast, olive rump, yellowish undertail-coverts.

Juvenile Yellow Wagtail. Note buff coloration, dull lemon underparts. Head pattern variable.

Yellow Wagtail in flight. Shortest tail of any wagtail. Light plain underwing.

Some late-autumn Yellow Wagtails are grey-and-white, lacking green and yellow tones. They are similar to Citrine Wagtail.

1st-winter Citrine Wagtail. Note heavy bill, broad supercilium extending around ear-coverts, wide white wing-bars, grey rump with blackish uppertail-coverts, white undertail-coverts.

163

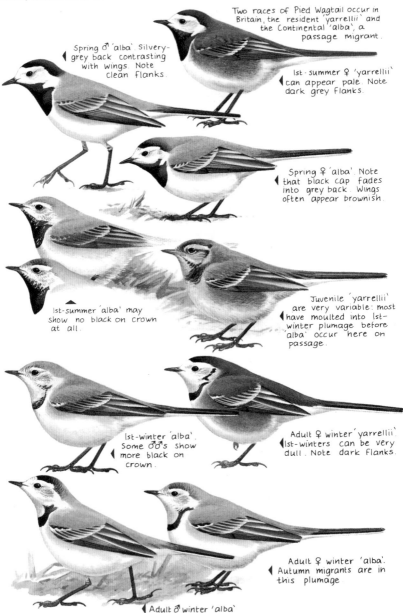

Two races of Pied Wagtail occur in Britain, the resident 'yarrellii' and the Continental 'alba', a passage migrant.

Spring ♂ 'alba'. Silvery-grey back contrasting with wings. Note clean flanks.

1st-summer ♀ 'yarrellii' can appear pale. Note dark grey flanks.

Spring ♀ 'alba'. Note that black cap fades into grey back. Wings often appear brownish.

1st-summer 'alba' may show no black on crown at all.

Juvenile 'yarrellii' are very variable: most have moulted into 1st-winter plumage before 'alba' occur here on passage.

1st-winter 'alba'. Some ♂♂'s show more black on crown.

Adult ♀ winter 'yarrellii'. 1st-winters can be very dull. Note dark flanks.

Adult ♀ winter 'alba'. Autumn migrants are in this plumage

Adult ♂ winter 'alba'

164

more of a 'z' in it: *tzzeup*. When identifying *feldegg*, great care is needed to eliminate grey-headed *thunbergi*, which can look dark-headed in certain lights (see van den Berg & Oreel 1985 and Svensson 1988 for discussion of this problem). Particularly grey-and-white autumn Yellow Wagtails, presumably eastern races, also occur in Britain: see below.

Summary of head patterns of spring male Yellow Wagtail races which have occurred in Britain and Ireland.

1 *M. f. flavissima* 'Yellow Wagtail'. Green head; yellow supercilium and centre of ear-coverts. **2** *M. f. flava* 'Blue-headed Wagtail'. Crown bluish-grey, ear-coverts darker; white supercilium, chin and throat often white. (Females may show bluish or greyish tint to head and ear-coverts, and white supercilium.) **3** *M. f. thunbergi* 'Grey-headed Wagtail'. Crown grey, ear-coverts dark grey or blackish; no supercilium, or very short one above or immediately behind eye. **4** *M. f. feldegg* 'Black-headed Wagtail'. Whole head black. See text for details. (Females very washed-out, with greyish or blackish head with whitish supercilium.) **5** *M. f. iberiae* 'Spanish Wagtail'. Similar to *flava*, but supercilium narrower and may be absent before eye. **6** *M. f. cinereocapilla* 'Ashy-headed Wagtail'. As *thunbergi*, but whole throat white; ear-coverts dark. **7** *M. f. beema* 'Sykes's Wagtail'. Incredibly striking, like a 'super' *flava*: blue-grey head, huge thick white supercilium bordered above by dark lateral crown-stripe, pale centre to ear-coverts, dark moustachial line. (So-called 'individuals resembling *beema*' in Britain are probably hybrid *flava* x *flavissima* or mutant *flava*; they resemble *flava*, but have lavender head.) **8** *M. f. simillima*. Similar to *flava*, but lores and ear-coverts darker.

Citrine Wagtail *Motacilla citreola*

Three races: adult male of northerly nominate race *citreola* has pale yellowish head and grey back, with a black collar between; male of southerly *werae* is generally paler yellow, rarely has black collar and has little if any grey on flanks; even more southerly *calcarata* is darker yellow and has black back. The only summer male recorded in Britain resembled *citreola*. Spring female similar in pattern to first-winter (see below), but shows bright yellow on face and duller yellow on underparts.

Citrine is similar in shape to Yellow Wagtail, but slightly shorter-tailed; bill may look longer and sturdier, and head shape may appear more angular. First-winter is grey above (later-moulting individuals may retain at least some browner juvenile feathering, producing browner cast), whitish below with, perhaps, a pale peachy tint to breast, and grey flanks (latter may be absent on *werae*); some may retain traces of juvenile's malar stripes and necklace; white tips to median and greater coverts and white tertial edgings are thick and very striking. Pay particular attention to head pattern; following features of Citrine should be carefully noted. **1** A thick whitish supercilium (sometimes tinged yellow) *extends right around ear-coverts to form complete ear-covert surround* (this, however, varies individually in its conspicuousness, while it may be obscured if, for example, head sunk into shoulders); **2** usually shows a pale centre to ear-coverts, often appearing as thick pale crescent below eye; **3** may also show a buff forehead (lacking on Yellow); **4** supercilium may be emphasised by a narrow dark lateral crown-stripe. Other key feature is call: Citrine has very distinctive, almost buzzing *dzzeeup*, *tzzeeeep* or *tzzeeeeup*, like a rasping Tree Pipit *A. trivialis*. Caution needed, however, as some calls of Citrine and some of those of eastern races of Yellow Wagtail are similar. Latter seem to appear mainly in October, whereas Citrines may appear from late August. Grey-and-white Yellows are similar to Citrine in overall plumage tone, with upperparts dull grey (darker than

Continental race of Pied Wagtail *M. alba alba*, or 'White Wagtail') and underparts dull greyish-white, but show only *narrow* white supercilium, with (most importantly) *no ear-covert surround*, solidly grey ear-coverts (at best, only narrow pale ring below eye) and narrow white wingbars and tertial edgings; structure typical of Yellow Wagtail. Particularly important, call is usually typical of Yellow, although some have more strident call with more of a 'z' in it (rather like race *feldegg* of Yellow

Wagtail: see above) while some give calls very like those of Citrine.

Above notes take a rather simplistic approach to identification of autumn Citrine. Note that problem may be complicated by individual variation and by possible hybridisation between Yellow and Citrine. *British Birds* Rarities Committee currently accepts only 'classic' Citrines which show combination of all key features. *References* Milne (1959), Svensson (1988), van den Berg & Oreel (1985).

Pied and 'White' Wagtails

Where and When Pied Wagtail *Motacilla alba yarrellii* breeds commonly throughout Britain and Ireland; in winter, withdraws from high ground and some emigrate. Continental race *alba* ('White Wagtail') is a passage migrant from mid March to May and from mid August to October, commonest in western areas; occasionally breeds in northern Scotland.

Spring

Adult male Pied has a black back, so black is continuous from crown to bib; on 'White', the black crown and bib are obviously separated. Female Pied's back varies from blackish-grey, with black feathers mixed in, to dark olive-grey; even the greyer females look dark and sooty, with little contrast between back and head. Both sexes of 'White' have a pale, clean-looking ash-grey mantle which, unlike Pied, contrasts strongly with wings and black-and-white head, producing smart, clean-cut appearance; their rump varies from medium to dark grey, whereas on Pied it is blackish or blackish-grey (although this area is often cloaked by folded wings). Pied is sooty along sides of breast and flanks; 'White' is pale grey, so that, even overhead, it looks a clean, contrasting bird with predominantly white underparts. Minor points include 'White's' duller, browner wings, and male 'White'

(because of greyer mantle and flanks) gives *impression* of having a larger bib.

Sexing spring adult 'White Wagtails' is often possible by reference to crown. On male, the black is clearly demarcated from mantle, whereas on female it is less clearcut, sometimes with grey mixed in. On first-summer females (and some males), the black is reduced or even lacking.

Autumn

After autumn moult, adults of both races are similar to spring birds, but full black bib is replaced by narrow necklace. Juvenile Pieds are olive-grey on crown and mantle, breast sides and flanks, have messy blackish gorget across breast and may show strong primrose tint to face. By time first-winter 'Whites' appear (mainly in September), juvenile Pieds have usually attained at least some black on forecrown and sides of crown. Some first-winter female Pieds have disconcertingly pale mantle, so identification in autumn requires more caution than in spring. Juvenile and first-winter 'Whites', like adults, are pale grey on mantle, but (unlike Pied) many first-winter 'Whites' (females and a few males) retain pale grey crown and this contributes to a more open-faced expression (young 'White', too, may show yellowish face at this time); also have greyer rump, paler wings, cleaner flanks and fainter wingbars.

Redstart and Black Redstart

Where and When Redstart *Phoenicurus phoenicurus* is a summer visitor to mature deciduous woodland, commonest in northern and western Britain (largely absent from Ireland); more widespread on migration, mainly April–May and July–October, not normally seen in winter. Black Redstart *P. ochruros* is a scarce breeder, mainly in southern England (urban areas, industrial buildings); commoner on migration and in winter, mainly in coastal areas of England, Wales and Ireland. Adult males easily separated, but females and immatures may cause problems.

Habitat Often the first clue to identity. Redstart is markedly arboreal and, even on migration, rarely found far from cover. Black Redstart prefers open ground, perches prominently on rocks and buildings; on migration, often in ploughed fields or along sheltered beaches.

Plumage *Females and first-winters* Both species have bright orange tails, but easily separated by plumage tone. Female and young first-winter male Redstarts grey-brown above and pale buff below, often with strong peach tint to breast and flanks; narrow buff edgings to tertials and faint dark malar stripes; eye large, with faint pale eye-ring. Very exceptional (presumably older) females have dark throat and strong orange tone to underparts. Female, juvenile and first-winter Black Redstarts are slate-grey at all times (never show pale buff or peach tones), but vary in plumage tone to some extent (beware slightly paler individuals); males do not acquire black on face and throat until first spring or later, so first-winter male impossible to separate from female (though some, with whitish tertial panel, no doubt are first-winter males).

Males of both species acquire full plumage by feather abrasion (not moult). In autumn, male Redstart's distinctive col-

Juvenile Redstart closely resembles juvenile Robin but note rusty tail with dark central feathers. Juvenile Black Redstart is not spotted.

♀ Black Redstart. Dark grey above and below, from chin to legs. Eye-ring thin. Some individuals paler, more like ♀ Redstart.

1st-winter ♂ Redstart. Buff feather fringing obscures smart summer dress.

♀ Redstart is warm brown above, creamy below, with whitish chin. Eye-ring obvious, making eye appear large.

ouring is hidden by buff feather tips, but, by late autumn, these often wear sufficiently to reveal traces of black throat and orange underparts (when, very rarely, misidentified as Bluethroat *Luscinia svecica*). *Juveniles* Easily separated. Black is *plain* slate-grey, similar to female. Juvenile Redstart is spotted and difficult to separate from juvenile Robin *Erithacus rubecula*, but is generally paler and shows orange tail (regularly quivered); all but earliest autumn migrants have lost all traces of this plumage before they migrate. Juvenile Nightingale *L. megarhynchos* is also spotted, but has duller, rounded, orange-chestnut tail (unlike Redstart,

lacks darker central feathers); is larger, very furtive (creeps around on ground, rarely straying from cover, and habitually raises and lowers tail), and gives deep *tuc* calls and variations, almost frog-like, including a deep, guttural, *turrrrr*.

Calls Redstart has a *hoo-eet* call (both on breeding grounds and on migration) resembling call of Willow Warbler *Phylloscopus trochilus*, but fuller, more deliberate and far-carrying, and sometimes precedes a *chuch chuck* note; often gives short, soft, *pit* and short, hard, scratchy note. Black Redstart generally silent on migration, but gives soft *pit* similar to Redstart, and also a *pit-it-it*.

Whinchat, Stonechat and 'Siberian' Stonechats

Where and When Stonechat breeds on rough ground, usually with gorse, heather and bracken, mainly in Ireland and western Britain (absent from much of east and central England); winter dispersal leads to desertion of upland breeding sites and then becomes more widespread in lowland areas. Whinchat is a summer visitor, breeding on rough ground mainly in upland areas of Scotland, northern and southwestern England and Wales (scarcer in Ireland and southeastern England); it is more widespread on migration, in April–May and July–October. 'Siberian' Stonechats occur mainly at coastal migration sites in northern and eastern Britain in October (a few have occurred in winter); there are currently about eight records a year.

Stonechat *Saxicola torquata* and Whinchat *S. rubetra*

Structure Stonechat looks more rounded than Whinchat, with shorter wings: the primary projection is only about half length of overlying tertials. Whinchat is flatter-crowned and more angular-headed (an effect heightened by supercilium), flatter-backed and longer-

winged (primary projection about three-quarters that of overlying tertials).

Plumage *Males* Stonechat is easily identified in spring and summer by the black head and white neck patches. This plumage is, however, acquired not by moult, but by wear, so that autumn and winter males have their distinctive plumage to a large extent obscured by orangy-brown feather tips, which gradually wear off. Male Whinchat is easily identified by bold white supercilium, brownish or blackish crown and ear-coverts, and prominent white tail patches (older males are brighter than younger ones); also shows noticeable white on inner wing-coverts and primary coverts. In autumn, male resembles female and first-winter individuals (see below under 'females'). Unlike Stonechat, male acquires summer plumage by a winter body moult. *Females* Stonechat is identified by rounded shape, brown head *lacking obvious supercilium*, darker upperparts, orange underparts, *lack of white tail patches*, and by larger white patches on inner wing-coverts (obvious in flight); throat colour varies from brown to whitish. Whinchat has a *prominent, thick, whitish supercilium* which curves from bill back

Autumn ♀ Stonechat. Darker than Whinchat with no supercilium. No white in base of tail. Primary projection short.

Autumn ♀ Whinchat. Paler than Stonechat with strong supercilium, long primary projection and 'droplet' effect on back. Note white in tail base.

Autumn ♀ 'Siberian' Stonechat. Paler than Stonechat. Often with strong supercilium and pale rump. Note pale wing panel and black tertial centres

'Siberian' Stonechat shows a pale rump in flight.

Note long primary projection of 'Siberian' Stonechat.

♀ Stonechat appears very dark in flight

1st-winter ♀ Whinchat. Note tail pattern. Adults show white on primary coverts and inner greater coverts.

Juvenile Stonechat. Darker than Whinchat, breast more orange.

Juvenile Whinchat. Paler than juvenile Stonechat, underparts especially so. Note supercilium and white tail base. Compare primary projection.

169

towards nape; both upper- and underparts are paler and buffer than those of Stonechat, less orange in tone. Note in particular that Whinchat has *large white patches at base of tail*; these can, however, be dull buff and inconspicuous on autumn individuals, prompting confusion with 'Siberian' Stonechat (see below). Female Whinchat lacks Stonechat's *extensive* white on inner wing-coverts. Ages and sexes similar in autumn, when all Whinchats resemble females but show crescent-shaped white tips to mantle and scapular feathers; also show pale tertial panel (cf. 'Siberian' Stonechat below). *Juveniles* Stonechat is generally very dark, streaked or speckled on head, breast and upperparts, the pattern recalling that of juvenile Robin *Erithacus rubecula*, but darker; has a dark orangy upper breast. Juvenile Whinchat is paler than Stonechat, light cream below, and, like adult, shows a paler wing panel; it has pale shaft streaks above, slight mottling on breast and ill-defined supercilia. This plumage lost before migrating.

Behaviour Both species sit prominently on the tops of vegetation, nervously flicking open wings and tail. Stonechat's short wings produce a rather whirring flight; Whinchat has stronger flight. On autumn migration, Whinchat is rather more catholic in choice of habitat, and often found in cabbage and kale fields.

Calls Similar. Stonechat has hard, emphatic *chit chit* or *swit, chit chit*. Whinchat has a softer, less emphatic *stit stit* or *hew*, *stit stit* (also a low *churr*, like a low-pitched Wren *Troglodytes troglodytes*). Songs of both species are unmemorable. Whinchat's is variable, but consists of short, rather feeble phrases which may suggest a *Sylvia* warbler (longer phrases may vaguely suggest Blackcap *S. atricapilla* or Garden Warbler *S. borin*); song also includes some mimicry. Stonechat's song is higher-pitched, consisting of short, repetitive phrases which suggest Dunnock *Prunella modularis* in quality.

'Siberian' Stonechats *S.t. maura/ stejnegeri*

Note that Svensson (1984) could not distinguish *maura* from *stejnegeri* in museum skins and regards the two races as synonymous. All references below to 'Stonechat' refer to British and western European races *rubicola/hibernans*, which may also be synonymous.

Autumn Very distinctive, and perhaps more likely to be passed off as Whinchat than as Stonechat. However, typically Stonechat-like in shape, though wings are slightly longer with primary projection about two-thirds that of overlying tertial length. Easily separated from Stonechat by pale, Whinchat-like plumage, which is grey-buff above, streaked darker (but looking relatively plain at distance), and pale buff below, with slightly paler throat and only *faint* orangy-buff tint to breast. (First-winter males gradually acquire black on head and throat through abrasion, not moult, so this usually obvious on later individuals.) Like Whinchat, shows prominent buffish tertial panel. When identifying 'Siberian' Stonechat, concentrate on rump, which is unstreaked, ginger or orange at first, wearing to white later in autumn and showing as a discrete patch, sometimes having a 'wrap-around' effect (Stonechat has chestnut rump, usually streaked darker). Males can be sexed by their black axillaries (difficult to see in the field). To eliminate Whinchat, concentrate on structure and: **1** SUPERCILIUM 'Siberian' has relatively faint supercilium and looks rather plain-faced at distance; Whinchat always shows a prominent supercilium. **2** TAIL 'Siberian' shows black tail with narrow white edges and tip; Whinchat has prominent white tail patches, but beware occasional individual which shows dull buff (see above). **3** MANTLE 'Siberian' Stonechat appears relatively plain; Whinchat is strongly patterned above.

Spring Males Similar to Stonechat, but usually more white on inner wing-coverts (sometimes forming large panel); neck patches often very large and may form collar, while underparts are paler and orange or pink wash on breast may be demarcated from white belly. In fresh autumn plumage, feather fringes are buff, rather than reddish.

Behaviour, Calls and Habitat Similar to Stonechat.
(*S. t. variegata* There is one British record of this distinctive race, which occurs between Black and Caspian Seas: it has white tail patches, massive white wing patch and larger white rump.)
References Robertson (1977), Svensson (1984).

Ring Ouzel

Where and When Ring Ouzel *Turdus torquatus* is very much the upland counterpart of Blackbird *T. merula*, occurring in summer on mountains and moorland in Scotland, northern England, Wales and (more sparsely) southwest England and Ireland. On migration, also at coastal migration sites and on high ground, mainly mid March–late April and late August–early November; late-autumn migrants (and very occasional winterers) may associate with Fieldfares *T. pilaris* and Redwings *T. iliacus*. Blackbird is familiar and abundant throughout British Isles.

General Features Ring Ouzel is easily identified by conspicuous large white crescent across breast. Note, however, that it is duller on most females, on both sexes in winter, and can be virtually absent on first-winter females and completely absent on juveniles. Conversely, some Blackbirds occasionally show white breast markings (can confuse the beginner). To be sure of identification, other features need to be considered.

Structure Although similar in size to Blackbird, Ring Ouzel is more streamlined and more upright, with flat back forming continuous line with head and nape (shape strongly resembles that of Fieldfare), longer legs and thicker and more wedge-shaped bill (Blackbird is altogether more rounded; differences obvious in direct comparison). Is also longer-winged, this being noticeable on high-flying migrants, which again resem-

ble Fieldfare in shape (can also look rather like Starling *Sturnus vulgaris* when seen from rear). On the ground, has longer primary projection than Blackbird: exposed primaries about equal to overlying tertials (on Blackbird about two-thirds tertial length).

Behaviour and Calls Very shy, particularly on migration, often flies far when flushed. Has loud, hollow chacking call, rather like two pebbles banged together. Usual song is a series of plaintive piping notes.

Plumage Apart from breast crescent, most significant plumage feature is wing colour: all wing feathers have whitish edgings, so wings appear generally whitish at distance (effect can be less obvious on first-winter females). In fresh plumage, underparts have whitish feather edgings, producing scaled effect (tends to be most prominent on females). Female lacks rufous tones sometimes shown by female Blackbird.

Many Ring Ouzels are difficult to sex. A few adult females resemble males, but females tend to look browner and show more obscure breast band. Note that, in autumn, male's white breast crescent is slightly obscured by pale brown feather tips, while first-winter females can virtually lack crescent, their whiter throat being more obvious: confusion could arise with first-winter male Blackbirds of 'Stockamsel' type, which has dull bill and eyering, browner wings, paler chin and heavy

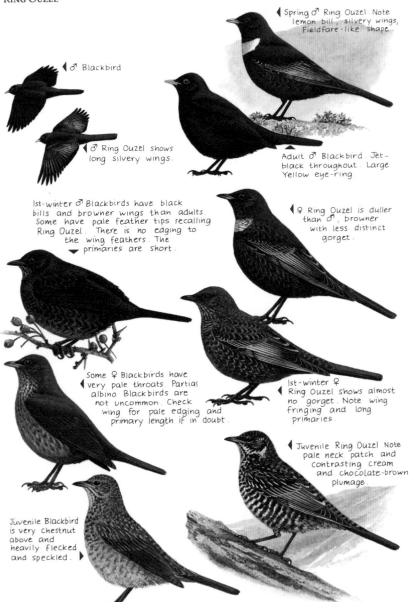

Spring ♂ Ring Ouzel. Note lemon bill, silvery wings, Fieldfare-like shape.

◀ ♂ Blackbird

♂ Ring Ouzel shows long silvery wings.

Adult ♂ Blackbird. Jet-black throughout. Large Yellow eye-ring.

1st-winter ♂ Blackbirds have black bills and browner wings than adults. Some have pale feather tips recalling Ring Ouzel. There is no edging to the wing feathers. The primaries are short.

◀ ♀ Ring Ouzel is duller than ♂, browner with less distinct gorget.

Some ♀ Blackbirds have very pale throats. Partial albino Blackbirds are not uncommon. Check wing for pale edging and primary length if in doubt.

1st-winter ♀ Ring Ouzel shows almost no gorget. Note wing fringing and long primaries.

◀ Juvenile Ring Ouzel. Note pale neck patch and contrasting cream and chocolate-brown plumage.

Juvenile Blackbird is very chestnut above and heavily flecked and speckled. ▶

pale fringing to underparts, but note Blackbird's plain wing, different shape and shorter primary projection. Juvenile Ring Ouzels are chocolate and cream (lacking rufous tones of juvenile Blackbird), completely lack breast cres-cent, but show pale throat, pale feather tips on underparts (producing rather barred effect), and usually whitish patch on sides of neck (can be virtually absent); they moult out of this plumage before autumn migration.

Song Thrush and Mistle Thrush

Where and When Both are common residents throughout Britain and Ireland.

Song Thrush *Turdus philomelos*
Habitat and Behaviour The most familiar thrush, common in gardens. More retiring, less demonstrative than Mistle, prefers to keep within easy reach of cover. **Structure and Plumage** More compact and evenly proportioned than Mistle, with warmer brown upperparts and rather buffy underparts, latter less boldly spotted, particularly on flanks. Juvenile yellower below, has buff streaks on mantle and scapulars.

Calls and Song Usual call an unobtrusive *tic*, often given by overhead migrants; also a harsh chattering alarm, *dji-dji dji djip djip djip djip*. Loud, clear song consists of varied series of repeated phrases, delivered with great gusto, often from prominent perch.
Flight Identification Similar to Redwing *T. iliacus* (latter slightly stockier, rather shorter-tailed, perhaps more consistent in habit of only partially closing wings between bouts of flapping). Has orangy-yellow underwing-coverts (Redwing's are reddish). Redwing also has whitish supercilium and breast is rather densely

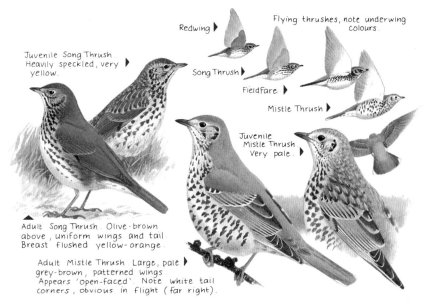

Redwing ▶

Flying thrushes, note underwing colours.

Song Thrush ▶

Fieldfare ▶

Mistle Thrush ▶

Juvenile Song Thrush. Heavily speckled, very ▶ yellow.

Juvenile Mistle Thrush. Very pale. ▶

Adult Song Thrush. Olive-brown above, uniform wings and tail. Breast flushed yellow-orange.

Adult Mistle Thrush. Large, pale ▶ grey-brown, patterned wings. Appears 'open-faced'. Note white tail corners, obvious in flight (far right).

streaked. Redwing's distinctive flight call (a thin, drawn-out *zeeeep*) is a familiar sound from nocturnal migrants on autumn nights.

Mistle Thrush *Turdus viscivorus*

Habitat and Behaviour Often occurs in pairs or small parties, usually in large gardens, parks and open countryside. Less retiring than Song Thrush, often found well away from cover.

Structure and Plumage Compared with Song, is a bold, upright, 'necky' thrush, much greyer-brown above and more boldly spotted below, particularly on flanks; has noticeable pale edgings to wing-coverts and tertials. Juvenile very pale, with whitish spotting and streaking and dark flecking on upperparts.

Calls and Song Most distinctive is its loud, angry, grating call *trrr-rr-rr-rr-rr-rr*, often quite persistent when alarmed. Wistful song is a series of disjointed phrases, mellow and ethereal in quality, rather more like Blackbird *T. merula* than clearer repeated phrases of Song Thrush.

Flight Identification Obviously larger, longer-winged and longer-tailed than Song, with slower, less hurried but more undulating flight, often at treetop height. White underwing-coverts obvious, while buffish-white tips to outer tail feathers may be obvious on take-off or landing. Can be confused with Fieldfare *T. pilaris* from below (note latter's dark undertail, heavily streaked throat and upper breast on peach or orangy background, and diagnostic *chack chack chack chack chack* call).

Locustella Warblers: Grasshopper, Savi's and River Warblers

Where and When Grasshopper Warbler is a widespread but scarce summer visitor throughout much of Britain and Ireland, frequenting overgrown tangled vegetation on downland and heathland, young forestry plantations and edges of marshland; has declined markedly in recent years. Savi's Warbler is a rare summer visitor to selected reedbeds, mainly in East Anglia; occurs rarely in other areas on migration. River Warbler is an east European bird, recorded in Britain on 12 occasions up to 1989; it is, however, expanding its range and seems likely to occur more frequently in future.

Grasshopper Warbler *Locustella naevia*

Behaviour All *Locustella* are extremely skulking and difficult to see. They *walk* furtively through low vegetation and may scurry off at speed when startled. All are more likely to be located by song.

Song Has distinctive, high-pitched reeling song, recalling an angler's fishing line.

Structure and Plumage A small-headed, scrawny warbler with markedly graduated tail and curved primaries, features shared by all *Locustella*. Olive-brown above, with faint supercilium, streaked crown and upperparts; breast often lightly streaked. Legs noticeably pale pink or orange. Adult's underparts vary from buffish-white to pale yellowish, but yellowish more normal on first-winters in autumn. Easily identified when seen well, but streaking on upperparts can be difficult to see, particularly in poor light or at distance, and this has led to confusion with Savi's Warbler (see below).

Savi's Warbler *Locustella luscinioides*

Behaviour Usually located by song, but, whereas Grasshopper Warbler tends to sing from drier areas (such as bramble bushes) within a reedbed, Savi's Warbler is most likely to be seen climbing to top of a reed stem in damper areas of reedbed itself.

Song Distinctly lower-pitched and more buzzing than Grasshopper Warbler's, which sounds high-pitched and more tinny or 'watery' in comparison. Tends to sing in shorter bursts but, like Grasshopper, may reel for considerable periods once underway; song is often preceded by accelerating sequences of hard ticking noises, similar to call, which is a quiet *tip tip* (reminiscent of Robin *Erithacus rubecula*). The songs of all three species covered here may be confused with various bush-crickets (Tettigoniidae): in particular, Roesel's bush-cricket *Metrioptera roeselii* has a song apparently similar to Savi's (see Burton & Johnson, 1984, for further details).

Structure and Plumage Visual differentiation from Grasshopper Warbler not difficult *once it is clearly established that there is no streaking*, but, as noted above, streaking on Grasshopper can be very difficult to detect. Grasshopper, however, has more buffish basic coloration, rather than dark brown tone of Savi's. Savi's has also to be differentiated from Reed Warbler *Acrocephalus scirpaceus*: in comparison, Savi's is quite a large bulky bird, with different shape, its small, rather rounded head and thin neck combining to produce rather an emaciated, scrawny appearance in the field; its most obvious feature, however, is a full, conspicuously rounded tail (quite a rich, dark brown colour), particularly obvious in flight. Note also Savi's curved primaries (straight on all *Acrocephalus*). Bill quite long, pointed and rather dagger-like: upper mandible black,

Savi's Warbler. Plain brown above. Note rounded tail, distinct supercilium, fairly plain undertail-coverts. Do not confuse with Reed Warbler.

Grasshopper Warbler. Darkish above and below. Streaks on back can be difficult to see.

River Warbler. Similar to Savi's Warbler, but note diffuse breast streaking and pale edges to undertail-coverts.

Grasshopper Warbler. Varies in colour, some greyer, others yellower. Grey birds often poorly marked.

lower mainly yellowy. Has very narrow eye-ring and narrow, pale supercilium (some individuals barely show latter in field). Overall plumage tone drabber, duller and darker than Reed: upperparts dull brown, lacking olivaceous tones, and underparts dingy buffish, but whiter on throat; cinnamon-buff undertail-coverts are plain, or lightly tipped pale buff (cf. River Warbler). Legs pinkish or brownish, paler than Reed Warbler's. Its typically furtive *Locustella* behaviour (*walking* up and down branches or reed stems) should also distinguish it from an *Acrocephalus*.

River Warbler *Locustella fluviatilis*

Behaviour Inhabits drier areas than Savi's (even cornfields); more terrestrial, creeping through tangled branches and among leaf litter rather like a chameleon, but, when startled, bolts into cover like a mouse.

Song Diagnostic: slower than Grasshopper's, more like a sewing machine, with syllables clearly articulated.

Structure and Plumage Similar to Savi's, but generally darker, particularly on underparts, which are dark grey-brown, slightly paler on belly. Two features must be clearly established when identifying this species: **1** breast is lightly streaked, and **2** undertail-coverts (often difficult to see in field) have noticeable pale crescent-shaped tips to all feathers (unmarked or with dull buff tips on Savi's).

Reference Burton & Johnson (1984).

Aquatic Warbler

Where and When Aquatic Warbler *Acrocephalus paludicola* is a very rare autumn passage migrant from eastern Europe, mainly in southern England; usually in reedbeds or rank vegetation, particularly sedges, but at migration points may resort to crops or bushes. Intensive ringing in suitable areas has revealed that it is more numerous than previously supposed; at Radipole Lake, Dorset, as many as 22 have been trapped in a single autumn. Almost all have occurred in August and early September, extreme dates ranging from late July to early November.

Identification

There is a popular misconception that Aquatic Warbler is basically 'a Sedge Warbler *A. schoenobaenus* with a crown-stripe'. This is not so. Aquatic is distinctive, and good views should reveal many subtle and not so subtle differences that combine to create a characteristic jizz (for the rarity-minded observer, Aquatic bears an uncanny resemblance to a miniature, thin-billed Bobolink *Dolichonyx oryzivorus*). The major pitfall is pale, buffy juvenile or first-winter Sedge, which may also show obvious crown-stripe. Aquatic should be identified with caution, and not claimed until all main differences have been noted. Most Aquatic Warblers occurring in Britain are first-winter individuals, and following details refer to that age group.

General Appearance Young Sedge are distinctly paler and buffer than adults, but Aquatic is yellower than that species. Upperparts are heavily striped black and yellowish-buff (giving a 'tiger-striped' appearance), with two rather broader, creamy 'tramlines' towards sides of mantle; rump is noticeably streaked black on a buffish background, in contrast to plain (or almost plain) chestnut-tinged rump of Sedge. Even in brief flight view, Aquatic looks a mass of streaks. Tail feathers are quite sharply pointed, giving Aquatic a spiky-tailed appearance (can at times be surprisingly different from Sedge, which has more rounded tail feathers); central pair protrudes beyond the rest, contributing to a more graduated tail shape.

1st-winter Aquatic Warbler.
Note rounder head, paler, thicker
bill, pale lores and broad
down-turned supercilium. ▶

Aquatic Warbler (left) and Sedge Warbler (right).
Note heavily streaked Aquatic Warbler with
spiky tail. Sedge Warbler shows warm brown
rump.

Juvenile Sedge Warbler. Breast
spotted not
streaked.
▼

1st-winter Sedge Warbler ▶
Note dark lores and 'sharper'
expression than Aquatic
Warbler.

1st-winter Sedge Warbler ▶
(top) shows pale median
crown stripe, it is
broad and clear-
cut on 1st-winter
Aquatic Warbler
(below) which also
shows bronze
forehead.

Worn adult Aquatic
Warbler in autumn is much
duller than 1st-winter and
may show dark lores.

Worn adult
Sedge Warbler in
autumn. ▼

1st-winter
Aquatic Warbler.
Shape and colour
distinctive as are
pale 'tramlines' on
mantle. Note clean
pink legs.

Head Pattern Given reasonable view of perched Aquatic, concentrate on head. Surprisingly, crown-stripe is not always obvious, particularly if head seen side-on, but note pale, unmarked lores (Sedge has dark line from bill to eye, producing 'sharper' facial expression reminiscent of Firecrest *Regulus ignicapillus*); prominent supercilium is yellowish-buff and rather downcurved (not so wedge-shaped as on Sedge), while black eye-stripe is rather stronger and thicker behind eye. Crown-stripe seen best when bird bends its head down: crown is very dark, almost black (browner on Sedge), contrasting strongly with thin, sharply defined crown-stripe, which broadens above bill into a small bronze patch (on well-marked juvenile or first-winter Sedge, crown-stripe is broader, messier and less sharply defined, while, unlike Aquatic, there may be intrusion of dark streaking, blurring demarcation between crown-stripe and crown itself). Bill of Aquatic is slightly shorter and thicker than Sedge's, while head may look more rounded. These features, combined with more curved supercilium and pale lores, create generally softer, more 'open' expression than Sedge Warbler.

Other Differences Aquatic has distinctly paler and brighter fleshy pink legs (darker and browner on Sedge). Subtle differences in overall shape may be perceived in prolonged views: Aquatic often looks rather more rakish, with proportionately smaller head, longer neck and, perhaps, slimmer body; first-winter may show narrow gorget of very faint black breast streaking (more spotted on juvenile Sedge and, to lesser extent, on first-winter) and thin black flank streaks.

Adults Adult Aquatics (much rarer here than first-winters) apparently do not complete post-nuptial body moult until winter quarters: in autumn may thus be heavily abraded, losing much of pale streaking and appearing peculiarly dark above; breast more streaked than on juvenile and first-winter, and may show better-developed loral line (more similar to Sedge).

Call Aquatic and Sedge Warblers may be quite vocal on migration, particularly early morning and late evening. Aquatic has *tucc* call, significantly deeper than that of Sedge (Rumsey 1984).

'Pishing' When faced with a potential Aquatic, the most immediate problem may be that of obtaining a good view. Flushing it into the open is often counterproductive. Since Sedge and Aquatic readily respond to 'pishing', it is advisable to retreat about 20m and try this technique: providing conditions are calm, this will usually bring the warbler into the open.

References Porter (1983), Rumsey (1984).

Reed and Marsh Warblers

Where and When Reed Warbler *Acrocephalus scirpaceus* is a common summer visitor, mid April to October, to reedbeds in England and Wales; largely absent from northern England, Scotland and Ireland. Marsh Warbler *A. palustris* is a summer visitor, late May to October, but is currently teetering on edge of extinction as a British breeding bird: former main breeding area Worcestershire, with occasional pair elsewhere, particularly in southeast England; migrants may also appear at coastal migration sites in spring (late May–June) and in autumn (mainly September–October).

Habitat May be first clue to identity. In summer Reed inhabits reedbeds, but Marsh breeds in rank vegetation, such as nettle beds, rosebay willow herb and osier beds. It should be stressed, however, that Reed frequently occurs in dryer habitats, sometimes breeding in dense shrubbery (usually near reeds), and on migration is often found well away from water.

Song The most reliable means of separation in the field. Reed gives a well-known grumpy chortle, including characteristic, repetitive *chara-chara-chara* or *crik-crik-crik* phrases, usually from depths of a reedbed; song can, however, become quite excited, and it may even mimic other species, although mimicry rarely persistent, is generally infrequent and unconvincing. Marsh, on the other hand, is a superb songster with very varied song (no two bursts are quite the same); a strong mimic, it is often difficult initially to be sure whether it is Marsh Warbler or 'the genuine article' that is starting to sing. The song is generally sweet and warbling, with chattering, grating and sweet, high-pitched sounds intermixed; although many phrases are unmistakably acrocephaline in quality, they are thinner and faster than those of Reed. The song phrases are long and frequently contain mimicry (extent of which varies individually): songs or calls of other species include

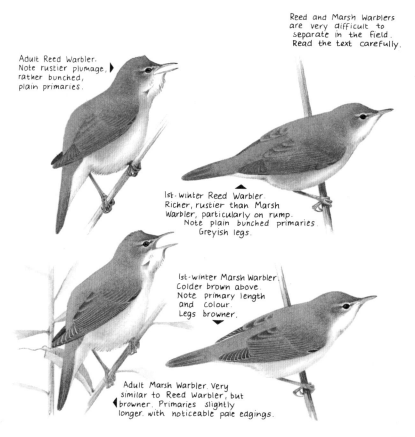

Reed and Marsh Warblers are very difficult to separate in the field. Read the text carefully.

Adult Reed Warbler. Note rustier plumage, rather bunched, plain primaries.

1st-winter Reed Warbler. Richer, rustier than Marsh Warbler, particularly on rump. Note plain bunched primaries. Greyish legs.

1st-winter Marsh Warbler. Colder brown above. Note primary length and colour. Legs browner.

Adult Marsh Warbler. Very similar to Reed Warbler, but browner. Primaries slightly longer, with noticeable pale edgings.

Skylark *Alauda arvensis*, Swallow *Hirundo rustica*, Yellow Wagtail *Motacilla flava*, Blackbird *Turdus merula*, Song Thrush *T. philomelos*, Whitethroat *Sylvia communis*, Great Tit *Parus major*, Starling *Sturnus vulgaris*, Chaffinch *Fringilla coelebs*, Bullfinch *Pyrrhula pyrrhula*, Greenfinch *Carduelis chloris*, Goldfinch *C. carduelis*, and even African species copied in their winter quarters. When singing, Marsh tends to be less secretive than Reed, regularly climbing to tops of plants or bushes and singing with bill wide open, revealing brilliant orange gape. Reed tends to sing well down in vegetation, opening bill only a few millimetres (fully only when 'getting carried away').

Calls Differences do not seem to be absolute, but Marsh gives soft *churr*, soft *stit* and stuttering *st-t-t-t-t*, whereas Reed's commonest call is a slurred *tchar*.

Plumage Separation of Reed and Marsh Warblers extremely hard (they undoubtedly represent one of the most difficult 'species pairs' on the British list). Nevertheless, to the experienced eye, Marsh *do* look different, though it is often difficult to claim a non-singing individual as anything other than a 'probable'. Following differences are most significant, but it should be stressed that Marsh Warbler should be identified by a *combination* of most of the characters. 1 PLUMAGE TONE Marsh is slightly, sometimes noticeably, paler than Reed, looking generally more pallid and lacking obvious rufous tones: rump especially is *usually* much less rufous than on Reed (particularly on adults), often appearing olive grey-brown; upperparts paler brown, even sandy-brown, and often show faint greenish or greyish tint; underparts creamy or yellowish-cream, not so buffy as Reed, and lacking rufous on flanks. Throat may look noticeably white, especially when singing. 2 WINGS Pay particular attention to

remiges: primaries generally look slightly longer, narrower and less bunched than on Reed, this leading to slightly longer-winged impression; more significantly, shows narrow pale edgings to tertials and secondaries, while whitish crescent-shaped tips to the seven or eight well-spaced primaries may stand out noticeably from darker background. On late-summer and autumn adults, however, edgings may, of course, disappear (adults, incidentally, do not moult these feathers until winter quarters). By comparison, most Reed show plainer, more uniform remiges, although faint pale feather edgings apparent when fresh. 3 LEGS Legs of juvenile and first-winter Marsh are paler than Reed, often noticeably orangy, brownish or straw-coloured, with yellower feet; legs of similarly aged Reed are darker, browny-grey (also with yellower feet). Legs of adult Marsh also slightly paler and browner, but closer in shade to Reed so differences not always especially striking. Marsh has pale claws (dark on Reed). 4 STRUCTURE Differences in shape very subtle, but Marsh may look somewhat *Sylvia*-like or even *Hippolais*-like about the head, with rather spiky rear crown and, particularly when singing, a more obvious 'jowl' (produced by bulging throat). 5 ALULA Marsh has more obvious dark alula, contrasting with paler wing-coverts, but, frustratingly, alula is often concealed by flank feathers. 6 OUTER TAIL FEATHERS In flight, Marsh may show faint *hint* of paler edges to outer tail feathers.

For differences from *Hippolais* warblers, some species of which can appear very similar to *Acrocephalus* in shape, see page 181.

Reference For further information on Reed and Marsh Warblers, and discussion of identification of Blyth's Reed Warbler *A. dumetorum*, see Harvey & Porter (1984).

Hippolais Warblers: Melodious, Icterine, Olivaceous and Booted Warblers

Where and When Melodious and Icterine Warblers are rare but regular autumn migrants (August–October). Coming from the east, Icterine is most regular down British east coast, from Shetland to Kent, but also annual further west at well-watched migration sites such as Isles of Scilly and Cape Clear Island, Co. Cork. Coming from the south, Melodious has a more southerly and westerly distribution and is most regular from Dorset westwards and at Irish Sea bird observatories, being very rare on British east coast. Small numbers of Icterines also occur in spring, but Melodious is very rare at that season. Olivaceous Warbler is a great rarity, with fewer than 15 records up to 1990. Booted Warbler has proved to be fairly regular in recent years, with 32 records up to 1991.

Melodious Hippolais polyglotta and Icterine Warblers H. icterina

Separation from Garden, Reed, Marsh and Willow Warblers Before separating them from each other, Melodious and Icterine have to be separated from other large, sturdy warblers (Garden *Sylvia borin*, Reed *Acrocephalus scirpaceus* and Marsh *A. palustris*) and also from Willow Warbler *Phylloscopus trochilus*. Separation from the first three is straightforward: Melodious and Icterine are essentially green and yellow (rather than brown and buff) and have long, pale, predominantly orangy bills. Garden is a podgy, featureless warbler, olive-brown above and pale buff below, with rather stubby, *blackish* bill, large, dark eye and rather plain-faced expression: as on Icterine, its primary projection is long, approximately equal to tertial length, but the wings are often slightly drooped to reveal rump; unlike Melodious and Icterine, it often feeds on berries in autumn. Reed and Marsh are more similar to *Hippolais*, but both have stronger facial pattern, with distinct eye-stripe and pale supercilium *before* eye (which is brown, not black), rounder tail and longer undertail-coverts; both are browner than Melodious and Icterine (Reed often showing rufous tones), are *far more vocal* and are more furtive, usually (but not always) feeding in lower vegetation. Willow Warbler is easily separated by its small size, more restless, flitting behaviour, strong facial pattern, weak bill, *hu-eet* call and, in autumn, by its yellower plumage.

Plumage Tone Virtually all autumn *Hippolais* warblers seen in Britain and Ireland are first-winters, so following details refer to that age unless otherwise stated. Icterine varies slightly, but is generally pale washed-out grey-green above (some are slightly more olive), this paleness noticeable even in flight (looks much paler than Willow Warbler); in the field, underparts are whitish-buff, with pale primrose on chin and throat. Melodious is similar, but less grey, being generally rather more olive-green above and more uniformly dull yellow below, richest on throat and upper breast. Spring adults of both species tend to look brighter and more uniformly yellow below.

Head Both have a long, hefty (long and wide-based) bill which is noticeably orange (apart from darker culmen), its size emphasised by the typical *Hippolais* head shape: a rather sloping forehead and a peaked crown. Unlike *Acrocephalus* and *Phylloscopus* warblers, including Willow, both have a bland, open-faced expression, lacking any dark between eye and bill and having only faint supercilium and eye-ring.

Wing Structure To separate them from each other, it is imperative to concentrate on the structure of the closed wing. On

Icterine, length of exposed primaries is approximately equal to length of overlying tertials; on Melodious, primaries are shorter and rather bunched and projection is only about half tertial length. Long-winged appearance of Icterine is usually very apparent in the field, even in flight, which is fast and rather flycatcher-like compared with the more fluttery flight of the shorter-winged Melodious.

Wing Panel Another good field character is Icterine's wing panel. This is usually conspicuous and is formed by broad pale edgings to secondaries (these are whitish in autumn, but may be yellower on spring adults). Melodious often looks completely plain-winged, but some individuals show paler edges to remiges (particularly in spring), though these edgings are narrower and less well marked than on Icterine and rarely stand out as a distinct panel.

Subsidiary Features Other differences subtle, but Icterine tends to show more obvious narrow pale edges to outer tail feathers in flight, and has bluer legs than Melodious.

Behaviour and 'Character' The two species tend to have different behavioural characteristics. Melodious is a more rounded-looking bird, tends to skulk, is more lethargic and is a rather slow and methodical feeder (often remains in same clump of bushes for considerable periods). By contrast, Icterine has rather long, slim appearance and is more lively and impetuous, shooting off over open ground when disturbed, with dashing, flycatcher-like flight, and swerving suddenly into back of a bush when alighting; often sits around in full view on tops of bushes, quite unlike the more reticent Melodious.

Voice Except when singing, neither is very vociferous so, if faced with a persistently calling *Hippolais*, check that it is not a Reed or Marsh Warbler. Icterine has a short, hard *teck*, and Melodious a low, brief sparrow-like chatter (which seems to be given mainly in presence of other

Melodious). Icterine's song is a hesitant, disjointed, high-pitched, sweet *Acrocephalus*-like refrain, perhaps recalling Marsh Warbler, but it contains discordant whistling, chacking, grating and squealing, as well as mellower, more thrush-like phrases; each sequence is often repeated before moving on to the next. Melodious starts hesitantly, but proceeds into softer, gentler, smoother but faster and more sustained musical rambling (also vaguely acrocephaline) but lacking Icterine's 'rough edges'.

'Brown-and-white' Melodious and Icterine Warblers There has been frequent reference in the literature to 'brown-and-white' or 'grey-and-white' Melodious and Icterine Warblers. Although some individuals (particularly Icterines) do look washed-out and lack *obvious* yellow, they still look essentially pale grey-green above and creamy or buffy below; paradoxically, examination in the hand always reveals a uniform pale yellow wash to underparts, even if this not obvious in the field. Although aberration is always possible, substantiated claims of colourless individuals have not come to light in recent years (indeed, two recent individuals claimed in Scilly turned out to be Olivaceous Warblers). If you have a totally 'brown-and-white' Melodious or Icterine, then the chances are that you have misidentified it.

Olivaceous Warbler *Hippolais pallida*

Structure, Plumage and Behaviour Structurally rather similar to Melodious, with similarly short primary projection (about two-thirds tertial length). Individuals of eastern race *elaeica* are generally smaller than western *opaca* and some are quite noticeably small, prompting confusion with Booted Warbler. Olivaceous is rather like a Melodious Warbler that is totally lacking in green and yellow: upperparts vary from pale brown to browny-

Characters common to Melodious and
Icterine Warblers; open-faced, yellowy base
to bill, square-ended tails with
outer feathers slightly paler,
short undertail-coverts.

1st-winter Melodious Warbler.
Dull green above, pale
yellow below.

Adult spring
Melodious Warbler.
Note structure;
visible primary tips
1/2 length of tertials.
Legs usually browner
than Icterine.

1st-winter Icterine Warbler.
Often dull. Note wing panel.

Spring adult
Icterine Warbler.
Brighter than 1st-winters.
Note structure; visible
primary tips equal
tertial length.
Pale wing panel often
obvious. Greyish legs.

Olivaceous Warbler.
Completely lacks green or
yellow. Note long pale bill
and downward tail
dropping. Short-winged
like Melodious Warbler.
Supercilium before
eye only.

Booted Warbler. Small
and Phylloscopus-like. Note
supercilium, widest behind
eye, dark coronal stripe
above. Legs dark horn.

183

grey, while underparts are strikingly pale, greyish-white; wings relatively plain, although narrow pale edges to remiges can give effect of a faint panel at times, rather like that shown by some Melodious. Olivaceous also needs to be separated from Marsh Warbler, but it shows typical *Hippolais* shape, often with slightly ragged effect to rear crown, a long, noticeably orange bill and a lack of warm buff plumage tones. Like Melodious and Icterine, Olivaceous has a bland face with plain, pale lores. A very faint suggestion of a supercilium may be slightly emphasised by vague *hint* of darkening along edge of crown. Pay particular attention to the tail. On Olivaceous, it looks very square with noticeably pale outer edges, but most useful is a significant behavioural trait: *Olivaceous continually and deliberately dips its tail downwards when feeding* (rather like Chiffchaff *P. collybita*), which Reed and Marsh do not. *Acrocephalus* warblers generally have longer undertail-coverts than *Hippolais*, but note that some Olivaceous can also show fairly long undertail-coverts. Olivaceous is a lively bird, and far more arboreal than either Reed or Marsh.

Voice More vocal than Melodious and Icterine, and gives a *tchak* or *chak*, weaker and less strident than Blackcap *S. atricapilla*. Song is a repetitive warbling and grating, continually and regularly rising and falling in pitch.

Booted Warbler *Hippolais caligata*

Quite different from preceding three species. Although confusion with small Olivaceous Warblers of race *elaeica* has occurred, Booted should not really cause difficulties. The following is, however, based on notes made on several Booted Warblers recently seen in October in England, and it should be noted that there is geographical variation in size and plumage tone, as well as in leg colour.

Size and Structure Smaller than other *Hippolais*, being closer in size to Chiffchaff,

but slightly larger and bulkier than latter. A small warbler with, in many ways, the character of a *Phylloscopus*. Bill, however, is longer and sturdier than Chiffchaff's (it is also rather pointed) and appears slightly angled upwards from face; as with other *Hippolais*, bill is pale, orangy-flesh or horn, with darker culmen and tip.

Plumage A strikingly pale warbler, upperparts being pale brown (frequently described as colour of milky tea) and underparts strikingly pale, off-white. Unlike other British *Hippolais*, has strong facial pattern, again rendering it more *Phylloscopus*-like in character: narrow dark eye-stripe, tapering behind eye and (unlike others of genus) may be apparent before eye, but note that gape line may give *impression* of darker lores; noticeable creamy supercilium, extending well behind rather beady eye, but fading at rear (although at times looks rather wedge-shaped). Another distinctive feature is a very faint, but quite definite, narrow dark lateral crown-stripe extending from bill and broadening to form a rather wedge-shaped line above supercilium. Other features include: thick and slightly ill-defined pale creamy edgings to greater coverts and secondaries, on latter forming fairly noticeable warmer-toned panel; short primary projection (about half to two-thirds tertial length) and distinct 'tertial step' between primaries and tertials; rump and rather square tail slightly darker and warmer than upperparts; very narrow pale edges to outer tail feathers (can be very difficult to detect in the field and are best seen in flight); and pale grey or greyish-horn legs.

Behaviour Feeding behaviour more deliberate than Chiffchaff, and does not habitually flycatch or hover. Unlike both Olivaceous Warbler and Chiffchaff, there is no persistent tail-dipping.

Separation from Bonelli's Warbler Surprisingly, there has been confusion between Booted and Bonelli's Warbler *P. bonelli* (page 192), even with individuals in the hand (partly as result of the two species having very similar wing formulae). Bonelli's should be readily separated by its fairly bland face, lacking strong super-cilium, its green edgings to wing and tail feathers and, when visible, a yellowy tint to rump. Being a *Phylloscopus*, Bonelli's is a daintier, more delicate bird and more arboreal than Booted, which is more likely to occur in weeds and low bushes. Also, Bonelli's Warbler is more vocal, those from the western part of the range (race *bonelli*) calling *poo-eet* and eastern *orientalis* calling *chip*.

Sylvia Warblers: Whitethroat, Lesser Whitethroat, Subalpine, Garden and Barred Warblers

Where and When Whitethroat is a common summer visitor (mid April–early October) to most of Britain and Ireland except Scottish Highlands and Northern Isles; in 1968/69 it suffered reduction in numbers of about 75% (considered a result of severe drought in the Sahel zone, south of the Sahara) and numbers have hardly recovered since. Lesser White-throat is also fairly common (mid April–October) but restricted mainly to England and east Wales. Subalpine Warbler is a rare vagrant (mainly April–June and again in autumn, mostly October), currently averaging about 17 records a year. Garden Warbler is another common summer visitor (mid April–October); rarer in north-ern Scotland and largely absent from Ireland. Barred Warbler is an autumn visitor (mid August–late October) mainly to Shetland and down British east coast, with smaller numbers along south coast and farther west; virtually unknown in spring.

Whitethroat *Sylvia communis*

Despite severe reduction since 1969, still a common and familiar bird and should be used as a yardstick when identifying rarer members of the genus. Easily identified: summer male has grey head and brownish back, buffish-white or greyish-white underparts and prominent white throat. Most significant are conspicuous rusty edgings to tertials and secondaries, distin-guishing it from all other British warblers (except Spectacled, see below); females, juveniles, first-winter and adult winter males are brown on head. Both sexes show a narrow white eye-ring which may be conspicuous (again suggesting Spectacled). A characteristic view is of a predominantly brown, rather long-tailed warbler, flying jerkily into cover, flicking tail and revealing narrow but conspicuous white outer tail feathers. An excitable bird: when breeding, is very responsive to human approach, often scolding the observer with body tilted forward, jerking tail upwards and constantly calling; when aggravated, raises crown feathers to pro-duce crested effect. Call is a distinctive soft, scolding *churrr* or *churrit*, but other calls include rapid, angry scolding *vit vit vit vit* (number of notes variable). Song defies description, but basically a short, throaty, scratchy *dji-do, ji-do ji-do ji-do ji-do*, very distinctive once learnt (varies con-siderably, however, in both content and length); is often given from a prominent perch, even telegraph wires, or from the air during jerky, dancing song flight.

Lesser Whitethroat *Sylvia curruca*

A slightly smaller, shorter-tailed, more compact, less excitable bird than White-throat and tends to be more arboreal. Easily identified by uniformly grey-brown upperparts, wings lacking Whitethroat's rusty tertial and secondary edgings. Head is grey, often with darker lores and ear-coverts, and lacking obvious eye-ring;

clean greyish-white or buffy-white under-parts contrast strongly with upperparts, and render it one of our smartest, most attractive warblers. Call is an abrupt, clipped *cht*, thinner and more abrupt than that of Blackcap *S. atricapilla*; also has a scolding *chr-r-r-r*. Song is a distinctive 'rattle' on one note (recalling Cirl Bunting *Emberiza cirlus* or even Yellowhammer *E. citrinella*), given with great gusto and often preceded by subdued, disjointed warbling and chattering.

'Siberian Lesser Whitethroat' *S. c. blythi*

In late autumn, Lesser Whitethroats of Siberian race *blythi* occur in small numbers, usually at well-watched coastal migration sites. Larger than nominate race, very brown on back and rather dark on head, contrasting strongly with throat; under-parts white, but may be sullied pinky-grey, particularly on flanks. Warmer brown edgings to tertials, and may show faint pale supercilium.

Subalpine Warbler *Sylvia cantillans*

In spring, easily identified by bluish-grey upperparts, red eye, and orange-brown or pinky-brown underparts which con-trast with white moustachial stripes; on adult males, underpart colour is intense, but females look more washed-out, the colour varying from creamy-buff to pinkish-buff. Some autumn individuals, however, may be far less distinctive. First-winter can be aged by the lack of pure white on outer tail feathers (are instead sullied brown). First-winter males acquire pinkish-brown underpart coloration after late-summer post-juvenile moult, but first-winter females often lack strong colour below and can be most puzzling. The following de-tails relate to such individuals.

Structure is distinctive: Subalpine looks a small, delicate, 'dinky' little warbler,

smaller and daintier than Lesser White-throat and rather more like a *Phylloscopus* warbler in character; has a small, dark bill, a rounded head, a rather plump body, a medium-length tail and short wings. Upperparts pale blue-grey, with faint brown tint which varies according to angle. Eye dark, but reddish coloration may appear during autumn; unlike Lesser Whitethroat, has noticeable pale eye-ring. Crown and ear-coverts are sharply demar-cated from white throat, while rest of underparts are also essentially white, but with very faint buffy tint, particularly on flanks. Wings are browner, with narrow buff tips to greater coverts and fringes to tertials. Unlike Lesser Whitethroat, legs are orangy-brown. Call is a soft *tac* and a *chur*, rather higher-pitched than corres-ponding calls of other *Sylvia* warblers. Song is a sustained warbling and chatter-ing, rather sweet and high-pitched for a *Sylvia* and mostly lacking harsher notes. Because of its shorter tail, the tail-cocking is less exaggerated than that of Dartford Warbler *S. undata* and body stays still while tail is cocked.

With their rather featureless appear-ance, 'colourless' first-winter female Sub-alpines have, in the past, often been misidentified as rarer *Sylvia*. Full treat-ment of the problem is beyond the scope of this book, but following extreme rarities could cause confusion. 1 SPECTACLED WARBLER *S. conspicillata* Only one or two British records. There should be no problem in separating Subalpine and Spectacled, but confusion has arisen probably because some field guide illust-rations show them as being far more similar than they really are. Spectacled is a small, energetic warbler, strongly reminiscent of a diminutive, brightly coloured Whitethroat. Like Whitethroat, it shows bright rusty edgings to secon-daries *at all ages* (although Subalpine has narrow buffish secondary edgings, they never give impression of a clear-cut rusty

Lesser Whitethroat in spring. Dark grey-brown above, with darker mask and white throat. Note grey rump, white outer-tail feathers and steel-grey legs.

Lesser Whitethroat in fresh autumn plumage. Lighter grey than in spring, some show a little white on 'face'

Lesser Whitethroat of race 'blythi'. Warmer brown upperparts, paler ear-coverts, pale forehead and short supercilium before eye.

1st-winter ♀ Subalpine Warbler. Small and dainty, light sandy-grey above, creamy below. Sandy tertials with diffuse dark centres, whitish eye-ring, horn-coloured bill. White undertail-coverts.

1st-winter Whitethroat. Larger than Lesser, with longer tail. Rufous above, brown rump and pink legs.

Garden Warbler. Large and stocky, with short unmarked tail. Short thick greyish bill, steel grey legs.

1st-winter Barred Warbler. Resembles huge Garden Warbler, but greyer or sandier above, with pale edges or tips to wing feathers. Variable amount of barring on scapulars, flanks and undertail-coverts. Outer tail feathers have whitish tips. Grey legs.

panel); rest of plumage is similar to, but brighter than, that of Whitethroat, but note Spectacled's generally more prominent eye-ring and, on spring males, a very black area on lores (latter useful when separating them from male Whitethroats). Spectacled has a different character from Subalpine and Whitethroat, preferring low, ground-loving vegetation, where it moves in quick, nervous manner, frequently shooting off across open ground with weak, tit-like flight. One of the best features is a characteristic grating call *trrrr*, very distinctive once learnt, and reminiscent of call of Wren *Troglodytes troglodytes*. **2** SARDINIAN WARBLER *S. melanocephala* Only 24 British records up to 1991. A larger, bulkier, much darker and duller warbler than Subalpine. Female has dark grey head, darkish grey-brown back and very dull underparts, being particularly dingy brownish or greyish on flanks (quite unlike Subalpine). Eye red, but dark on juvenile. Typical call is a rhythmic, stuttering *st-t-t-t-t*, recalling a football rattle, but also gives a more Whitethroat-like *chur* and other grating noises. **3** RÜPPELL'S WARBLER *S. rueppelli* Only four British records. Female has grey head, sharply demarcated from white throat; underparts also white, sullied grey only on rear flanks. Most distinctive plumage feature is narrow grey-white edgings to all wing feathers, contrasting with rest of upperparts, which are grey. Tail very black. Eye red. Some females have a blackish throat, like subdued version of male's. Structurally, Rüppell's is quite different from Subalpine, being rather a large, streamlined warbler, with a long bill which looks distinctly decurved (owing to . decurved upper mandible). Whereas Subalpine may recall a *Phylloscopus* in behaviour, Rüppell's is slow and deliberate, rather like an *Acrocephalus* in its movements, often craning forward carefully to inspect foliage. Usual call a rapid stuttering chatter.

Garden Warbler *Sylvia borin*

Often causes problems for beginners and, sometimes, more experienced observers, because it is a featureless bird. Paradoxically, its lack of features becomes a feature in itself. It is worth spending time familiarising yourself with Garden Warbler, so that, when you eventually come across something rarer, you will be in a better position to identify it. Garden Warbler is a large, bulky, but unobtrusive warbler. It looks rather podgy and rounded, often with drooped wings, has a thick, rather stubby dark bill and dark grey legs. Plumage is a warm olive-brown, lacking strong characters (only very faint hint of a supercilium and a slight eye-ring). Large, round eye stands out strongly in a plain face, giving it a pleasant, gentle expression. In spring and summer, best located by song: a jumbled warble, superficially similar to that of Blackcap, but deeper and fuller, containing mellow phrases, quality of which recalls Blackbird *Turdus merula*, and lacking high-pitched discordant whistling of Blackcap. Full songs are easily separated once learnt, but note that Blackcap will often introduce its song with a weaker, more subdued preamble similar to song of Garden Warbler, so caution is required. Call is *chack*, softer and quieter than equivalent call of Blackcap; also has quick, rhythmic alarm, *chur chur chur chur chur*. Begging juvenile has loud *chip chip chip chip chur-ee*. Like Blackcap, feeds extensively on berries in autumn, a habit not readily associated with *Acrocephalus* or *Hippolais* warblers.

Barred Warbler *Sylvia nisoria*

Adult Barred Warblers (i.e. ones with bars) are extremely rare in Britain and Ireland; overwhelming majority of records relate to first-winter individuals in autumn, to which following details refer. A large, hefty warbler, with slightly ragged effect to head, and a rounded back. Often shows a pronounced 'jowl', has strong, sturdy, grey legs and a full tail, and is quite slow and heavy in its movements. General appearance vaguely recalls a shrike *Lanius*. Head and upperparts pale grey; face plain except for slightly darker line through eye and slight eye-ring. Unlike adults, eye is brown. Very white below, but with buffer wash on flanks. Features assisting identification: **1** most noticeable are white tips to median coverts and pale grey edges to greater coverts, forming double wingbar; **2** less conspicuous, pale

edges and tips to tertials and whitish edges and tips to primaries; **3** dark bases to median coverts which highlight pale wingbar; **4** unlike Garden Warbler, has narrow white outer tail feathers; and **5** bill is strong and pointed, dark but with pale grey base to lower mandible. Call a loud chacking, very chat-like and very different from Blackcap and other common *Sylvia* warblers.

Reference Baker (1988).

Phylloscopus Warblers: Willow Warbler, Chiffchaff, Wood, Bonelli's, Greenish and Arctic Warblers

Where and When Willow Warbler is an abundant summer visitor throughout Britain and Ireland, late March–September, with stragglers into October; does not normally occur in winter. Chiffchaff is also common, mid March–October (absent from much of Scottish Highlands), and small numbers winter, mostly in southern areas; browner or greyer Scandinavian Chiffchaffs (race *abietinus*) occur on migration, while grey Siberian Chiffchaffs (race *tristis*) are rare in late autumn and winter. Wood Warbler is a summer visitor associated with mature deciduous woodland, particularly sessile oakwoods of western Britain (rare in Ireland); unaccountably rare on migration, being infrequent at coastal migration sites. Bonelli's Warbler is a rare vagrant, mainly August–October, also occasionally in spring; currently averages four or five records a year, mostly in southern England. Greenish Warbler is a rare autumn vagrant, currently averaging about ten records a year, mostly along British east coast, with peak in late August and early September; a few spring and summer occurrences. Arctic Warbler currently averages about six records a year, with peak in September (has never occurred in spring); most are seen in eastern counties and, particularly, in Orkney and Shetland.

Willow Warbler *Phylloscopus trochilus* and Chiffchaff *P. collybita*

General Features Field identification of these two common species, which may at first appear very similar, becomes much easier with practice. Apart from song (see below), following features are most useful. **1** SHAPE Although subtle, Willow is rather more attenuated, sleeker and long-winged compared with rounder-headed, rounder-bodied, 'podgy' Chiffchaff. **2** PRIMARY PROJECTION Pay particular attention to extension of primaries beyond overlying tertials (can be frustratingly difficult to see on a rapidly moving warbler). Willow is longer-winged than Chiffchaff and primary projection is about three-quarters of, or equal to length of tertials. On Chiffchaff, wings are shorter and less pointed and exposed primaries are only about a third to half tertial length. **3** LEG AND BILL COLOURS Willow has paler, orangy legs and often has obvious orange at base of bill; Chiffchaff has dark legs and darker-looking bill (usually with little orange evident). Leg colour differences, however, not absolute since some Willows have blackish legs (although usually still show dark orange feet). **4** TAIL-DIPPING One significant behavioural trait is Chiffchaff's habitual downward tail-dipping when feeding. Willow does not do this *persistently* (usually just one desultory dip after alighting) and, when feeding, usually holds tail still. 5 FLIGHT The idea of separating these species in flight may seem fanciful, but, because of its longer wings, Willow has a more dashing, flycatcher-like flight compared with weaker, more tit-like flight of more pot-bellied Chiffchaff. Differences of course subtle, but again become more apparent with practice.

Plumage Plumage differences are both subtle and variable, but an understanding of ageing and moult times helps considerably. Following differences apply to all ages. 1 FACIAL PATTERN Willow has 'sharper' facial expression, with stronger eye-stripe and longer, more definite supercilium; cheeks are blotchy. Chiffchaff has weaker head pattern, but (particularly autumn and winter) often shows well-marked upper and lower eye-crescents which form noticeable eye ring; cheeks more smoothly buff. 2 WING PANEL Willow *tends* to show better-marked green panel on tertials/secondaries; Chiffchaff looks uniform and plain-winged. 3 ALULA Chiffchaff shows contrasting blackish alula. Following differences are related to time of year. Note in particular that *the two species are relatively easily separated in autumn*. 1 SPRING ADULTS Plumage differences most subtle in spring, but Willow is typically paler and more washed-out than Chiffchaff, with greener upperparts and a primrose-yellow tint to supercilium, throat and upper breast. Chiffchaff is darker, more olive-green above and olive-yellow below. 2 JUVENILES Compared with summer adults, juvenile Willows are noticeably primrose-yellow about the supercilium and underparts, and very green on upperparts; both bill and legs are very orangy compared with Chiffchaff. Juvenile Chiffchaffs have very fine wispy plumage and often manage to look scruffy: greener above than adults, lightly

streaked yellow below (yellowest on sides of breast), and slightly greyer on head; extensive dull orange at base of bill. Juvenile Chiffchaff's calls are monosyllabic (see below). 3 FIRST-WINTERS AND WINTER ADULTS Juvenile Willows have a body moult in late summer, while adults can begin a complete body moult by early July. Moult quickly so that, by early August, both adults and young can be in fresh plumage and cannot be safely aged in the field (indeed some are difficult in hand). Fresh autumn plumages of adults and first-winters are similar to juvenile and, consequently, *Willows are distinctly green above and evenly yellow on supercilium and underparts*, thus much easier to separate from Chiffchaffs in autumn (adult Willow, however, may be whiter on belly). Chiffchaffs moult slowly in autumn, so individuals still in wispy juvenile plumage can be encountered in September; first-winter and adult winter Chiffchaffs are much less yellow than Willow, being olive above and rather buff below.

Song Diagnostic: Willow has a familiar, pleasant, soft, descending refrain, whereas Chiffchaff's song repeats its name (this usually preceded by peculiar nasal wheezing). There are several recorded instances of Chiffchaffs finishing their song with the tail of a Willow Warbler's: this may be due to individual idiosyncrasy, but probable hybridisation has been recorded. Chiffchaffs of Iberian race *ibericus* also have an intermediate song.

Call Differences subtle, but Willow's *hoo-eet* is more penetrating, more emphatic and slightly more disyllabic than Chiffchaff's. Juvenile Willow has squeakier, fuller, more monosyllabic call than adult, while juvenile Chiffchaff gives monosyllabic *hoot* in late summer/early autumn. **Alien Races** Scandinavian Chiffchaffs of race *abietinus* are similar to nominate, but more colourless, being greyer or browner above, paler below, and have

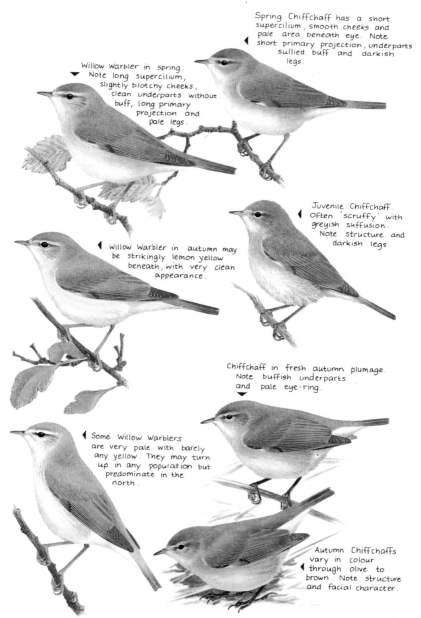

Spring Chiffchaff has a short supercilium, smooth cheeks and pale area beneath eye. Note short primary projection, underparts sullied buff and darkish legs.

Willow Warbler in spring. Note long supercilium, slightly blotchy cheeks, clean underparts without buff, long primary projection and pale legs.

Juvenile Chiffchaff. Often 'scruffy' with greyish suffusion. Note structure and darkish legs.

Willow Warbler in autumn may be strikingly lemon yellow beneath, with very clean appearance.

Chiffchaff in fresh autumn plumage. Note buffish underparts and pale eye-ring.

Some Willow Warblers are very pale with barely any yellow. They may turn up in any population but predominate in the north.

Autumn Chiffchaffs vary in colour through olive to brown. Note structure and facial character.

191

better supercilium. Greyer eastern individuals of race *tristis* ('Siberian Chiffchaff') rather more problematical, are dealt with below. Northern Willow Warblers (race *acredula*) may appear particularly pale and washed-out, but there is much gradation between *trochilus* and so-called *acredula*.

Wood Warbler *Phylloscopus sibilatrix*

Plumage Once known, a very distinctive *Phylloscopus*, but beginners often mistake brightly coloured Willow (particularly in autumn, when much yellower), while out-of-context Wood at, for example, a coastal migration site may confuse even more experienced observers. Wood is, however, very much a 'super *Phyllosc*': very bright green above, colour recalling that of Firecrest *Regulus ignicapillus*, it has obvious narrow green edgings to black-centred remiges; underparts a clear, silky white, and throat and supercilium bright primrose-yellow (does not, however, normally show the *clear-cut* intensely yellow throat illustrated in most field guides). Head pattern strong, with clear-cut yellow supercilium and a clear-cut green eye-stripe; ear-coverts yellow (blotchy green on Willow).

Structure Compared with Willow, is a sleek, attenuated, streamlined bird, and always looks long-winged (wing length 70–81mm, compared with Willow's 59–72 and Chiffchaff's 53–68: Svensson 1984).

Behaviour A typical view is from below, with bird high in tree canopy, where silky white underparts and long undertail-coverts most obvious. When feeding, often falls and glides through canopy with wings half open. No tail-dipping.

Song Diagnostic: a beautiful fast, dribbling trill, often preceded by clear, piping *pew pew pew pew* notes, highly evocative of mid-summer mature deciduous woodland.

Call Clear, piping *pew*, quite unlike Willow.

Bonelli's Warbler *Phylloscopus bonelli*

Closely related to Wood Warbler, and song similar.

Structure In shape and structure more similar to Willow Warbler, but often looks rather round-headed.

Plumage Superficially, a rather nondescript warbler, but looks distinctly pale greyish, with pale, greeny-grey head and upperparts and buffy-white underparts. Large black eye stands out prominently from a bland face, which lacks strong eye-stripe; only faint pale supercilium. Most likely to attract attention are narrow green edgings to tail and to remiges, latter forming a rich green panel on closed wing, contrasting with dark-centred tertials. Rump pale yellow, but can be very difficult to see in the field (best seen when hovering) and is in any case duller on first-winter individuals. Bill has orangy cutting edge and lower mandible, and legs are grey-brown.

Call Varies according to race: western individuals (race *bonelli*) give a *poo-weet*, similar to Willow but with a consonant at beginning and rising more sharply; eastern race *orientalis* gives an abrupt *chip*. One recent English vagrant, however, gave both calls, so there may be degree of overlap.

Song A quick trill, like start of Wood Warbler's song, but slower and more liquid.

Pitfalls There are at least three recorded cases of peculiar Wood Warbler-like birds that have very strongly resembled Bonelli's. Like Bonelli's, they were very grey above and white below, with strong green edgings to wing and tail feathers, but stronger eye-stripe and supercilium, structure (particularly very long wings) and call indicated that they were probably aberrant Wood Warblers or possibly Wood x Bonelli's hybrids. Such freaks, although very rare, need to be borne in mind when identifying vagrant Bonelli's. Other confusion species are Chiffchaff of race *tristis* (see below) and Booted Warbler *Hippolais caligata*. Latter has been confused with Bonelli's on several occasions, even in the hand: separation is not helped by fact that they have very similar wing formulae (see page 184).

Greenish Warbler *Phylloscopus trochiloides*

Two important confusion species must be eliminated when identifying Greenish Warbler. The most obvious is the similar Arctic Warbler, but there has been considerable past confusion with Siberian race of Chiffchaff *tristis*, which is not only rather grey, but may also show a wingbar (see below). Note, however, that *tristis* Chiffchaffs do not usually appear in Britain and Ireland until late autumn (October onwards), well after Greenish peak (August/September).

Structure Smaller than Willow and more Chiffchaff-like in shape, and may look rather short-tailed. Bill small compared with Arctic, but deeper and broader than that of Chiffchaff and rather more 'parallel' when viewed from side.

Plumage Autumn adults very rare in Britain and Ireland, so following details relate to first-winter unless otherwise stated. Upperparts green with distinctive grey cast, but exact shade may vary according to light; underparts whitish with duller greyer flanks but, at *close range*, diffuse yellow streaking may be discernible on breast and belly; bright green edgings to tail feathers and to remiges, latter forming wing panel, but again this will vary according to light. Four important features stand out. 1 HEAD PATTERN Most obvious is a prominent, clear-cut, long whitish or yellowish supercilium, broadest behind eye but dulls as it fades into nape: is usually straight, but there may be a slight up-kink at rear (although this less pronounced than that shown by

Arctic). Supercilium is emphasised by dark olive-grey eye-stripe, which fades behind eye into olive-grey ear-coverts. 2 WINGBAR Narrow but noticeable clear-cut wingbar, formed by white or yellowish-white tips to outer four to six greater coverts, is sharply defined (unlike more diffuse bar on some *tristis* Chiffchaffs). Very rarely shows trace of a second bar on median coverts. 3 BILL Dark along culmen, but *cutting edge and lower mandible (except tip) yellow or pinkish-orange*: an important difference from mainly dark bill of *tristis* Chiffchaff. 4 LEGS Darker than Arctic, generally looking quite dark, medium brown (are in fact brownish-grey at front but pinkish-grey at back and sides), but note that in bright sunlight or at certain angles can look quite pale, even taking on a yellowish tint (prompting confusion with Arctic).

Voice One of the best differences from Arctic. Greenish gives distinctly disyllabic note variously rendered as *soo-wit, ch-wee* or *tis-wee*, has been likened to soft conversational call of Pied Wagtail *Motacilla alba*, but can be louder and more explosive when agitated. Spring birds often sing a high-pitched, rapid musical chattering jangle, often with trills reminiscent of Wren *Troglodytes troglodytes*.

Behaviour Extremely active, moving quickly through foliage, constantly flicking wings, and occasionally flicking tail in nervous downward dipping (unlike more consistent dipping of Chiffchaff).

Late-summer/Autumn Adults Worn adults, between June and early August (when they moult), may lose fresh olive tone to upperparts and become relatively dull grey-brown; wingbar may abrade away or become irregular. Such individuals can be identified by combination of head pattern, bare-part colour, structure and call. Note that adult Greenish Warbler has only a body moult in late summer, so in autumn shows abraded remiges and rectrices.

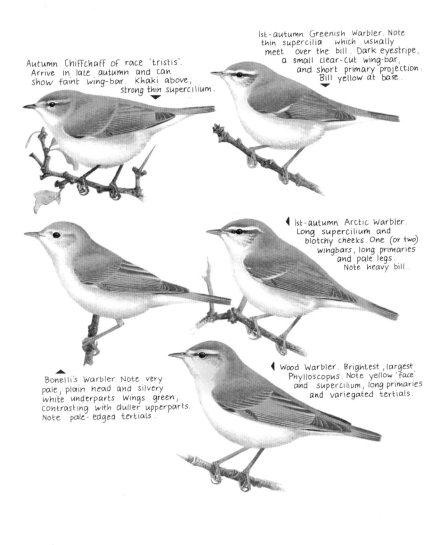

1st-autumn Greenish Warbler. Note thin supercilia which usually meet over the bill. Dark eyestripe, a small clear-cut wing-bar, and short primary projection. Bill yellow at base.

Autumn Chiffchaff of race 'tristis'. Arrive in late autumn and can show faint wing-bar. Khaki above, strong thin supercilium.

1st-autumn Arctic Warbler. Long supercilium and blotchy cheeks. One (or two) wingbars, long primaries and pale legs. Note heavy bill.

Bonelli's Warbler. Note very pale, plain head and silvery white underparts. Wings green, contrasting with duller upperparts. Note pale-edged tertials.

Wood Warbler. Brightest, largest *Phylloscopus*. Note yellow 'face' and supercilium, long primaries and variegated tertials.

Two-barred Greenish Warbler *P. t. plumbeitarsus* There has been a recent British record (October 1987) of this eastern counterpart of Greenish. The taxonomic position of *plumbeitarsus* has, however, been the subject of debate, and it is now treated as a race of Greenish. It is, perhaps, most likely to occur in late autumn, and any apparent Greenish Warbler showing a strong bar on median coverts should be very carefully scrutinised and, if possible, trapped and photographed and a full description taken.

Arctic Warbler *Phylloscopus borealis*

Structure Larger, chunkier and heavier-headed than Greenish, and often looks rather short-tailed. Intermediate in size between Willow and Wood Warblers, indeed overall shape and long-winged appearance recall Wood. Bill substantial and hefty for a *Phylloscopus*, is noticeably broad at base.

Plumage Overall plumage tone similar to Greenish, but upperparts a richer green; upperpart tone does, however, vary, some having slight greyish cast, others being dull grey, washed with olive. Following differences should, in combination, separate it from Greenish. 1 HEAD PATTERN Supercilium is longer, passing beyond ear-coverts and virtually reaching nape, where it often kinks upwards, but up-tilt is dependent on posture (Greenish can also show an up-kink). On Greenish, supercilia *often* meet over bill, but often stop short on Arctic. Lores often have a dark smudge on Greenish, less distinct on Arctic, which has lores unbroken from bill to eye. Arctic usually shows prominent pale mottling on ear-coverts, with a darker border. 2 WINGBARS Frequently a suggestion of a second wingbar on median coverts (rare on Greenish). 3 LEGS Paler than on Greenish, looking orange, orange-yellow or even pinkish-yellow in some lights; at closer range may look yellow with browner wash, but yellowest at rear.

Voice The best difference: a hard, metallic *dzik* or *chick*, quite unlike Greenish.

Late-summer/Autumn Adults Like Greenish, worn adult Arctics can lose one or both wingbars and they also have only a body moult in late summer, so autumn adults can have worn remiges and rectrices.

'Siberian Chiffchaff'

Chiffchaffs show a reduction in yellow and green coloration towards east of their range. Scandinavian individuals (race *abietinus*) tend to be greyer or browner on head and mantle, have a buffer supercilium and are paler below, but these grade into Siberian race *tristis*, which is greyer. Latter can be confused with both Greenish and Bonelli's Warblers, but are unlikely to be found in this country except in late autumn and winter. 'Siberian Chiffchaff' is like nominate race, but upperparts are a cold beige or khaki (also described as 'mackintosh colour') and underparts are cold whitish, with some beige across breast and on flanks; under-tail-coverts cream. May show some yellowish at bend of wing, and has green edgings to remiges and rectrices, but is otherwise devoid of yellow or green. Has distinct pale supercilium, strong and narrow to end of ear-coverts, and a white-lime eye-ring; cheeks are rather rusty. Often has slight, but noticeable, pale wingbar, and it is this feature that has caused past confusion with Greenish, but 'Siberian Chiffchaff's' wingbar is less well defined and not clear-cut. Bare-part colours as nominate race: note in particular that bill is mainly dark, unlike Greenish or Bonelli's. Call particularly distinctive: a plaintive, piping, monosyllabic *peep*, recalling a lost chick or, vaguely, a Bullfinch *Pyrrhula pyrrhula*.

References Dean (1985), Svensson (1992).

Marsh and Willow Tits

Where and When Both species occur throughout England and Wales; Willow Tit *Parus montanus* reaches southwest Scotland, but is comparatively rare in southwest England. Marsh Tit *P. palustris* prefers deciduous woodland, especially beech and oak, whereas Willow prefers damp woods, carr and lowland coniferous forest.

Voice Unless they call, the two species are very difficult to separate (not until 1900 was it realised that Willow Tit occurred in Britain). Like all tits, both have a variety of calls; fortunately, those most frequently given are diagnostic. Marsh has very distinctive high-pitched, sneezing *pitchou*, which may be extended into a nasal *pitchou-chu-chu-chu-chu*. Willow has a loud, deep, buzzing scold: *si-zur-zur-zur*. Although heard less frequently, their songs are also different. Marsh has a rapid, ringing, typically tit-like *swe swe swe swe swe swe swe*, while Willow has a slow, clear, melancholy *tsui tsui tsui tsui*, recalling piping song of Wood Warbler *Phylloscopus sibilatrix*. Willow gives various other songs, including a series of thin, high-pitched phrases, and thin, wistful *si si si soo soo soo*, descending at end. Young Willow have a descending three- or four-note begging call *jzee jzee jzee*, which young Marsh do not give.

Structure and Plumage Differences in plumage and structure subtle, should be used with care. Willow has a larger head and is bull-necked, with less 'mantle', while head plumage is more loosely textured. It has a dull, matt crown, a larger swept-back area of white on cheeks and a larger throat patch. Marsh has a glossy crown and a smaller 'Hitler moustache' but note that juvenile Marsh has dull crown. Willow has pale edgings to secondaries and tertials which, in fresh plumage, produce distinctive pale wing panel; this may be lacking in worn plumage in late summer, while, conversely, fresh-plumaged Marsh may show a subtle panel. Willow has buffer flanks, and shows more obvious white in outer tail feathers and slightly rounder tail tip.

Behaviour Unlike Marsh, Willow excavates its own nest hole (beware Willow Tit excavations taken over by Marsh Tits).

Marsh Tit has slightly glossy cap, white cheeks which become dusky behind ear-coverts. Note uniform tertials and square tail.

Willow Tit has dull black crown which sweeps back onto mantle, cheeks wholly white and also sweep back onto sides of neck, giving bull-necked appearance.

Note pale wing-panel.

Willow Tit has slightly larger black bib, the tail is slightly rounded, with paler outer feathers.

Treecreeper and Short-toed Treecreeper

Where and When Treecreeper *Certhia familiaris* is a common resident throughout most of Britain and Ireland. Short-toed Treecreeper *C. brachydactyla* breeds on Channel Islands of Guernsey, Jersey, Alderney and Sark, and is a very rare vagrant to southern England (eleven records up to 1991).

It is probably true to say that Short-toed Treecreeper is the most difficult British bird to identify. Plumage differences are very subtle, and only the calls are likely to attract attention in the field. Anyone faced with a possible Short-toed Treecreeper should take very detailed notes on plumage, listen to calls over a long period and then endeavour to enlist the cooperation of a ringer. In the hand, hind claw: bill ratios are useful and fine details of wing pattern and structure are important (see summary in Svensson, 1992). Untrapped individuals are much less likely to be accepted by *British Birds* Rarities Committee. A good series of photographs would also prove beneficial.

Plumage Plumage differences very subtle, but following are most important. **1** PLUMAGE TONE Short-toed is noticeably greyer above than Treecreeper, sometimes hardly showing any hint of brown; upperparts tend to look more untidy and coarsely marked, with irregular dark streaking. Treecreeper has uniformly rich brown upperparts with narrow pale feather shafts producing prominent fine white streaking, particularly on nape and upper mantle. On Short-toed, greyer upperparts contrast with distinctly browner rump and tail, this contrast being perhaps most obvious initial plumage difference in the field. Note, however, that some Short-toed from southern Europe have upperpart coloration very similar to Treecreeper, while Treecreepers from northern Europe of race *familiaris* (have occurred in this country) show

colder, more spotted upperparts (but, unlike Short-toed, they show prominent white supercilium and very clean white underparts). **2** SUPERCILIUM Subtly different. On Treecreeper, supercilia are longer and broader and pure white, usually extend to base of bill, and on race *familiaris* often join as a white line over bill. Supercilia of Short-toed always short, but often prominent, being well defined and wide behind eye, but often fading away towards bill (never join above bill); unlike Treecreeper, supercilium greyish-white or yellowish-white, and does not contrast so much with rest of head. **3** UNDERPARTS Short-toed has dingier underparts than Treecreeper, being browner or greyer towards belly, vent and undertail-coverts. On Treecreeper, underparts are silvery-white, but may show faint brown wash to vent and undertail-coverts (particularly further to south and west of European range).

Voice More useful than plumage are calls. Both species utter a variety of calls, some so similar as to be of no value in the field. Short-toed has, however, a consistently louder, *more varied*, *more tit-like* vocabulary than Treecreeper and this should be readily apparent if an individual is listened to over a long period. Note, however, that calls of both vary considerably in both volume and composition and many 'intergrades' can be heard, but following represent the main types. **1** Most familar call of Treecreeper is a weak, unobtrusive *see*, often protracted into descending sequence, *see see see see see*; at close range may sound quite loud, while at other times individual notes sound more disyllabic: *tui tui tui tui tui*. Short-toed gives a very similar call, a rather weak *suup*, often several together in descending sequence; these calls are, however, generally louder and more strident than Treecreeper. **2** Short-toed often gives a loud

Bills of Treecreeper (above) and Short-toed Treecreeper (below). The latter tends to have longer bill, often with pale extending to tip.

Treecreeper. Browner above, stronger supercilium, neater upperpart streaking, whiter below.

Both species similar in field. Pay careful attention to calls.

Short-toed Treecreeper. Greyer mantle contrasts with browner tail. Duller supercilium, messier upperpart streaking. Dusky flanks.

tsui, similar to, but higher-pitched than, Coal Tit *Parus ater*, again often in series to form descending sequence; this call is similar to variation described above for Treecreeper, but is characteristically very loud and almost 'ringing' in quality. **3** Coal Tit-like phrase of Short-toed may be followed by loud, ringing *chink* or *tink*, recalling Chaffinch *Fringilla coelebs*; these notes may also be given separately. **4** Short-toed may also give loud, shrill, piping *peep*, vaguely similar to call of Dunnock *Prunella modularis*; again, several of these may be strung together. **5** Both species give a thin, high-pitched *sit . . . sit*, frequently in flight. Treecreeper's song is unobtrusive, yet very distinctive once learnt: begins with series of call notes *swee swee swee*, followed by trill recalling song of Blue Tit *Parus caeruleus*, and ends with emphatic, almost Coal Tit-like *stoo-eet*. Song of Short-toed is reminiscent of Treecreeper, but begins with loud, ringing, Coal Tit-like *spee spee spee* notes, accelerating into loud, tit-like trill.

References Identification of treecreepers has, over the years, generated considerable correspondence in *British Birds*. The paper by Mead & Wallace (1976) is the standard reference, but following are also useful: Chapman (1984), Hirschfeld (1985), Pym (1985), Rodriguez de los Santos (1985), Tucker (1984).

Red-backed, Woodchat and Isabelline Shrikes

Where and When Formerly a common summer visitor, Red-backed Shrike is currently teetering on the edge of extinction as a British breeding bird; now most likely to be seen as a scarce spring or autumn coastal passage migrant. Woodchat Shrike is a rare spring and autumn vagrant, occurring mainly on south coast of England, and currently averaging about 18 records a year. In Asia, Red-backed Shrike is largely replaced by the closely related Isabelline Shrike, a very rare late-autumn vagrant to this country, just about annual in recent years.

Red-backed Shrike *Lanius collurio*

Adult male, with its grey head, black facial mask, reddish back and white bases to tail, is easily identified; female and immature are less distinctive. By the time migrant Red-backed appear in late August, young birds will have lost their strongly scalloped juvenile feathering; first-winter plumage is essentially rusty-brown above and the scalloping, although still present, is rather more subdued. Adult females are plain on upperparts, and greyer on head and rump. Note that some females and immatures show a distinctly redder tail, which may suggest Isabelline (see below).

Woodchat Shrike *Lanius senator*

Adult easily identified by its black-and-white plumage and chestnut rear crown. Young retain much of their juvenile plumage well into the autumn: compared with Red-backed, they lack strong rufous tones and are messily scalloped on a colder, paler, buffy-grey background. Three features suggest their future adult patterning and are diagnostic: **1** whitish rump; **2** whitish scapulars/median coverts; and **3** a buffy-white patch at base of primaries. All three characters vary individually, and whitish scapulars may not be as easy to see in the field as some guides suggest. Some

autumn juveniles may show a faint rusty tint to nape, again suggestive of their future adult finery.

Isabelline Shrike *Lanius isabellinus*

Specific Status Has been traditionally treated as conspecific with Red-backed Shrike, but is now given full specific status. Identification complicated, not only because there are four recognised races, but also because western birds may interbreed with Red-backed and produce hybrids that could conceivably occur in western Europe.

Juvenile and First-winter The first point to remember is that a proportion of female and immature Red-backed Shrikes show a decidedly rufous tail, so it is essential to concentrate on other features to confirm identification of Isabelline. Like Red-backed, juvenile Isabellines are scalloped, but, by time late-autumn migrants reach western Europe, they will have moulted into first-winter plumage, which (unlike first-winter Red-backed) is *plain* on upperparts, with *inconspicuous* and delicate scalloping largely confined to forehead, sides of crown, breast and flanks. It should be remembered, however, that *adult* female Red-backed is also plain above, but, if in doubt, both species can be aged by fact that juveniles and first-winters have a blackish subterminal bar behind the pale tip of each greater covert, tertial and tail feather. Upperparts of first-winter Isabelline are uniformly pallid, varying individually from pale sandy, through cinnamon-buff to pale grey-brown. In all cases, this contrasts strongly with strikingly rufous or cinnamon-orange rump and tail (perhaps suggesting oversized female Redstart *Phoenicurus phoenicurus*); even underside of tail is rufous (greyish on almost all Red-backed). Other points to watch out for are a distinct pale wing panel (caused by pale secondary

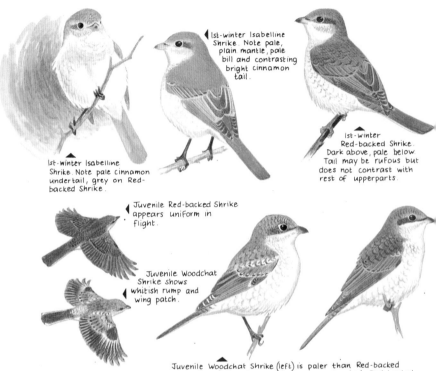

1st-winter Isabelline Shrike. Note pale, plain mantle, pale bill and contrasting bright cinnamon tail.

1st-winter Isabelline Shrike. Note pale cinnamon undertail, grey on Red-backed Shrike.

1st-winter Red-backed Shrike. Dark above, pale below. Tail may be rufous but does not contrast with rest of upperparts.

Juvenile Red-backed Shrike appears uniform in flight.

Juvenile Woodchat Shrike shows whitish rump and wing patch.

Juvenile Woodchat Shrike (left) is paler than Red-backed Shrike (right), its plumage is more variegated. Red-backed Shrike lacks white centres to scapulars.

edgings), a paler-based bill (usually with a pink component), and a distinctive whitish patch at base of primaries (although not all individuals show this). Subtle structural differences, such as a thicker bill and a slimmer tail, should be discernible in prolonged field views. It should be noted that some Isabellines, particularly extreme examples of western race *phoenicuroides*, may approach less well-marked Red-backed in mantle colour and prominence of underpart barring. Observers are advised to exercise caution with non-classic individuals and to consult Dean (1982) for clarification.

Adult Adult male has variable whitish patch at base of primaries and a black or blackish-brown 'eye-patch'; on adult female, wing patch may be subdued or absent and eye-patch is less prominent. Whereas first-winter Isabelline has a pale base to bill, it may be mainly blackish on adults (particularly males). Adults of race *phoenicuroides* usually have a rather rufous crown, contrasting with a greyer nape and mantle, and a white supercilium. Other races are generally less strongly patterned on head: see Dean (1982) for details of racial differentiation.

Reference Dean (1982).

Great Grey and Lesser Grey Shrikes

Where and When Great Grey Shrike *Lanius excubitor* is a rare autumn and winter visitor, mainly October–March, to wild, open country. Lesser Grey Shrike *L. minor* is a very rare vagrant from southern and eastern Europe, averaging three records a year in May–November (most in spring and early summer).

Plumage *Adults* Adult Lesser Grey is easily distinguished from Great Grey by broad area of black over forecrown (slightly less extensive and less solid on females than on males). Also, males have beautiful soft, salmon-pink flush on breast (greyer on females). *Juveniles and first-winters* Young Lesser Grey lacks adult's black forehead, may be passed off as Great Grey. Juveniles (slightly browner than adults and lightly barred) do not occur in Britain, but first-winters do: they bear strong superficial resemblance to Great Grey, and need to be identified by following features, which apply to all ages. *General plumage features* Note Lesser Grey's lack of white supercilium, its indistinct white scapular edges and, particularly, its larger white primary flash. Both species have white in outer tail: on Great Grey, this widens at tip to produce white tail corners; on Lesser Grey, it broadens at

Juvenile /1st-winter Lesser Grey Shrike

1st-winter Lesser Grey Shrike. Mask resembles Great Grey Shrike. Note large white wing patch, shorter tail and long primary projection.

Adult ♂ Lesser Grey Shrike. Broad black forehead, pinkish breast.

Adult Great Grey Shrike Note white line above black mask.

Adult Great Grey Shrike Note long tail and short primary projection.

base to produce two basal tail patches (as male Red-backed Shrike *L. collurio*).

Structure Without direct comparisons, plumage assessments may be rather subjective. Concentrate on structure and, in particular, on length of exposed primaries: on Great Grey, primaries are short, appearing to be about two-thirds to three-quarters length of overlying tertials; Lesser Grey has long primaries, appearing perhaps 1¼–1½ times tertial length (fresh-plumaged Lessers also show noticeable

pale edges and tips to primaries). Other differences include Lesser Grey's smaller size, thicker, stubbier bill and proportionately shorter tail (latter no doubt explains its tendency to adopt more upright posture than its long-tailed relative).

'Steppe Grey Shrike' Only nominate race of Great Grey is discussed above. There are two Fair Isle and one Suffolk records of pale, eastern race *pallidirostris* ('Steppe Grey Shrike'): see *British Birds* **50**: 246–9; **66**: 401–2.

Crows: Carrion Crow, Rook, Raven, Jackdaw and Chough

Where and When Rook and Jackdaw occur throughout Britain and Ireland, except in Highlands of Scotland. Carrion Crow is similarly widespread, but is replaced in northwestern Scotland and Ireland by grey-and-white 'Hooded Crow' (race *cornix*). Raven is absent from most of lowland England, being confined to Scotland, northern and southwestern England, Wales and much of Ireland. Chough is found on rocky coastlines in west Wales, Isle of Man, southwest Scotland and Ireland (excluding east coast).

Carrion Crow *Corvus corone* and Rook *C. frugilegus*

Adults When seen well, adult Rook is easily separated from Carrion Crow by bare, whitish face (Carrion Crow has completely feathered face); also has a throat pouch which, when full, appears as prominent lump.

Immatures Juveniles are rather browner and duller on body than adults. Juvenile Rooks have fully feathered faces and appear Crow-like: only late in first winter or spring (i.e. when one year old) do they start to lose both facial feathering and the wedge of feathering along top of bill base. When separating juvenile/first-year Rooks from Crows, overall shape is particularly important (see below): note

steep forehead, peaked crown and 'trousered' thighs, all typically Rook-like.

Shape and Structure Particularly useful when separating Crows from juvenile and first-year Rooks. In particular, Carrion Crow has rather flat crown and low forehead, which merge into rather blunt-looking bill to produce wedge-shaped profile with bill appearing as continuation of head. When at ease, Rook has a steep, even vertical, forehead and peaked crown, creating distinctly dome-headed profile. At rest, it is a less compact, more emaciated bird than hefty, powerful Crow: has ragged 'trousered' effect to thighs, and full, rather mobile, rounded tail (often partially spread and angled downwards at rest). In flight, differences subtle, but Carrion Crow has slightly broader, more rounded wings and shorter, squarer tail; Rook's wings are slightly more tapered, and tail appears distinctly more graduated. Crow's flight is slightly flappier, but differences are slight and depend largely on weather conditions and on what bird is doing. Young Rooks are smaller and skinnier than adults and, by late winter, are heavily abraded about wings and tail (latter often showing protruding feather shafts); growth of new central tail feathers in late winter will briefly accentuate graduated look to tail.

◀ Carrion Crow. Note heavy black bill, flat crown, lack of shaggy thighs and more tidy compact shape.

◀ Adult Rook Note whitish bill and face, steep forehead, shaggy thighs and less compact shape.

Note difference in calls:
Carrion crow 'caw' whereas Rook gives a gruff 'arrgh'.

Carrion Crow

Juvenile Rook

Juvenile Rook ▶ resembles Carrion Crow until one year old. Note steeper forehead, slimmer, scrawnier shape and feathered thighs. The bill is more slender and pointed.

Jackdaws. Adult (right) ▶ easily identified by small size, pale eye and grey nape. Juvenile (below) has duller eye and lacks the obvious grey nape until autumn moult.

◀ Raven. Huge, similar in size to Buzzard. Note heavy powerful bill and shaggy throat. Deep croaking calls.

203

Raven in flight. Huge crow with diamond-shaped tail. Note shaggy 'beard' and huge black bill.

Rook in flight. Note straighter rear edge to wing, slightly rounded tail and more pointed narrower wings than Carrion crow.

Carrion Crow has square-ended tail and bulging rear edge to wing.

Some Carrion crows and Rooks show silvery-white speckling to wings and tail.

Carrion Crow of the 'hooded' race 'cornix'. Grey body, black wings, tail and head.

Chough. Large rounded wings. Buoyant, stylish flight. Noisy and acrobatic.

Jackdaws are small with pointed wings and short tail. They appear blunt-headed.

Calls An important distinction: Crow has a characteristic *caw*, while Rook has gruff, strangled *aargh*.

Behaviour Rooks are, in general, more gregarious, but such differences not absolute and large flocks of Crows may be frequent in favoured areas. Rooks usually breed in colonies (rookeries); Crows are solitary nesters.

White Plumage Both species sometimes acquire white feathering (especially in wings), but this trait is fairly common in Crows, which sometimes show large white wingstripe.

'Hooded Crow' Easily separated by grey belly and mantle, and black head, breast, wings and tail. Intermediates between 'Hooded' and Carrion Crows are frequent in zone of overlap between the two races.

Raven *Corvus corax*

Compared with Carrion Crow, Raven is huge (size of Buzzard *Buteo buteo*). Seen high in air, however, its enormous size is not always apparent, but shape then more significant: Raven is long-winged and (unlike Crow) the 'hands' are rather tapered and angled back in flight; tail is strongly graduated but, surprisingly, this is not always obvious at distance; it has a longer head-and-bill profile, and huge, deep bill projects conspicuously from powerful head, whole effect often emphasised by shaggy throat feathering. Very vocal, its loud, croaking *cok cok* is diagnostic, as is an evocative, ringing,

bell-like sound. Often indulges in spectacular aerial displays, twisting, tumbling or rolling in mid flight. Nests singly on cliffs and in trees.

Jackdaw *Corvus monedula*

Much smaller than Carrion Crow, unlikely to be confused at rest because of its grey nape and pale eye (juveniles have a darker nape and a dark eye until early autumn). In · flight, is a small, compact, short-winged corvid, with tapered primaries and energetic, flapping flight; often associates with Rook flocks. Has a wide vocabulary, but the familiar, excitable *jack jack* is diagnostic. Nests in holes in cliffs and trees, also in chimney pots.

Chough *Pyrrhocorax pyrrhocorax*

Similar in size to Jackdaw. A stunning bird, easily identified by red legs and long, curved red bill; juveniles have orange legs and shorter orange bill. Unlike Jackdaw, wings long, broad, square and prominently fingered: fingered primaries may be noticeably kinked backwards in certain conditions, this characteristic most marked when adjacent inner primaries missing or partly grown during summer moult (Grant 1988). Choughs are absolute masters of the air: twist and swoop over favoured cliffs, often plummeting earthwards with wings partially closed and swept back close to body. Loud *chee-aah* calls distinctive.

Reference Grant (1988).

Rose-coloured Starling

Where and When Rose-coloured Starling *Sturnus roseus* is a rare vagrant, averaging about seven records a year: adults occur mainly in late spring and summer, juveniles in autumn (particularly October).

Adult Easily identified by pink mantle and belly, and black head, breast, wings and tail; has pink bill and elongated rear crown feathers. In winter plumage much of pink obscured by buffish feather tips (eventually wear off); first-summers tend to be a buffer pink. Occasional 'washed-out' partially leucistic adult Starlings *S. vulgaris* have shown patterning very similar to Rose-coloured: look for latter's shorter, pale pink bill.

Juvenile A rounded, pleasant, bland-faced, innocent-looking bird, easily identified by very pale, sandy plumage: sandy-grey above and pale buffy below (rump somewhat paler; wings darker, with feathers noticeably edged pale). To eliminate aberrant sandy, leucistic juvenile Starling (essential), check bill: shorter and stubbier than Starling's, pale–bright yellow at base, graduating towards pink, dull reddish or brownish at tip (juvenile Starling's bill uniformly blackish). Any pale juvenile seen before end of August will undoubtedly prove to be leucistic Starling. Juvenile Rose-coloureds occur when young Starlings mostly have adult-like first-winter plumage.

Juvenile Starling.
Note sharp all-dark bill. Uniformly dark plumage.
Dark legs.

Juvenile Rose-coloured Starling.
Note pale plumage below, darker wings. Blunt yellowish bill, often with pinkish tip, pale pinkish legs.

Beware of pale leucistic Starlings in late summer.

Green Finches: Greenfinch, Siskin, Serin and escaped green finches

Where and When Greenfinch is a common resident throughout Britain and Ireland, though shuns very high ground. Siskin breeds in coniferous woodland mainly in Scotland, Ireland and Wales, but also thinly (increasing) in England as far south as North Devon and Hampshire; more widespread and often common in winter, although annual numbers fluctuate considerably; feeds in alder, birch and larch and increasingly regular in suburban gardens where, like Greenfinch, feeds on peanuts. Serin is a very rare visitor, mainly to southern coastal counties (where occasionally breeds), mostly in spring and summer (although recorded throughout year); tends to occur in weedy fields and gardens.

Greenfinch *Carduelis chloris*

Structure and Plumage A familiar garden bird. A large, bulky, sparrow-sized finch with thick, pale conical bill. Male green, brightest in summer; female generally duller, sometimes suggesting female House Sparrow *Passer domesticus* in plumage tone. Both have yellow flashes in primaries and tail, again generally duller on females. Juveniles (often confused by beginners) are browner and streaked, both above and below, with a brown rump, but wings and tail show adult-like yellow patches.

Voice Call a rather deep, but soft, rippling *djit djit djit*. Male has twittering song which includes call notes, soft trills and very distinctive loud nasal *djuwee* (very similar to song of Brambling *Fringilla montifringilla*); often sings in bat-like display flight, with slowly flapping wings.

Siskin *Carduelis spinus*

Behaviour Gregarious, often in large flocks with Redpolls *C. flammea*. Markedly arboreal, feeding in alders, birches and larches where, like Redpoll, hangs tit-like from ends of branches. Flight light and undulating (recalling Goldfinch *C. carduelis*).

Voice Most common call a very distinctive loud, ringing musical *sweeeloo*, or variations thereof; also gives hard chattering and twittering, particularly when feeding. Song contains trills and twitters and, like Greenfinch, is often given in bat-like display flight.

Structure and Plumage A small, delicate finch, easily separated from larger Greenfinch by its wingbars, plumage streaking and calls. Predominantly green and yellow, male brighter and less streaked than female; main features include two thick yellow or yellowish-white wingbars, greeny-yellow rump and yellow patches at base of tail. Male has black on crown and chin (sometimes grey on first-years). Juvenile resembles female, but rather duller and browner.

Serin *Serinus serinus*

This small, yellowy finch needs to be separated from Siskin, and also from other small finches that escape from captivity.

Behaviour Markedly more terrestrial than Siskin, usually feeding on ground or among vegetation (although Siskins often feed in fields in absence of suitable trees).

Voice Readily separates Serin from Siskin. Particularly at migration watchpoints, Serins may be detected by call as they fly overhead in fast, direct, but undulating flight, uttering quick, dry *tillil-lit* or *psit-it-it-it*, totally different from Siskin. Once known, flight call diagnostic. Occasionally gives other calls, including nasal *tchoo-it*, metallic *twing* (recalling Goldfinch), single, sweet, tuneful *pwuu*, soft *zit* and metallic *chidick chidick*.

Juvenile Greenfinch. Large and bulky with yellow in primaries and tail. Juvenile is browner than adult and lightly streaked on breast.

♂ Siskin. Note black on crown and chin, strong wing-bars, black legs. ▶

♀ Siskin. Note long pointed bill, long primaries, thick wing-bars and yellow at base of tail.

♂ Serin. Yellow on head and breast. Prominent yellow rump in flight. Note small conical bill.

Juvenile Serin. Much buffer than ♀.

♀ Serin. Note bill and facial pattern, yellowish rump in flight.

♂ Yellow-fronted Canary or Green Singing Finch. Escaped finches need to be eliminated when identifying Serin.

Canary in natural colours. Note short primary projection, and longer tail than Serin.

Juvenile's begging calls include a *dzeep*, vaguely recalling Tree Pipit *Anthus trivialis*, and a high-pitched *seee seee*. Male's song (one of most familiar sounds of Mediterranean) may be first clue to species' presence during breeding season: a rapid, prolonged, jangling (vaguely suggesting high-pitched speeded-up Corn Bunting *Miliaria calandra*), often delivered with great gusto with bill fully open, tail half cocked and head stretched up and jinked from side to side. Also has bat-like display flight. Some individuals have phrases remarkably similar to song of Wren *Troglodytes troglodytes*.

Structure and Plumage A small, rather dumpy, round-headed finch, with rather short tail and short, stubby, conical bill. Male has bright yellow forehead, supercilium, ear-covert surround, throat, breast, wingbars and (very important in flight) rump; yellow at rear of ear-coverts may stand out as a rather distinct neck patch. Also has yellow crescent below eye, yellow patch at bottom of ear-coverts, and variably prominent yellow median crownstripe; belly white, with streaking on sides of breast and down flanks. Female is a rather duller, less intense yellow, with rather plain face in which beady eye prominent. Juvenile duller again, with yellows replaced by buff. Serins differ from Siskins in following respects. **1** BILL Small and stubby (long and pointed on Siskin). **2** WINGBARS Narrow (broad on Siskin), can be virtually lost through wear by mid summer. **3** RUMP Yellow rump prominent, clear-cut and rather rectangular, positively 'glows' on adult male; duller on female and rather buff on juvenile, but still stands out as distinct pale patch, prominent in flight. (On Siskin, rump more greeny-yellow, less clear-cut and altogether less eye-catching.) **4** TAIL Siskin shows yellow bases to tail sides, readily apparent if looked for. **5** HEAD Male Siskin shows black or blackish on crown and chin. **6** TERTIALS, SECONDARIES AND PRIMARIES

On Siskin, edged yellow, forming panel against which plain primary coverts stand out as black patch. **7** PRIMARY LENGTH Serin's primaries are relatively short (less than or equal to tertial length), do not extend down tail; Siskin's primaries long (longer than overlying tertials), appear to extend well down tail. **8** MANTLE AND BACK Serins are browner, Siskins greener. **9** LEGS Pinkish (blackish on Siskin).

Escapes

It is essential to consider possibility of escaped cagebirds, most likely of which is Canary *S. canaria*. Most escaped Canaries will have plumage abnormalities: many are completely yellow and unstreaked, while some have yellow or whitish patches in wings and tail. Those resembling their wild ancestors are easily confused with Serin, but following features should assist recognition. **1** SIZE AND SHAPE Canary is distinctly larger and more attenuated than Serin. **2** PRIMARY AND TAIL LENGTH Canary has short primaries, only about two-thirds length of overlying tertials; Serin's are three-quarters to equal to tertial length. Partly as result of this, Canary appears to have a much longer tail. **3** BILL Canary's is not so stubby as Serin's. **4** CALL Canary has soft *sweet* or *tsooeet*, as well as pleasant twittering contact call. **5** PLUMAGE Wild-type Canaries tend to be greyer above, yellower on belly and duller on rump than Serin.

Another problem is Yellow-fronted Canary or Green Singing Finch *S. mozambicus*, which shows bright greeny-yellow rump, is yellow below and green above (lightly streaked) and has green wingbars and tertial edges. Male has grey rear crown and rear ear-coverts (grey varies racially), tapering yellow supercilium and black malar stripe. Female has similar but duller, greener facial pattern. Heavier-billed than Serin, primary projection is only half tertial length, and tail is tipped white. See Holman & Madge (1982, 1983).

Brown Finches: Linnet, Twite, Redpoll and Scarlet Rosefinch

Where and When Linnet is a common, widespread but declining breeding bird, absent only from higher ground in northern Scotland; in winter, avoids upland areas and concentrates in flocks on farmland, rough ground and saltmarshes. Twite replaces Linnet in upland Scotland and the Scottish islands, and also breeds in western Ireland, the Pennines and North Wales; in winter, descends to lower areas, particularly coastal saltmarshes, with large concentrations on the Wash and in Essex. Redpoll breeds throughout much of Britain and Ireland, particularly in upland areas, but thin on the ground in southwestern England; widespread in winter. Scarlet Rosefinch is a rare spring and autumn migrant, with most seen at well-watched coastal migration sites; September is peak month and most records have been in Shetland (bred in 1982 and 1992).

Linnet *Carduelis cannabina*

Plumage The familiar Linnet should be treated as a yardstick in the identification of the other three species in this group. With red on forehead and breast, the attractive summer male presents no identification problem, but females, winter males and juveniles are less distinctive. Upperparts are relatively uniform warm brown, even chestnut-tinged, while underparts are rich orangy-buff, streaked darker. Head has strong olive-grey tint, with pale areas both above and below eye, as well as on cheeks, creating distinctive facial expression; juvenile, however, has a rather peach-coloured face. Bill grey, but may look pale at certain angles or in certain lights. White flashes in outer primaries and tail distinctive, particularly in flight (but similar white flashes shown by Twite: see below).

Calls Flocks feeding on ground among low vegetation rise with a distinctive dry twittering. Has a variety of calls, but single individuals passing overhead give soft, rather musical *djit . . . djit djit*. Begging juvenile gives persistent chirruping.

Twite *Carduelis flavirostris*

Structure and Plumage Superficially similar to Linnet, and also has prominent white flashes in primaries and tail (especially noticeable in flight), but readily identifiable in a good view. Somewhat slimmer, more compact and slightly longer-tailed than Linnet. Plumage rather nondescript, but dark brown upperparts strikingly streaked, the stripy appearance recalling Redpoll rather than Linnet. Concentrate in particular on rather plain 'face' and throat, which are a beautiful rich orangy-buff; dark streaking at base of the buff extends less strongly down whitish flanks. Unlike Linnet, bill is pale yellow in winter, contrasting with rest of head; bill blackish in summer. Has a more conspicuous wingbar than Linnet, tips of greater coverts varying from rusty to whitish. Male has pink rump, but in autumn and winter the pink is often obscured by pale feather tips (and even in summer it can be surprisingly easy to overlook).

Calls Has variety of calls. Diagnostic is a harsh, nasal *tchooik*, often the first indication of presence of a Twite in Linnet flock. Other calls include twittering noises similar to, but slightly harder than Linnet, and a soft Linnet-like *tweep tweep tweep*.

Redpoll *Carduelis flammea*

Size, Structure and Behaviour Compared with Linnet and Twite, is a smaller, dumpier, short-tailed finch, far more arboreal in behaviour (although will feed in low vegetation and on ground). Typi-

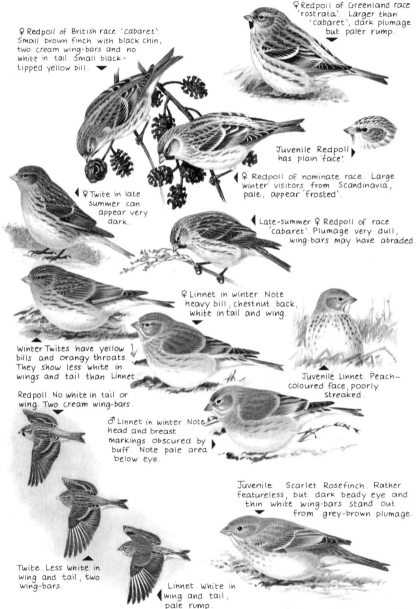

♀ Redpoll of Greenland race 'rostrata'. Larger than 'cabaret', dark plumage but paler rump.

♀ Redpoll of British race 'Cabaret'. Small brown finch with black chin, two cream wing-bars and no white in tail. Small black-tipped yellow bill. ▼

Juvenile Redpoll has plain 'face'. ▶

♀ Twite in late summer can appear very dark. ◀

♀ Redpoll of nominate race. Large winter visitors from Scandinavia, pale, appear 'frosted'.

◀ Late-summer ♀ Redpoll of race 'cabaret'. Plumage very dull, wing-bars may have abraded.

♀ Linnet in winter. Note heavy bill, chestnut back, white in tail and wing.

Winter Twites have yellow bills and orangy throats. They show less white in wings and tail than Linnet.

Juvenile Linnet. Peach-coloured face, poorly streaked.

Redpoll. No white in tail or wing. Two cream wing-bars. ▼

♂ Linnet in winter. Note head and breast markings obscured by buff. Note pale area below eye. ▶

Juvenile Scarlet Rosefinch. Rather featureless, but dark beady eye and thin white wing-bars stand out from grey-brown plumage. ▼

Twite. Less white in wing and tail, two wing-bars.

Linnet. White in wing and tail, pale rump. ◀

211

cally seen in small flocks, often with Siskins *Carduelis spinus*, feeding in tit-like manner on outer twigs of birches and alders, or at tops of tall weeds.

Plumage Compared with Linnet, is darker and more heavily streaked, both above and below. Lacks white primary and tail flashes of Linnet and Twite, instead *shows two narrow buffish or whitish wingbars*. Adults show a red 'poll' and black bib, but juveniles (before late-autumn moult) lack these. Adult male shows strong pinkish-red tinge to breast, rump and sides of head. Adult female can show traces of this colour, whilst first-winter male may lack all red except the 'poll'. Bill pale yellow.

Call Perhaps easiest way to detect Redpolls is by their distinctive flight call, a staccato, rhythmic *chi chi chi chi chi*, usually heard as bird bounces high overhead in light, buoyant, undulating flight. Other calls include a soft nasal *tchewick*.

Other Races Most Redpolls seen here are of the small, dark, west and central European race *cabaret* ('Lesser Redpoll'), but variable numbers of Continental immigrants of race *flammea* ('Mealy Redpoll') appear in autumn and winter, particularly on British east coast. 'Mealy' is typically larger and paler than 'Lesser', whiter below and buffer above, with two pale lines down middle of back being more obvious than on most 'Lessers'; rump often whitish, streaked darker, while the rhythmic flight call is rather deeper. Greenland race *rostrata* also occurs in northern and western Scotland and in Ireland: is dark and heavily streaked, but larger and bulkier than 'Lesser' (almost Linnet-sized), with obvious pale wingbar and whitish rump; like 'Mealy', its call is distinctly deeper than that of 'Lesser'.

Note, however, that not all Redpolls are racially identifiable in the field.

Arctic Redpoll *C. hornemanni* Has not been covered here as there is still uncertainty over identification of 'intermediate' individuals. *British Birds* Rarities Committee currently accepts well-described classically white Arctic Redpolls, and observers faced with such a bird are urged to make very detailed notes on plumage, and check in particular: **1** exact extent of white rump, noting carefully presence or absence of streaking; **2** size and shape of bill; **3** exact extent of streaking on flanks; and, very importantly, **4** *exact* pattern of streaking on undertail-coverts. Anyone finding a potential Arctic would be well advised to enrol the services of a friendly ringer and, if possible, photograph the bird.

Scarlet Rosefinch *Carpodacus erythrinus*

Nondescript, but identification is straightforward. Adult males in distinctive red plumage (not acquired until second summer) very rare in this country; most are autumn juveniles. (Incidentally, juveniles and adults apparently do not moult until in winter quarters, so autumn adult females are less olive in tone than juveniles, with more heavily abraded remiges and rectrices.) A sparrow-sized, thick-set, bull-necked bird, rather like Bullfinch *Pyrrhula pyrrhula* in shape, particularly in flight. Rather bland and featureless: upperparts cold grey-brown and underparts cold greyish-white, both faintly streaked; thin, double white wingbar; dark, Bullfinch-like bill. Perhaps most distinctive feature is the dark, beady eye set in a pale, featureless face. Call a soft, piping *teu-eik*.

Crossbills

Where and When Crossbill occurs in suitable habitat throughout much of British Isles, but numbers fluctuate and distribution varies; much more numerous during periodic invasion years. Scottish Crossbill (promoted to specific status in 1977) occurs only in Scottish Highlands. Parrot Crossbill is a very rare vagrant from Scandinavia and Russia, recorded almost exclusively during periodic invasions (e.g. 85 in 1962/63, over 100 in 1982/83); most have been in northern Scotland and eastern England (following latter invasion, bred in East Anglia). Two-barred Crossbill is the rarest (67 records 1958–91, but small invasions in 1987 and 1990); it originates in northeastern Europe and Siberia.

Crossbill *Loxia curvirostra*

General Features Generally found only in coniferous woodland. Large, bulky, short-tailed, with rather sparrow-like wingbeats and undulating flight. Gregarious.
Bill Thick, with tips noticeably crossed, but slimmer than Scottish and Parrot Crossbills (see below). Young juveniles of all species do not have crossed bill tips.
Voice Very noisy, easily identified by distinctive *chip chip* calls. Song high-pitched and twittering, interspersed with variety of harder *tiwee tiwee* notes and more nasal sounds; thinner, faster, more ethereal than Parrot Crossbill.
Plumage *Adult* Male mainly reddish, but some resemble females, showing little red, while others appear distinctly orange in tone (variability apparently unrelated to age); female mainly grey-green or yellowish-green, yellower on rump. Note that a very few show prominent whitish wingbars (see Two-barred Crossbill). *Juvenile* Well streaked, greyish above and greyish-white below; rump slightly paler, and usually has thin buff double wingbar.

Crossbills often breed in mid winter and juvenile plumage is retained until June–October.

Parrot Crossbill *Loxia pytyopsittacus*

Structure Noticeably larger and heavier than Crossbill, but note that adult males average larger than females and juveniles. Large bill (see below) and thick neck (recalls Hawfinch *Coccothraustes coccothraustes*) contribute to front-heavy appearance. Large-billed individuals often seem to lack a forehead, show very flat crown, but crown feathers can be raised to produce dome-headed appearance. Smaller-billed females and juveniles generally show more pronounced forehead.
Bill Key to identification is an accurate evaluation of bill structure (*detailed* description of bill a prerequisite to acceptance by *British Birds* Rarities Committee). Compared with Crossbill's, it is noticeably heavier, deeper (indeed, more parrot-like), also *proportionately* shorter and deeper. Upper mandible prominently but evenly arched, while lower bulges at base of gonys before angling up to tip. Note in particular that, compared with Crossbill, tips *do not look obviously crossed in profile*, so bill looks blunter and stubbier; tip of upper mandible, however, more obvious than that of lower. Seen front-on, bill is broader-based than Crossbill's. It must be stressed that bill size increases with age, and males have larger bills than females, so it is adult males that are most likely to have classically huge 'parrot-like' bills, but even females usually look larger-billed than male Crossbills. Juveniles in particular may be altogether less impressive, so careful assessment of bill *shape* essential. Parrot Crossbill also shows noticeable pale ivory cutting edges to the mandibles (these being more pronounced than on Crossbill).

All three species share the same plumage characteristics, they differ consistently only in bill size.

Adult ♂ Crossbill

Adult ♂ Crossbill. Typically orange-red, some will show odd yellowish or greenish feathers irrespective of age.

◀ Crossbill has long evenly curved mandibles.

Juvenile Crossbill

Scottish Crossbill has very limited range. The bill is intermediate between Crossbill and Parrot Crossbill.

Adult ♀ Crossbill. Greyish-green ▶ upperparts, yellowish underparts, strong yellow rump. Note stocky build, short notched tail.

Adult ♂ Scottish Crossbill

Adult ♂ Parrot Crossbill

Juvenile Crossbills are heavily streaked. Bill not fully developed.

1st-winter ♂ Crossbills are variable, showing some orange or red feathers.

Juvenile Parrot Crossbill

Parrot Crossbills are bull-necked and very large headed. Note bulging lower mandible and straighter culmen. Bill tips not obviously crossed in profile.

Some Crossbills ▶ (1 in 1000) show whitish wingbars. These are narrower than Two-barred, and diffusely bordered. They are sometimes pink not white.

◀ Adult ♂ Two-barred Crossbill. Note pinkish rather than orange-red plumage and shape of white wing patches, especially the tertial tips.

Voice Call slightly deeper than Crossbill's, but interpretation depends on familiarity with latter's. Most distinctive call is a definite *choop choop*, distinctly lower and deeper than Crossbill; also *quop* or *gop*, more similar to deeper calls of Crossbill. Juvenile's calls may be higher-pitched than adult's. Song weak and hesitant: *chit, chit, chit-chit-chit tcho-ee tcho-ee* (with calls interspersed), deeper, slower and better enunciated than Crossbill's.

Plumage No reliable differences from Crossbill, but male usually a duller, deeper crimson with greyer nape and mantle. Females tend to appear duller and greyer, especially on head and mantle (Catley & Hursthouse, 1985).

Scottish Crossbill *Loxia scotica*

Intermediate in size and structure between Crossbill and Parrot Crossbill, bill therefore thicker than Crossbill's. Best identified by locality, but note that Crossbills may also occur in same area. Has at various times and by various authorities been considered a subspecies of either Crossbill or Parrot Crossbill, but currently regarded as a full species. Bill intermediate in size between the two, and seems (like Parrot) to be adapted to feeding in pines (Crossbill shows preference for spruce). Taxonomic relationship of the three is discussed by Dr A.G. Knox in Nethersole-Thompson (1975).

Two-barred Crossbill *Loxia leucoptera*

Owing to occurrence of Crossbills with wingbars, identification of this species far from straightforward.

Structure Generally looks smaller, slimmer, more compact than Crossbill, with smaller, flatter head; also rather less bull-necked, while wings and, particularly, tail usually look proportionately longer. Note, however, that there is size overlap with Crossbill.

Bill Usually looks slimmer than Crossbill's, but again overlap.

Call A *tyip tyip*, distinctly higher-pitched than Crossbill.

Plumage Has double white wingbar and white tertial tips, but it must be stressed that Crossbills can also show these features (indeed, in 1850, Crossbills with wingbars were described as a separate species: '*L. rubrifasciata*'). It is, therefore, essential to note *exact size and shape* of wingbars and tertial tips, and also differences in structure and plumage tone. Two-barred should be identified by a *combination* of all relevant features. Adults have *thick*, pure white wingbars that *bulge prominently on inner coverts* but taper to point on outers (upper median-covert bar may be obscured by overlying feathers): wingbars are 5–12mm deep at their broadest (Svensson, 1984) and consist of white feather tips generally neatly squared off, creating solid-looking wingbar; also shows prominent white tips to tertials. Juvenile shows narrower wingbars (2.6–6mm), also has white tertial tips. On Crossbill, any white wingbars and tertial tips are usually narrower (1–2.5mm) and normally consist of relatively narrow crescentic fringes to feather tips generally not linking to form solid bar (thus appears diffuse, blurred). It may be helpful to gauge wingbar depth by reference to exposed darker base of feathers. In the hand at least, Crossbill's wingbars tend to be slightly buffer than those of Two-barred. There appears to be overlap in the exact *pattern* of white on both wing-coverts and tertials: on both species, white may extend slightly up outer web of feather. Male Two-barred tends to be slightly paler and more *pinky*-red than Crossbill (but some more similar in tone to Crossbill) and to show pale-edged brownish scapular feathers (can lack these).

References Catley & Hursthouse (1985), Nethersole-Thompson (1975), Svensson (1984), van den Berg & Blankert (1980).

House and Tree Sparrows

Where and When The familiar and abundant House Sparrow *Passer domesticus* can be met with almost anywhere, but is usually associated with man. Tree Sparrow *P. montanus*, although often common in central and eastern arable regions, is scarcer in some parts of Britain, particularly the damper pastoral areas of the southwest, west and north (in Ireland, it has a localised, mainly coastal distribution), and is prone to cyclical fluctuations in population level.

Identification Female House Sparrow is a dowdy, rather plain grey-brown, tinged olive and streaked black above, with unobtrusive pale supercilium. Male House and both sexes of Tree are more similar, but separation straightforward: note Tree's brown crown, black ear-covert spot, white collar and buffer plumage tones. Both species fly fast and direct, give muffled chirps in flight, but harder, more abrupt flight notes of Tree distinctive once learnt, as are its hard, dry 'tecking' and chattering noises at rest.

Hybrids Hybrids between the two species are rare. That illustrated below is based on one seen in Somerset which showed characters obviously intermediate between the two.

Tree Sparrow (sexes similar). Slightly smaller and neater than House Sparrow. Note buffer underparts, brown rump, chestnut-brown crown, white collar and black 'cheek spot'.

♂ House Sparrow. 'Bib' more extensive during summer. Note grey crown and rump, dull underparts and plain dull 'cheeks'.

Tree Sparrow. Bill black in summer. Note short black 'bib'. Never shows white above eye.

Tree Sparrow × House Sparrow hybrid (April), showing mixed characters of both species.

Tree Sparrow × House Sparrow hybrid. Note grey fore crown, larger 'bib' and white fleck over one eye.

♀ Cirl Bunting has strongly streaked 'face', fine streaking below, olivey rump, underparts less yellow than Yellowhammer

Adult ♀ Yellowhammer. Strong yellow 'face' and breast. Rump chestnut, underparts more heavily streaked than Cirl Bunting.

Juvenile Yellowhammer. Duller than adult, with finer streaking below. Rump chestnut.

Female Cirl Bunting and Yellowhammer

Where and When Yellowhammer *Emberiza citrinella* is common and widespread in all kinds of open country; in winter, it withdraws from high ground and concentrates in flocks, mainly on arable farmland. Cirl Bunting *E. cirlus* is rare and now unlikely to be encountered away from a narrow coastal belt in South Devon, between Exeter and Plymouth, where it has, surprisingly, recently shown signs of an increase; outside this area identification, particularly of females, should be attempted with caution.

Structure and General Hints Compared with Yellowhammer, Cirl is a rather slimmer, more compact, flatter-headed bunting. Females of the two are superficially similar: pay particular attention to call, plumage tone, facial pattern and rump.

Plumage Unlike Yellowhammer, female Cirl is basically a buffy-brown and grey-brown bird, lacking strong yellow or chestnut tones. Its rather distinctive stripy facial pattern strongly reflects the male's: a brown stripe from eye back, a brown moustachial stripe extending back along lower border of ear-coverts and a narrow malar stripe all contrast strongly with the buff or dull yellow supercilium, lores/cheek line, submoustachial stripe and throat. In comparison, female Yellowhammer's face is messier, the yellow background coloration considerably reducing the stripy effect of the brown facial lines (which are, in any case, rather less sharply defined). Unlike Yellowhammer, female Cirl Bunting lacks an obvious crown-stripe: crown appears relatively uniform, evenly and finely streaked darker. The eye is dark and prominent and

217

surrounded by a diffuse buffy eye-ring. On female Yellowhammer, underparts are essentially yellow, with diffuse brown or chestnut-brown breast and flank streaking; on juveniles and some first-winter females, however, the amount of yellow may be severely reduced but still readily apparent about face and neck. On Cirl, underparts vary from dull buff to dark, deep yellow (never attaining the bright, intense yellow of Yellowhammer), with streaking fine and pencil-like. Cirl's upperparts are also duller and browner, the only real chestnut being confined to scapulars; in particular, rump is a dull olive-brown or greyish-brown, quite unlike the bright chestnut of Yellow-hammer's.

Call The most useful character: Cirl has a soft, barely audible *sip*, occasionally strung out to *sissi-sissi-sip*; this is totally different from familiar loud, hard, metallic *tchik*, *tzik* or *tillip* of Yellowhammer.

Song If lone female Cirl is encountered, a nearby male's song may assist identification. It is a fast, high-pitched, dry, insect-like trill, or a slower, lower-pitched, more Yellowhammer-like 'dribbling' trill. May recall Lesser Whitethroat *Sylvia curruca*.

Behaviour Cirl is more elusive than Yellowhammer, often feeding unobtrusively in secretive, mouse-like manner, hidden even among short vegetation.

Reference Davis (1982).

Reed, Little and Lapland Buntings

Where and When Reed Bunting is a common and widespread breeder in all kinds of marshy habitats, and even in dryer areas (such as young conifer plantations); in winter, retreats from high ground and concentrates in freshwater and coastal marshes and on farmland. Little Bunting is a rare but increasing autumn migrant, currently averaging about 25 records a year, mostly in Shetland and at coastal migration points west to Scilly; there are several spring and winter records, the latter among finch and bunting flocks, closer scrutiny of which would undoubtedly produce more. Lapland Bunting is a scarce autumn coastal passage migrant, but small numbers winter, mainly along east coast of Britain from southern Scotland to Kent; has also bred several times in Scotland in recent years.

Reed *Emberiza schoeniclus* and Little Buntings *E. pusilla*

Out-of-context Reed Buntings may be confused with both Little and Lapland Buntings. When seen well, Little is not difficult to identify but, since it is still a *British Birds* rarity, a detailed description is essential to ensure acceptance. Pay particular attention to call and fine details of head pattern.

Size and Structure On first view, Little will appear a small, delicate, compact bunting, creeping around rather like a Dunnock *Prunella modularis*, a similarity enhanced by nervous wing-flicking. Crown is rather less rounded than Reed's, while bill has a straight or slightly concave culmen, combining to produce more pointed head-and-bill profile.

Head Pattern Little's facial pattern and colour will initially attract attention, and following differences from female Reed Bunting (in rough order of significance) should be carefully noted. 1 LORES AND EAR-COVERTS Distinctly chestnut in tone, but intensity of chestnut variable; note also that lores are plain, lacking a dark loral line. 2 EYE-RING Has thin, but obvious buff eye-ring, presence of which should be clearly established before claiming a Little. 3 EYE-STRIPE Black eye-stripe encircles rear of ear-coverts (thickening at rear), but peters out on lower border of ear-coverts roughly below eye. 4 MOUSTACHIAL STRIPE

◄ Winter ♂
Reed Bunting

♀ Reed Bunting ►

Detailed examination of
head pattern is critical. Note
Little Bunting's culmen shape,
central crown-stripe. The
moustachial and malar
stripes do not reach
the bill. ▼

Little Bunting.►
Some lack chestnut
on 'face'.

♀ Reed Bunting. Bulkier than Little
Bunting. Note 'face' pattern,
bolder flank streaks.

Little Bunting. Small and ►
compact. Noticeable wing-bars.
Note head pattern, particularly
pale eye-ring, chestnut cheeks
and lores.

Little Bunting

♀ Lapland Bunting (left) with
winter ♂ (right). Note pale
crown-stripe and 'open face'.
♂ has black blotching across
breast. ▼

♀ Lapland Bunting. Large, bulky and
lark-like. Note yellow bill, pale lores,
beady eye and chestnut panel between
wing-bars. Note long primary projection.

Because ear-covert border peters out below eye, this means that there is *no dark moustachial stripe* from base of bill backwards along lower border of ear-coverts. (Do not confuse the moustachial and malar stripes: see section on 'Topography' on endpapers.) **5 EAR-COVERT SPOT** Usually has distinct pale spot at rear of ear-coverts. **6 SUPERCILIUM** Buff supercilium is most prominent behind eye and is squarer-ended than on Reed.

The combination of pale eye-ring, pale lores and lack of a dark moustachial stripe produces a distinctly more 'open-faced' look than the rather streaky-faced Reed.

Other Plumage Features Wingbar differences are useful: on Reed, wingbars are buff and do not stand out from the buff tones of rest of plumage; on Little, whitish tips to median and, sometimes, greater coverts produce obvious wingbar(s). Lesser coverts of Little are dull olive-brown (chestnut on Reed), though these feathers are usually hidden in the field. Upperpart tone of Little is variable, but underparts have finer, neater and more delicate breast streaking.

Call The most useful character. Little typically gives a *tic*, reminiscent of Robin *Erithacus rubecula*, or a slightly softer *tsip*, perhaps more suggestive of Song Thrush *Turdus philomelos*. This is totally different from the familiar *tsew* or *swee* of Reed Bunting. The Robin-like call will enable confident identification even if all the fine detail is not observed (but note that rarer Rustic Bunting *E. rustica* has a similar call).

Tail-flicking A behavioural difference between the two is Reed's habit of flicking open tail sideways, revealing white outer tail feathers. Although Little occasionally does this, it is not so deliberate and it is not habitual.

Lapland Bunting *Calcarius lapponicus*

Once known, Lapland is simply not confusable with Reed, but the less experienced observer unfamiliar with Lapland may be thrown by out-of-context Reed.

Size and Structure Compared with Reed, Lapland is a large, bulky, broad-beamed, almost lark-like bunting, usually found on coastal saltmarshes, coastal fields or on windswept headlands during migration, often feeding among short heather; often very approachable. Long wings clearly apparent at rest, and *primary projection is long, approximately equal to length of overlying tertials* (on Reed, projection is only about half length of tertials).

Plumage *Autumn and winter* Head pattern distinctive, with black eye-stripe extending back to surround ear-coverts (thickest at corners) and extending forwards along lower edge of ear-coverts to bill; lores plain buff, as is centre of ear-coverts and the supercilium, producing very open-faced expression in which dark eye is prominent. Has chestnut or buffish 'shawl' over nape. White tips to median and greater coverts form double wingbar, and sandwiched between the bars is a distinctive chestnut panel. Male usually shows extensive areas of black on throat but, as these feathers have pale tips in winter, the obviousness of the black depends on amount of abrasion. Bill pale, yellowish. *Summer* Summer male very striking, with black 'face', throat and breast, creamy supercilium which extends in a thick white line bordering sides of black breast, chestnut shawl across lower nape/upper mantle, and yellow bill.

Calls When flushed, often gives a dry, rattling call, variously transcribed as *ti-li-li-lit*, *t-t-tip* or *ticky ticky*. This is often followed by soft, clear *peu* or *teu*. Note that Snow Bunting *Plectrophenax nivalis* has a similar call, *teu*, but this is loud and ringing and is often preceded by a soft, liquid rippling.

Flight Identification A long-winged, blunt-headed, bulky, lark-like bunting, with strong, purposeful flight. Smaller Reed Bunting has very distinctive action in which short wings are erratically closed into body to produce very hesitant flight. *Reference* Wallace (1976).

General bibliography

Cramp, S. & Simmons, K.E.L. (eds.) (1977–88) *The Birds of the Western Palearotic*, Vols I–V. Oxford University Press, Oxford.

Grant, P.J. (1986) *Gulls – a guide to identification*. 2nd edition. Poyser, Calton.

Harrison, P. (1983) *Seabirds: an identification guide*. Croom Helm, London.

Hayman, P., Marchant, J. & Prater, T. (1986) *Shorebirds: an identification guide to the waders of the world*. Croom Helm, London & Sydney.

Madge, S.C. & Burn, H. (1987) *Wildfowl: an identification guide to the ducks, geese and swans of the world*. Christopher Helm, London.

Porter, R.F., Willis, I., Christensen, S. & Nielsen, B.P. (1976) *Flight Identification of European Raptors*. 2nd edition. Poyser, Calton.

Svensson, L. (1992) *Identification Guide to European Passerines*. 4th edition. Stockholm.

Specific bibliography

British Birds is *the* monthly magazine for the keen birdwatcher and, over the years, it has made a unique contribution to bird identification. Unless otherwise stated, all the following references relate to that journal. Those marked with an asterisk have also been published in *Frontiers of Bird Identification* by Sharrock (Macmillan, 1980).

Appleby, R.H., Madge, S.C. & Mullarney, K. (1986) Identification of divers in immature and winter plumages. **79** 365–91.

Baker, K. (1988) Identification of Siberian and other forms of Lesser Whitethroat. **81** 382–90.

Bourne, W.R.P., Mackrill, E.J., Paterson, A.M. and Yésou, P. (1988) The Yelkouan Shearwater *Puffinus (puffinus?) yelkouan* **81** 306–19.

Britton, D.J. (1980) Identification of Sharp-tailed Sandpipers. **73** 333–45.

Broome, A. (1987) Identification of juvenile Pomarine Skua. **80** 426–27.

Burn, D.M. & Mather, J.R. (1974) The White-billed Diver in Britain. **67** 257–96.

Burton, J.F. & Johnson, E.D.H. (1984) Insect, amphibian or bird? **77** 87–104.

Catley, G.P. & Hursthouse, D. (1985) Parrot Crossbills in Britain. **78** 482–505

Chapman, M.S. (1984) Identification of Short-toed Treecreeper. **77** 262–3

Davenport, D.L. (1987) Behaviour of Arctic and Pomarine Skuas and identification of immatures. **80** 167–8.

Davis, A.H. (1982) Mystery photographs 66: Cirl Bunting. **75** 283–5.

Davis, A.H. & Prytherch, R.J. (1976) Field identification of Long-eared and Short-eared Owls. **69** 281–7.

Dean, A.R. (1982) Field characters of Isabelline and Brown Shrikes. **75** 395–406.

Dean, A.R. (1985) Review of British status and identification of Greenish Warbler. **78** 437–51.

Dennis, R.H. & Wallace, D.I.M. (1975) Field identification of Short-toed and Lesser Short-toed Larks. **68** 238–41.*

Dubois, P.J. (1986) Mediterranean races of Manx Shearwater in British waters. **79** 352–4.

Dubois, P.J. & Yésou, P. (1984) Identification of juvenile Yellow-legged Herring Gulls. **77** 344–8.

Gillham, E., Harrison, J.M. & Harrison, J.G. (1966) A study of certain *Aythya* hybrids. *Wildfowl Trust Seventeenth Annual Report 1964–65* 49–65.

Grant, P.J. (1972) Field identification of Richard's and Tawny Pipits. **65** 287–90.

Grant, P.J. (1981) Mystery photographs 51: Brünnich's Guillemot. **74** 144–5.

Grant. P.J. (1983) The 'Marsh Hawk' problem. **76** 373–6.

Grant, P.J. (1987) Wing shape of Chough and Alpine Chough. **80** 116–17

Grant, P.J. & Jonsson, L. (1984) The identification of stints and peeps. **77** 293–315.

Grant, P.J. & Scott, R.E. (1969) Field identification of juvenile Common, Arctic and Roseate Terns. **62** 297–9.*

Grant, P.J., Scott, R.E. & Wallace, D.I.M. (1971) Further notes on the 'portlandica' phase of terns. **64** 19–22.*

Harrison, J.M. & Harrison, J.G. (1968) Wigeon x Chilöe Wigeon hybrid resembling American Wigeon. **61** 169–71.

Harrison, P. (1983) Identification of white-rumped North Atlantic petrels. **76** 161–74

Harvey, W.G. (1981) Pallid Swift in Kent. **74** 170–8.

Harvey, W.G., Porter, R.F. & Tucker, L.A. (1984) Field identification of Blyth's Reed Warbler. **77** 393–411.

Hirschfeld, E. (1985) Further comments on treecreeper identification. **78** 300–2.

Holman, D.J. & Madge, S.C. (1982) Identifying Serins. **75** 547–53 (with correction in **76**: 317–18).

Hume, R.A. (1975) Identification and ageing of Glaucous and Iceland Gulls. **68** 57–67.*

Hume, R.A. (1978) Variations in Herring Gulls at a Midland roost. **71** 338–45.

Hume, R.A. & Grant, P.J. (1974) The upperwing pattern of adult Common and Arctic Terns. **67** 133–6.*

Johnson, I.G. (1970) The Water Pipit as a winter visitor to the British Isles. *Bird Study* **17** 297–319.

Jonsson, L. (1984) Identification of juvenile Pomarine and Arctic Skuas. **77** 443–6.

Kemp, J.B. (1982) Field identification of Long-eared and Short-eared Owls. **75** 227.

Knox, A (1988) Taxonomy of the Rock/Water Pipit superspecies. **81** 206–11.

Lansdown, P.G. (1985) Identification pitfalls and assessment problems No. 8: Purple Heron. **78** 97–102.

Marquiss, M., & Newton, I. (1982) The Goshawk in Britain. **75** 243–60.

Mather, J.R. (1981) Mystery photographs 54: Long-tailed Skua. **74** 257–9.

Mead, C.J. & Wallace, D.I.M. (1976) Identification of European treecreepers. **69** 117–31.*

Milne, B.S. (1959) Variations in a population of Yellow Wagtails. **52** 281–94.

Mullarney, K. (1987) Mystery photographs 124: Tree Pipit. **80** 158–60.

Nethersole-Thompson, D. (1975) *Pine Crossbills*. Poyser, Berkhamsted.

Oddie, W.E. (1980) Leg colour and calls of Spotted Sandpiper. **73** 185–6.

Ogilvie, M.A. & Wallace, D.I.M. (1975) Identification of grey geese. **68** 57–67.

Olsen, K.M. & Christensen, S. (1984) Field identification of juvenile skuas. **77** 448–50.

Pym, A. (1982) Identification of Lesser Golden Plover in Britain and Ireland. **75** 112–24.

Pym, A. (1985) Bill coloration of treecreepers. **78** 303.

Robertson, I.S. (1977) Identification and European status of eastern Stonechats. **70** 237–45.*

Robertson, I.S. (1982) Field identification of Long-eared and Short-eard Owls. **75** 227–9.

Rodriguez de los Santos, M. (1985) Notes on Short-toed Treecreepers from southern Spain. **78** 298–9.

Rumsey, S.J.R. (1984) Identification pitfalls: Aquatic Warbler. **77** 377.

Scott. R.E. & Grant, P.J. (1969) Uncompleted moult in *Sterna* terns and the problems of identification. **62** 93–7.*

Svensson, L. (1988) Field identification of black-beaded Yellow Wagtails. **81** 77–8.

Thorpe, J.P. (1988) Juvenile Hen Harriers showing 'Marsh Hawk' characters. **81** 377–82.

Tucker, L.A. (1984) Possible use of bill colour in separating Short-toed Treecreeper and Treecreeper. **77** 263–4.

Ullman, M. (1984) Field identification of juvenile Pomarine Skua. **77** 446–8.

van den Berg, A. & Blankert, J.J. (1980) Crossbills with prominent double wing-bar. *Dutch Birding* **2** 33–6.

van den Berg, M. & Oreel, G. (1985) Field identification of black-headed Yellow Wagtails in Western Europe. **78** 176–83.

Vinicombe, K.E. (1980) Tern showing mixed characters of Black Tern and White-winged Black Tern. **73** 223–5.

Vinicombe, K.E. (1988) Unspecific Golden Plover in Avon. *Birding World* **1** 54–6.

Wallace, D.I.M. (1970) Identification of Spotted Sandpipers out of breeding plumage. **63** 168–73.*

Wallace, D.I.M. (1976) Distinguishing Little and Reed Buntings. **69** 465–73.*

Williamson, K. (1963) The identification of the larger pipits. **56** 285–92.*

Williamson, K. (1965) Moult and its relation to taxonomy in Rock and Water Pipits. **58** 493–504.

Yésou, P. (1986) Mediterranean races of Manx Shearwater in British waters. **79** 354.

Index of vernacular and scientific names

Figures in italic refer to the illustrations; figures in bold to main text references. Significant subspecies have been included (vernacular names in inverted commas).

Median crown-stripe
Eye-ring
Lateral crown-stripe

The Eye-ring is made of feathers. The Orbital-ring is the bare ring of flesh shown by some birds, such as large gulls.

Supercilium
Eye-stripe
Moustachial stripe
Submoustachial stripe
Malar stripe

Coronal stripe

Primary projection
Tertial step
Carpal bar

Emargination
Notch
Outer web
Shaft
Inner web

'Saddle'
Carpal bar
Shoulder patch
Leading edge
Trailing edge
Carpal joint

Culmen
Upper mandible
Lower mandible
Gonys
Gonydal angle

Lores
Forehead
Crown
Ear-coverts
Nape
Scapulars
Mantle
Secondaries
Tertials
Back
Rump
Uppertail-coverts
Tail
Primaries
Undertail-coverts
Vent
Chin
Throat
Lesser coverts
Median coverts
Breast
Greater coverts
Alula
Greater primary coverts
Flanks
Belly
Thigh
Tarsus

Primaries
Greater primary coverts
Alula
Secondaries
Lesser coverts
Median coverts
Greater coverts
Tertials

UPPERWING

Axillaries

UNDERWING